Ownschooling

Bitcoin, Sovereignty, and Education

Ownschooling

Bitcoin, Sovereignty, and Education

Deanna Heikkinen

ISBN: 978-196-4944-012

Library of Congress Control Number: 2025914421

Published by Deanna Heikkinen
Edited by Heart and Quill Editing
Book layout by Deanna Heikkinen
Cover design by Deanna Heikkinen

Visit the book website at www.ownschooling.com

Dedicated to the memory of my mom, the original ownschooler.

Table of Contents

Preface

This book is a culmination of my experience as an educator, my educational path from kindergarten to my doctorate, and my journey of learning about money, including its history and inner workings, which led me to Bitcoin.

This book serves several purposes. First, it recounts my educational journey, both as a student and a teacher. It is also a sort of memoir, reflecting on how my mother was present in my education and how, through that and my own experiences, I developed the concept of ownschooling. Throughout my life, I was primarily educated in public or government-run schools. It was not until the 2010s, when I returned to school to pursue my doctorate, that I attended a private school.

Furthermore, I was not homeschooled in the traditional way. However, my mother was a type of homeschooler, a parent who was always present in our learning, actively encouraging me to follow my curiosity and enabling me to become a lifelong reader and student. In fact, as I write this, I am considering returning to school to receive further training as a classical educator. I currently have subscriptions to three online course platforms, where I sign up and attend classes on topics that interest me, such as AI in education, literature, and dance, among others.

Much of the content in this book is derived from my years in education. Some of the chapters included information from my dissertation and research papers, which I wrote while pursuing my doctorate in education. Some portions originated from years of consulting with families seeking alternative educational paths for their children. Some parts came from my own teaching experience, where I counseled students and families on test preparation for private school and college examinations, or discussed pathways for young adults outside of college.

Ultimately, I conducted extensive research and summarized my previous book on the history of money. My goal in consolidating all this information is to help families understand the available options, to illustrate the importance of money and education in achieving sovereignty, and to inform people about how both money and education are being manipulated to serve other agendas.

This book is intended for parents, aunts, uncles, grandparents, friends, and anyone who has children in their life. It is intended to inform, inspire, and even infuriate, all in the effort to protect and preserve the minds and futures of children.

In sovereignty,

Deanna Heikkinen
El Salvador, July 2025

Acknowledgements

There are so many people who helped inspire this book, but none more than my mom. I am grateful every day for her and the way she raised me. I am also indebted to my father, even through the hard times. If I had different parents, I would likely not be where I am today. I am also thankful for my sister. Without her excelling at everything she did growing up, I may not have pushed myself so hard, nor been so inspired to be both like her and as different as I could be. We have always been close and remain that way today, even with the thousands of miles between us. She has also served as an editor for this book, for which I am so appreciative.

Without the support of my husband, this book would not be finished. His constant encouragement, openness to discussing these ideas over the years, and his finding Bitcoin have led us on our own path to find sovereignty.

I am also indebted to my friends who supported me during this endeavor. To Ollie and Sydney, your comments on the draft were remarkably insightful. I appreciate you taking the time from your busy lives to read through it and provide feedback. To my friend, Magda, who continually shopped and took care of me while I was feverishly writing and not leaving my little bungalow. To Grace and Belinda for continually checking in on me and inviting me to do things even though the answer was always the same: “I can’t. I’m writing.”

I am also grateful to all the parents out there who continually seek ways to keep their children curious and to actively participate in their children’s education. You are the reason why I have hope. You are how we, as humans, continue to flourish, rather than becoming complacent with our minds, letting others or even AI do all the thinking for us. You will ensure that future generations embrace their humanity, utilize their rational faculties, and remain curious.

Finally, to Satoshi Nakamoto, thank you for inventing the first decentralized money. And to everyone working to spread Bitcoin adoption, thank you for giving others hope and freedom.

Part 1: Foundations of Money and Education

Chapter 1: My Path to Ownschooling

We must be present with our children, not just physically but emotionally. We must make time to connect and listen, to be available and responsive.

- Gordon Neufeld & Gabor Maté, *Hold On to Your Kids*

I have been an educator for quite some time, teaching homeschool kids, tutoring publicly and privately schooled children and teens, and serving as a tenured professor. I have witnessed many ways students can learn and how the schooling they receive impacts them. However, the one thing that stands out as the most critical factor in whether a student will succeed or not is parent involvement.

In fact, extensive research consistently shows that parental involvement is one of the most significant predictors of student success. Meta-analyses and longitudinal studies, such as those by Henderson and Mapp (2002) and Jeynes (2007), have found that when parents are actively engaged in their children's education, students achieve higher grades, have better attendance, display improved behavior, and are more likely to graduate and pursue higher education. These positive effects are consistent across different age groups, socioeconomic backgrounds, and school types, with evidence indicating that early and sustained parental involvement not only boosts academic achievement but also fosters motivation and positive attitudes toward learning throughout a child's educational journey.

Ownschooling is a term I coined to describe an intentional way of educating children. It simply means you actively choose and engage in your children's education, rather than outsourcing it to others.

Looking back, ownschooling is what my mother always did for my sister and me, even though we attended public schools all the way through high school, and even college. It is parent involvement that led me to be a curious, lifelong learner. It was parent involvement that enabled me to attend good schools, even though they were public institutions. It was parent involvement that saved me from being another statistic in a small town with not many options out of poverty. This first chapter describes my educational experience from first grade to my current role as a teacher. With that story comes the need to describe how money plays a role in a child's development, and how a parent's understanding and relationship with money can impact a child's education, whether they are aware of it or not.

I grew up in a small town in Central California in the 1970s. We were a traditional, middle-class family, where my dad worked and my mom stayed at home. My sister is three years older than I, and when I was born, my mother moved us to a neighboring, smaller town that had better schools. This became her pattern whenever we moved, which has turned out to be a frequent occurrence throughout my childhood and into adulthood.

My first school experience was fantastic. I loved learning, something my mother instilled in my sister and me from an early age. Books were an integral part of my everyday life, even before I started attending school. A trip to the library was typical, and I have so many memories of being this tiny little girl, carrying as many books as I could hold from the children's section to my mom when it was time to check out. Then, the bartering came.

My mom always made me put some back! I would lay them out and really think about which ones I wanted to read now versus later. It was painful, and sometimes I would cry over not being able to check them all out. I still do not know why she made me limit my stack; perhaps it was to save some for other kids, or maybe there was a limit on the number of books I could check out. As I write this, I wish she were still here so I could ask her.

Nevertheless, books were always in our house. Reading was always encouraged. Learning was just there.

I have such vivid memories of my elementary school education. From my kindergarten years, I recall the smiling teacher letting us explore our passions, supporting us when we faced challenges, and encouraging our curiosity as she guided us through our first level of public school. When I evoke those thoughts of her classroom, I feel a sense of safety and calm that I fear many students no longer experience.
My all-time favorite teacher was Mrs. Hall, my second-grade teacher. She was one of the loveliest women I have ever known. She had dark hair, and I thought she was the most remarkable and beautiful human ever to walk the planet. She let me shine, this curious little girl who was always thinking, always asking why, always learning. I stayed after classes, asking for more worksheets, asking questions, needing to know more, and wanting to understand everything on a deep level.

My first experience with having my curiosity squashed came about a year or so later when I attended a fundamentalist, hell-and-damnation church with some baton corps friends. Although I was christened Lutheran, like any good American-Scandinavian child would be, I did not grow up in a religious household. We celebrated holidays, but it was not in a religious manner.

There was an understanding that God exists, but it was not something we discussed extensively. We did not attend church as a family. Yet, living in a very traditional, small town surrounded by farmland, many of my friends came from extremely devout families. One such family always invited my sister and me to attend Sunday school with them. We would go on occasion; for us, it was mainly for the social aspect.

I remember that I was learning about dinosaurs in third grade at the same time one of the Sunday school lessons was teaching about Adam and Eve. As my curious self, I asked my regular school teacher which came first: the dinosaurs or Adam and Eve. He kindly told me to ask my parents. Now, as an educator, I realize he wanted to be respectful of my family's beliefs and did not see it as his place to weave religion into his science lesson. I did not ask my parents, though; I wanted an expert to tell me!

The following week, I was ready to revisit the subject. When I went to Sunday school, I raised my hand as any good, curious child would do and asked the Sunday school teacher, "Who came first: the dinosaurs or Adam and Eve?" She was aghast… I was sent to sit in the corner and was belittled for even questioning anything relating to the Bible. I felt shame and an overwhelming need to cry. But, being a good girl, I sat quietly, lip trembling, holding back tears. I had never had anyone shut my curiosity down so harshly, let alone in front of my friends and peers.

I did not understand what had happened. It just did not compute. I was not a troublemaker; I was a model student. I did not tell anyone until many years later, the shame of that day darkening a bit of my curiosity. However, thanks to my mother's and many school teachers' continued kindness and support. I bounced back and continued to learn, filling my knowledge cup and trying many new things.

Yes, I was that kid. I was the insatiable why child. My mother once said that if I were born first, I would be an only child. That may not sound kind, but I got it. I was a lot (I still can be). I exhausted her with my questions, driven by my need to keep my mind satisfied and to know more. As a result, in most of the candid photographs I have of myself from my childhood, I am not smiling.

My sister later coined it as my "dumb look" in all those photos. After showing these pictures to others as an adult and explaining my lack of smile using that disparaging term, which only an older sister who you adored could get away with, I came to realize that it was not a dumb look on my face. Rather, it was my thinking look. My active brain would never shut off; in fact, it still does not.

Photo of my sister and me with my thinking look at Disneyland, circa 1976.

This makes me think of that old debate… nature versus nurture. Was I born as a curious thinker, or was it instilled in me by my amazing mother, teachers, and upbringing? Perhaps, it is both.

My education in early elementary school was marked by excellent, supportive teachers who genuinely cared about their students and the lessons they shared. Furthermore, my parents were also quite active in the school. My mom was a member of the Parent-Teacher Association (PTA) and even served as president for a while. My dad ran the school carnival, and although he never embraced school himself, he supported his daughters wholeheartedly in their own pursuits.

My parents did everything they could to help my sister and me have an adventurous and fun childhood. While my dad was fun-loving, and although he was not academically inclined, he was curious. He had a zest for life and a deep appreciation for American ideals that he passed down to me. He loved model trains, collected vintage toys, and went to flea markets. I learned about early Americana from him. I helped him build train layouts and shelves to display his collections. He taught me how to bargain at flea markets and garage sales, and how to navigate and exit thrift stores quickly when searching for something in particular. He taught me to be a kind and honorable person. He taught me the reason to be a patriotic American, because of the values instilled by the Founding Fathers. He taught me my work ethic. He was actively present in my formative years.

On the other hand, my mom nurtured my creative and intellectual side. She would take us to a local museum, where I became fascinated with an Egyptian mummy. She enrolled us in art classes, where I learned to appreciate color theory (even though I would not understand what that was until much later). She let me try everything and then allowed me to quit if it did not hold my interest. She taught me that being curious is okay and to explore what makes me happy. Both my parents chose happiness in their own way, instilling in me the same value.

I loved my first school and thought I would stay there until it was time to go to high school. But, in my third-grade year, we moved across town. I was in a different neighborhood and attended a different school. I had to adjust to being the new kid. I no longer had the security of my older sister paving the way for me, telling me about the teachers and having them familiar with my family. Nobody there knew my parents. I figured it out, though. I had learned how to be optimistic through stories like *Heidi* and *Pippi Longstocking*. I was also alright because my mom was being proactive, present, and intentional when it came to our education. In other words, she was ownschooling. She purposefully moved us to an area with one of the better schools in town.

This became a familiar pattern throughout my young life. I know my resilience was due to my mom vetting schools and advocating on my behalf. She always nurtured my love of learning and curiosity, and she met and communicated with my teachers. It was these traits that helped me navigate attending numerous schools by the time I graduated from high school.

When I was in fourth grade, my parents separated, and my mom moved us to Southern California, away from my safe hometown. I adapted. I made friends. I continued to be curious. As I had always done, I stayed after class to hang out with my teacher as much as possible. I asked questions and for additional assignments on topics I loved.

Moving became the norm as my mom, a single parent, tried to keep my sister and me sheltered, fed, and safe. This was a shift in my world, especially after my father met someone, and it became serious. She had her own children, two of whom still lived at home, including a daughter six months younger than me.

I spent my fourth-grade year in a wonderful school in northern San Diego County. I won a grade-level spelling bee, and my teacher took me and the other winner to McDonald's to celebrate (it was the early 80s: times were different, and things like this were allowed!). The school also had a wonderful music program, where I had the opportunity to experiment with various instruments and fell deeply in love with the violin. My sister, being three years older, had three more years of security, living with both parents. She was able to play the flute with the band. I was not so lucky.

My mom could not afford to buy me a violin, and my dad had a new family. He and his new wife chose not to help me pursue music. This was the first time I realized, I think, that he was no longer a part of my daily life, that he was no longer involved in my education. Unbeknownst to me, I was competing with his new family for his time, love, and financial support. It ultimately put a strain on the relationship between my father and us, his daughters, for two decades. This conflict would also have some educational repercussions when I tried to attend college after high school. However, looking back, I still came out the winner, as my curiosity and love of learning have never waned.

While visiting my dad the summer between fourth and fifth grade, my mom moved from Southern California to the outskirts of Phoenix, Arizona. I was devastated. I loved my school and the experience I had near San Diego. I was initially angry about moving before attending the school, but once I arrived, I realized I would be alright. My mom was supportive and nurturing. Once again, I found friends who could appreciate my quirkiness. I had a place to learn. I quickly made friends. I remained curious. This pattern happened a few times from sixth grade through high school. I would go to visit my father in my hometown, and my mom would move. There were reasons that I understand more now, but I survived, and by many standards, I thrived.

I spent most of my middle school and high school years in the same area on the border of Phoenix and Scottsdale, Arizona. Although I disliked high school for reasons related to my social standing, I still enjoyed learning. My mom encouraged me to be curious, to discover things I was passionate about, and to explore the world around me. In high school, I lettered in theater, choir, and badminton (I know, I just admitted what a nerd I was, and honestly, I am still proud of it!). I was in a sorority, albeit the one for not-so-popular girls. I was a cheerleader for the wrestling team. I did makeup for a local professional theater. I was a member of the Masonic organization, Job's Daughters. I participated in Junior Achievement. I even sheepishly sang in my choir classes to be close to my theater friends, where we all went on a performance trip to Southern California. I participated in the school lip-sync competition. I hiked Camelback Mountain. The list goes on and on. Looking back, I'm not sure how I managed to fit it all in, but I wanted to learn and experience as much as I could. I had inherited my dad's zest for life, but explored it in my own unique way!

In high school, I took all the required classes and as many additional ones as I could fit in to delve into subjects that interested me. Unlike my sister, whose electives tended to be the same from semester to semester, I tried a lot of different subjects. I learned a little bit of German. I took theater classes, where I fell in love with improv techniques and realized that I was horrible at acting from a script. I loved my English classes, especially reading Shakespeare, poetry, and literature, which came easily to me as I had been a reader of classics for as long as I can remember.

Once again, it was my mom had fostered this love over and over again. I remember some of my favorite gifts were copies of *The World's 200 Greatest Poems* in fifth grade and *The Complete Works of Shakespeare* for my sixteenth birthday. I still have both of those books, and looking back, that book of Shakespeare is better than the car I wanted at the time! I would have long ago parted with the car, but I still have that book. In my pursuit of knowledge and curiosity, I excelled in high school.

Even so, I still struggled in high school. My love of learning was not shared by many of my peers. I felt alone in my passion for learning. I wanted to stay and talk with my teachers after class. But peer pressure for a teenage girl was real. I went to a school that could have been a model for the schools in a 1980s John Hughes movie. There was definitely a hierarchy, and although I found my tribe in theater, it could still be lonely when I was in my classes. I also had integrity.

I recall a couple of students cheating by peeking at my paper in English class. I decided to take matters into my own hands, so I placed the incorrect answers on the front and the correct answers in the margin on the blank side. When I turned in my exam, I quietly told my teacher that people were cheating off me, so my correct answers were on the back. She smiled and nodded. I was happy. Honestly, I just could not understand why people did not love learning as much as I did. It was a hard pill to swallow. It still is.

Additionally, my mom was a single parent. Whereas my dad remained middle-class with his new family, we did not. My mom struggled with money, and it was one reason we moved around so much. Moving often became my norm; even still, it is not unheard of for me to move from house to house, town to town, country to country. Yet, there were times of stability. I grew up in the same house until I was in third grade. I stayed in the same school district from middle school to most of high school, despite moving several times in that area. I survived, and by many standards, I did more than that. I had love. I had my curiosity. I had a passion for learning.

Yet, I did not have financial security. As part of my reflection on my schooling, this is a significant component. Part of the mindset of ownschooling is to have autonomy for your family. This is something that requires parents to take charge not only of their children's education but also of their finances. I now see that families need financial **sovereignty**, or the freedom from someone or an entity taking away the value of what you earn through your time and energy.

When I was growing up, financial sovereignty in its truest sense did not exist. In fact, this concept is less than twenty years old. (I will explain this more in the chapters on money and Bitcoin.) In retrospect, there were significant gaps in my learning. For all my curiosity, it was never directed towards money or finances. I did not have healthy role models for money. When I was old enough to truly understand money, my parents had separated. After that, my mom scraped by, and my dad became a miser towards my sister and me. I would learn that this was largely due to the influence his wife had over him.

Like many single parents and even two-parent families today, my mom could never save money. She lived paycheck to paycheck. When money came in, we spent it. We would go to the store and stock up on essentials. We would treat ourselves to a dinner out, often fast food, as that was what we could afford. By the time high school came around, she would try to give me a little spending money, but the money was always tight. I went to school with very wealthy kids. In fact, the cars in the student parking lot were sometimes nicer than those in the teacher's lot. Designer clothing, handbags, and shoes were everywhere. My Payless Shoe Source clearance shoes and Sears clothing put me in a different class. Mean girls are real. Class awareness by teens is a thing.

It was not a secret that I was poor. Yet, I found solace with theater kids. And even though some came from money, they were kind. We had a shared love of the performing arts, and that was enough. I was the poorest of my closest friend group, but they did not care. They loved my mom; they loved that they could come over and hang out at my house without expectations. They could be curious. They could be happy. They could just be. This is how I grew up, yet money, or the lack thereof, always weighed me down.

In my junior year, I went behind my mom's back and got a part-time job at a dry cleaners. We had moved again, downgraded to an apartment complex that was not as nice as our last one. It was also just outside the school district. I could no longer walk to school (which was still embarrassing to my teenage self as I could see my peers driving by in their fancy cars). I took the city bus to school and could walk to my new job right after it ended. My mom was livid when she found out I had taken an after-school job. She had told me she did not want me to work in high school. She wanted me to have fun, learn, and enjoy my teenage years. However, we were struggling, and she could not afford to give me spending money.

I also wanted to help her out by buying my own bus pass. I wanted to go to dinner and the movies with my friends, and afford to get a meal when someone went out to grab food during rehearsals. I wanted to be independent and to earn it myself. Yet, I did not save. I had not learned that. I worked. Got paid. Spent what I earned. However, at least I was paying for my own social life, which made me happy. It was enough at that time. But in retrospect, I wish I had been taught to save, had learned the art of delayed gratification. I had only learned the concept of spending as soon as you earn it. It would take me much longer than I care to admit to learn those tough money lessons.

Growing up, money was a taboo subject. We never earned an allowance or got money for good grades. My parents didn't distribute money for my sister and me to decide how to spend it on our own. If we wanted something, we could sometimes ask. I say sometimes because we were often told before going to a store not to ask for anything. My mom always knew what I wanted, but my dad was always strict with money and didn't talk about it.

After my parents separated, my dad rarely helped outside of his regular child support check. He always paid on time, and for that, I am extremely grateful. However, it was not a lot, and to my knowledge, my mom never requested more from him. He paid the same $200 per month per kid for over ten years. When my sister went away to college, so did that $200 for her.

Things got tougher financially for my mom and me at that point. Dad was no help. When asked if he could help me with something specific, like the violin when I was younger, he always said he needed to check with my stepmother. She almost always said no, and he would come back saying he could not help right now. Because of this, I conflated his money with his love. Both seemed absent. It would take years and my mother's eventual death to repair this damage.

During this time when my sister was away at college, things got even worse for my mom and me. Money was scarce, and honestly, it became a shameful topic. In essence, I was not taught to be curious about money. Even in my high school economics class, surrounded by students who came from more financially secure families, some of whom were quite wealthy, all I could feel was shame. I felt like this class was something outside of my life, and it just did not apply to me. It was one of the few subjects in my entire academic life where my curiosity did not prevail. I just shut down.

There are terms we hear in society, one of which is the cycle of poverty. After high school, I lived this cycle. Like my mom and dad, I did not go to college. It was not for a lack of trying. I applied and got into two schools I wanted to attend. I was set to go, but panic set in when it came to paying for it. While my sister graduated from high school with a higher GPA and attended a state college in Arizona, I wanted to stretch my wings and attend an out-of-state college in the Southern United States. When it came time to pay for the housing and tuition, I realized I would not be able to make it work.

My dad would not contribute enough for me to attend. Due to the way financial aid was structured, I had to include my dad's income on my application, even though he was not contributing much. This meant that I did not qualify for enough financial assistance, and my mom did not qualify for a loan. I had to cancel my acceptance. Being resilient, I made the most of it. I stayed in Phoenix and found a roommate. I worked at a dry cleaner, had friends, and decided to go to the local community college. I was able to get some tuition assistance, but I still needed $200 for books and fees. My mom could not help.

Previously, my mom had been offered a job in Florida between my junior and senior years of high school. We drove across the country in a U-Haul, and I spent one semester there attending one of the better public schools in the area. Although it was one of the better schools, I think for the first time in my life, my mom did not make a decision about where to work and live based on which school I would be attending. I mean, I just had one more year left, and she had been struggling for years. She was tired, and although the reasons why are not relevant here, she needed a clean break away from her own toxic mother and siblings.

For the first time in my life, I was in culture shock at a new school. I had come from an excellent school in an affluent area of Phoenix, where, due to AP classes, the valedictorian often had a GPA above 4.5. The new school had much lower academic standards. I was shocked to hear that the valedictorian had a grade point average below a 4.0. It was disorientating. On the first day of English class, I sat behind a guy who seemed bigger than the entire football team from my old school in Arizona put together. He had the Batman insignia shaved into the back of his head. Football was no joke here. It was so different from the high school I knew. And, even though I struggled due to my socio-economic status in Arizona, it was familiar. I had friends, I had my place in the theater.

Within the first month at my new Florida high school, I was asked, while excitedly awaiting my history class to begin, "What do you do with your horses?" The girl sitting next to me was earnest in her question, but I had no idea what she was talking about. I asked her to clarify what she meant. She said, "What do you do with your horses when you go into the store?" I came to find out that she thought we still rode horses everywhere in Arizona. I was stunned that she still believed it was the Wild West out there. She had no idea Phoenix was a large city, larger than almost all of the cities in Florida.

Within a few weeks, there was a drug bust, and weapons were found on campus. I was a good girl. I did not do drugs. I realized that, despite having lived in Phoenix and moved around a lot, I was still very innocent. I had heard of the parties happening in Arizona, like you see in an 80s movie, where the rich kids did drugs and illicit activities happened, but I was so far removed from that scene. Those parties were never even appealing to me. Furthermore, I was insulated from much of the weekend's goings-on by my high school peers, as I preferred to hang out with my small group of misfit theater kids. I was grateful for that, and I still am to this day.

Needless to say, my mother was concerned about my schooling in Florida. So was I. And, although I had been in to see my guidance and school counselors during my middle and high school years in Phoenix, I sought out therapy to deal with being at that school in Florida. Well, that and issues with my dad and being poor. My mother refocused on my education; she was ownschooling to find a solution. Luckily, my best friend's family was extraordinarily kind, and my mother's main concern was my safety, education, and happiness. So, I moved back to Arizona and lived with my best friend and her family to complete my high school education.

This is how I ended up living in Phoenix, wanting to attend college, but unable to afford it. With no help from my dad to pay for books and fees, I spent one semester at Phoenix College, taking classes to fulfill my love of learning and curiosity. I felt like I could never get enough of school, but I had to survive. So, I left school and settled into working various retail and restaurant jobs. I also moved back and forth between Phoenix, where my friends lived, and Florida, where my mom was, just trying to find my way. I made money and then spent it. I never saved, not that I earned a lot. I was not thinking long-term, and I was not learning anything in a profound way. But I remained curious.

After a few years, I ended up moving between Northern and Southern California for most of my twenties. I finally landed a decent job in San Diego after spending time in and around San Francisco working at various retail chains. Yet, I wanted more. I knew I wanted to be in school. I craved it. I also wanted to travel. So, I decided to be a travel photojournalist!

Growing up, my dad dabbled in photography, and his best friend was a photographer for the police department. I remember going into his friend's darkroom where he'd print shots for my dad. It was the coolest place. That, along with having a French exchange student when I was in kindergarten and first grade, had planted the seeds long before my twenty-seventh year when I decided to enroll in a photography program. I knew I wanted to explore the world with a camera in my hand. I thought I had finally found a way to fulfill my insatiable curiosity.

While living in and attending school in San Diego, I had a friend who worked for a suite of local newspapers. She connected me with the editor, and I landed a part-time freelance photography job. The newspapers gave me assignments, but I could also take my own shots to highlight the beach communities as well. Between that, taking photos for my classes, and building my portfolio, I knew I had found a passion. If only I could figure out how to financially support myself doing it.
I soon realized that being a travel photojournalist was a long shot. After having a decent-paying job in retail management, I began to crave financial security more than I did adventure. Freelance photojournalists rarely had a regular, secure paycheck, and that scared me. Do not get me wrong, I still had not learned how to manage money very well. I just knew that I no longer wanted to have to decide between having something decent to eat or paying the electric bill.

So I found a compromise. I quit my decent-paying job and signed up to be a cruise ship photographer for a river-based cruise line in the United States. What could go wrong? It blended travel and photography; it was, after all, my dream! However, I lasted just a couple of months. Remember that value of being happy that my parents instilled in me? Well, unlike them, I applied this to every facet of my life, including my job. I realized that taking photos of passengers was not what I wanted to do. I had never aspired to be a portrait photographer, and although I spent my time off in various ports pursuing my passion for photographing landscapes and architecture, I knew this was not the life for me. So, I left the river life and headed to spend some time with my mom, who was now in Wyoming. I was back to seeking a path that would allow me to continue learning while also supporting myself. I still feared poverty more than anything.

It was while living in Wyoming that I really became aware of homeschooling. It was through some of the friends my mom had made in church. She had become a born-again Christian, returning to her roots after spending a significant amount of time with her grandparents during her childhood. One day, while hanging out with her friends, I met their 10-year-old daughter. Being an avowed book nerd myself, I asked her what she enjoyed reading. Her mother said that she could not read, that God had not yet wanted her to read. I was floored. Reading had been my constant companion since I could remember. But beyond that, I thought to myself, "How could the family not teach her how to read?" Her younger siblings could read; it was later remarked that she did not want to read. I was utterly turned off by the idea of homeschooling at that point. I was sure that it was the worst thing a family could do to their children, and I held that belief for a long time.

Yet Wyoming was not all bad. My mom had gone back to school to earn a degree in Christian counseling, and she once again instilled in me a love of learning. She listened to my dreams, my reservations. She was present even when I was an adult working and trying to find my path.

Driven solely by curiosity, rather than a lofty career goal this time, I enrolled in community college courses again, taking classes in world religions, Western civilization, and geology. I loved photography, but had decided it would be a lifelong hobby. The world was my oyster once again, and I was thrilled to be learning new subjects once more.

I loved school, just like I did when I was a kid. Just for fun, I would visit the campus bookstore, much like I used to visit the library, browsing through textbooks and taking in all the different subjects I could learn about. It was on one of these occasions when I stumbled upon an art history textbook. It was a massive book. I spent a long time in the store that day, thumbing through it, feeling like my soul had taken off.

Memories of visiting the local museum as a kid, heading into the historic school building in my hometown for a summer art class, and watching my mom paint scenes from books on our walls flooded my mind. I fell in love that day. I knew what I wanted to study, but it was not to be an artist, like I had wished with photography. Spending so many years in financial uncertainty, I knew that being a struggling artist was not for me. I wanted, no, I needed some sense of financial security that I could provide for myself. It occurred to me that I wanted to learn about the great works of art and find a path to pursue that. I loved museums. There had to be jobs. I just knew I could find a way to support myself with this major.

After a harsh winter and realizing that snow and I are not that friendly, I decided to move back to California to be near my older sister again. I also needed to go back to college to study art history. Once again, I set my sights on the local community college in the small city a couple of hours from Los Angeles, where my sister lived. That summer, just two weeks after returning, I enrolled in math and cultural anthropology classes for the first term.

The curiosity that my mom had repeatedly sparked in me was fueled again that first summer in that anthropology class. I would call my mom after classes as I waited for my sister to pick me up from school. (I was still poor and did not have a car, but I was certain I was finally on the right path.) I told my mother everything I was learning. I was like a child who had just discovered their favorite thing in the world. Talking in run-on sentences, I could not contain my excitement during those weeks in summer school. It was during the last week of the summer session that my mother died unexpectedly. It was the most devastating thing that had ever happened to me. I took my finals in a fog the day after she died. But I finished my semester. I took all of my sadness and I dove into school with a fury for nearly a decade.

That fall, I declared myself an art history major and had the most remarkable professor. I would later travel with her on a student trip to Egypt, and she would eventually become my mentor and friend. Upon having enough credits to graduate with an Associate's degree in art history, I then transferred to the local state university to finish my undergraduate degree. By that time, I had also decided to study anthropology, so I double-majored in art history and anthropology with a focus on archaeology.

I was a first-generation college student and the first in my family to graduate from college, even beating my studious older sister to it! Just like I set out to do with taking the travel photojournalist world by storm several years earlier, I was determined to be an Egyptologist. The museum with the mummy that my mom took me to decades ago had made a lasting impression. The fact that there was no Egyptologist that I could study with at my college was never an issue in my mind. I had been raised to believe that I could do what I set my mind to; I was curious, resourceful, and smart enough to find a way. Well, in this case, the way found me. One of my archaeology professors was asked to join a dig in Egypt as part of a team affiliated with another university. He knew my goal and work ethic, so he asked me to join the project as well. I was ecstatic. I was on my perfect educational path, and nothing could stand in my way.

It was during this time that my dad re-entered my life in a new way. Even though they had been divorced for a long time and he had been with my stepmom for much of that period, my mother's death deeply impacted him. He showed up for my sister and me like he had when we were little, before my parents went their separate ways. Like high school, I was significantly involved in my college. However, this time it was less about extracurricular activities and more focused on academics. I competed in campus and state-wide research competitions, gave talks and lectures in various capacities, started a chapter of the anthropology honor society, and joined other academic and honors organizations.

My dad was present; I remember him cramming his large frame into student desks at various college campuses to hear me present my research at state-wide competitions. Afterwards, noting that he understood what I was talking about (mummies), but a lot of the other anthropology papers were lost on him. He would smile and say, "I knew that one was about monkeys," or smirk and ask if I could follow the statistical studies. He helped fill the gap of losing my mother during that time. Even as an adult, I still wanted parental support for my academic endeavors. It had always been there, with my mom, and now with him.

After getting my bachelor's degree, I enrolled in not one but two Master of Arts programs: history and anthropology. Remember how I mentioned that I took out the devastation of losing my mom by focusing on my education? Well, this is how I coped. I learned, I studied, I excelled in school. I stayed at the same university where I received my bachelor's degree for graduate school. And, like my conviction to be an Egyptologist, I knew I could be a classical historian even though the history department focused more on modern history.

Once again, fate or perhaps just pure luck was on my side. I found two scholars in the history and religious studies departments to work with… a Roman historian and an early Egyptian Christian (Coptic) scholar. This was like striking gold! The archaeological site I was now working on in Egypt had an early Christian component, and I was able to work with my archaeology mentor on the burials. I spent three years working on my master's thesis in archaeology, only to discover my true calling at the end: teaching. I switched to a teaching master's in anthropology and continued to work on my history master's degree and thesis.

Seven years after earning my bachelor's degree, two years after completing my master's degree in anthropology, and two and a half years as an adjunct professor, I earned my second master's degree in history.

I was then determined to pursue my passion for learning even further with a doctorate in Coptic Studies. My specialty was the study of burial techniques in early Christian Egypt. I focused on early Christianity, late antiquity, Greco-Roman Egypt, and ancient Rome itself. I read Gibbon, learned the liturgical language of Coptic, and even gave lectures on Coptic history for the local Coptic church. I attended conferences in Egyptology and Coptic studies, where I shared my research. I was ready for this next step and received a full-ride scholarship to a university in Australia, where I would work with one of the leading scholars in the field.

However, this time, fate was not on my side. Just as I was finishing my master's in history, my dad was diagnosed with Parkinson's disease. I could not leave him. We had repaired our relationship, and I was not willing to move around the world for what I knew would be the best years he would have left. To this day, I have no regrets about that decision. I got to spend eight years seeing him as often as I could, sharing trips to Disneyland, and having him get to meet the man I married. My path changed, but my love of learning and curiosity never wavered.

From the time I was finishing up my graduate degree in anthropology, I worked as an online adjunct professor for California Community Colleges, spanning from San Diego to north of San Francisco. At the same time, I also taught in person in southern California, driving as far as two and a half hours away to take any class I could, teaching anthropology and history. I loved teaching and consistently applied for adjunct and full-time positions. I needed to make sure I could pay my bills, and adjunct classes were never guaranteed. I also yearned for the Holy Grail of teaching: a tenured position. The year after I earned my master's in history, I landed my dream job as a tenured humanities professor in Los Angeles.

Teaching humanities courses elated me. It blended all my passions: art history, cultural history, anthropology, philosophy, and music history. The classes I was assigned could not have been more perfect. I taught courses on ancient Mesopotamia and Egypt. Ancient Greece and Rome, great minds across the ages, women in the humanities, as well as special topics I got to choose and explore.

Every semester, I reworked my core classes to improve them, learning more and challenging myself to make the classes better and better. I stretched my comfort zone and read philosophy, primary sources, and literature I had never thought I would read. Each semester, I took students to Los Angeles area museums. Intellectually, I had never been happier. However, as the saying goes, all good things must come to an end.

In just a short time, I started taking on leadership roles on my campus. I joined multiple committees, was elected to the academic senate, and even held committee appointments on the state level. I observed how academia functioned, and I realized I could no longer ignore some trends that were disturbing to me. The first was the underpreparedness of students for college. I taught humanities, history, and anthropology and had been teaching at the community college level for over five years. The students were becoming less motivated and more frequently lacked basic skills.

I became certified and a trainer for a reading program that many California colleges began using to teach their adult students reading comprehension. This approach was originally designed for middle school students but is now being applied to college students. I spent more than one class period showing students how to write an essay and an exam response. Honestly, I did not mind trying to help my students, but most of them were disinterested in improving their skills.

Most students never took advantage of my office hours or open-door policy. They did not bother to read the extensive comments I made on their papers, nor did they read the books I assigned. They only cared about what was on the exam and whether I gave extra credit. I realized that I taught a few students, and the rest just paid my salary. So, I focused on those few, the best I could, but it was still a little soul-crushing. Like in high school when those guys were cheating off of me, I was sad that my students did not care to learn.

In addition, I had colleagues who were just as complacent. They used the same multiple-choice exams each semester, the same lectures year after year. They themselves seemed to lack intellectual curiosity. Furthermore, the environment for anyone who did not share the post-modern, victim versus oppressor, identity politic groupthink would be marginalized or even ostracized by their colleagues. Intellectual homogeneity prevailed, and if you did not align with it, the work environment was not pleasant.

I remember the day after a presidential election, a colleague came skipping and hollering down the hall, "We won, we won!" The assumption that "we," being faculty, all felt the same and were elated with the election results. Four years later, when the other side won, a different colleague was in despair, questioning what she would tell her daughter now that the opposition was in office.

I remember Union propaganda being so far left-leaning; flyers with whom to vote for on the local, state, and federal levels were handed out. Lobbying dollars would be deducted from your check as union dues. A colleague told me that one could opt out of that portion of the fees, but I was warned against it, as it would be perceived as a sign that you were not on "their side." He had done it, and his choice was not kept confidential; rather, he was known to be a dissenter.

Although I did not always disagree with everyone, I began to view academia in a different light. It was not a place for curiosity. It was for ideological conformists. Blatant Marxism was all around me. One of my colleagues, a rather popular professor, bragged about a birthday cake her students made for her. It featured a rendering of Karl Marx on it. On one faculty opening day, professors were to participate in the privilege walk, a group activity where participants step forward or backward in response to statements about life experiences, visually revealing disparities in privilege among them. This activity labels people as victims or oppressors, often inducing guilt or shame in those identified as more or less privileged.

Another time, I recall discussing educational philosophy with one of the deans. She mentioned that she loved Paolo Freire. I was not that familiar with him at the time. I was curious, so she shared an article of his with me. I was shocked that he was her inspiration. His ideas about the purpose of education were not to learn, to be curious, to acquire knowledge, but rather to teach kids to be activists, to teach them that they were either an oppressor or the oppressed. It was shocking to see it laid out so blatantly before me. As a historian who was familiar with the history of Marxist ideas and the millions of lives lost as a result, I was unsettled by these and many other disturbing examples.

I felt a shift in how I saw the academy. Personally, I taught ideas from different viewpoints and incorporated readings and art in my classes based on their contributions to the time period in which they lived, regardless of their sexuality or ethnicity. I did not teach from a Marxist lens, nor was I focused on identity politics. But this was not the norm. In fact, it was not how most teachers, particularly in Los Angeles felt. It was even transmitted to the students.

I recall being asked by a student in my course on ancient Greece and Rome why I had not included any readings by an African-American writer. Inside, I was stunned; outside, I merely mentioned that America had yet to be founded; therefore, there were no African American writers at the time. Yet, in the back of my mind, I feared she would complain to the school, and I could be reprimanded.

I felt I had to hide the fact that I was teaching a lot of classic literature, philosophy, and art by those old, dead white guys. I did not want to be shunned or, worse, fired. I was friendly, but like high school, I also felt like I was different. There was a disconnect. There was a lack of curiosity. There was just identity politics and a victim/oppressor mindset.

So, being my idealistic and optimistic self, I thought I could change it from the inside. I decided to return to school to pursue my doctorate in education. With my credentials, certainly people would listen to me. I could share how objectively disheartening it was to see the decline in standards, the lack of meritocracy, and the absence of curiosity. I applied to a couple of programs in the area and settled on a small liberal arts college near Los Angeles. I enrolled in a doctoral program for educational leadership.

I was at my first private school, and wow, could I tell. The common areas were clean, and the chairs were comfortable. You could see the difference between this and the public college I had attended and the one I was currently teaching at. Furthermore, the program was filled with educators; they all wanted to be there. I was thrilled to be surrounded by others who wanted to learn and excel in the program.

I remember discussing with my dad the idea of returning to school. He was supportive, but joked that he did not know where I got my academic drive. I smiled at the phone, thinking it was my mom, but it was also in a way my dad. I learned my sense of justice from him after all. When it came down to it, they had both been there, encouraging my thirst for knowledge in their own ways. They nurtured my interests and lovingly challenged me to do my best constantly.

However, the doctorate program was not what I expected. Like in my teaching career, I soon learned that I was the outlier in my thinking. It was uncomfortable at first, as I had not felt like the student who could ruffle feathers since that day in Sunday school as a child. But by now, I had more conviction in my knowledge, in my values, in my philosophical ideas. Instead of feeling shame, I leaned into it. I had my secret little talismans I could wear or put in my bag to protect me from the stares, the eye rolls, and the homogeneous ideas of both my professors and peers.

In most of my classes, we focused on diversity, mainly gender or ethnicity. I would raise my hand and ask about intellectual diversity every chance I got. I argued that since we were in the business of learning, the various ideological viewpoints should be primary to the diversity discussions. I was shut down, but this time, I smiled through it. I was the rebel now, and whereas in my job as a professor I hid, in my doctorate program, I thrived. Yet, in hindsight, getting my doctorate was not worth the time and money. During the three years I spent in the program, I did not learn how to expand my practice or become a better educator; instead, I was taught that everything boils down to a Marxist, oppressor/oppressed mindset.

Additionally, I struggled to find an advisor and get my dissertation topic approved. Initially, I wanted to focus my dissertation research on educational policy in America, specifically examining how education evolved over time, tracing its roots back to the founding fathers and their arguments, and exploring why it was not included in the Constitution. I wanted to explore how education had shifted in practice and its purpose. I examined policy changes that affected education on both the federal and state levels over more than 200 years. Yet, I was told that I had to do a qualitative or quantitative study on some aspect of education. I had to use a postmodern theoretical perspective. So I decided to throw their lack of intellectual diversity back at them. I would study the presence of intellectual diversity in higher education.

It was not an easy path. I struggled to find an advisor and committee members, but luckily, they hired someone open to my research. With a committee in place, I used critical race theory with Ayn Rand as my data point and as the oppressed class. As I write this, I still cannot keep the smirk off my face. I ended up graduating, with my principles intact, my head held high, and my curiosity unscathed.

Even so, realizing how my values no longer aligned with those of academia, along with seeing instances of professors around the country being canceled by students, and even tenure professors losing their jobs for not being part of the main ideological leanings of their campuses, I decided to leave my six-figure, tenured, once upon a time, dream job. My dad questioned this decision. He was pragmatic about money after all, and had worked in passionless jobs his whole life. I was not built that way; I wanted to be happy in all aspects of my life.

I had decided. I wanted to leave teaching on my own terms before someone else made the decision for me. My husband and I moved to the Pacific Northwest to be closer to his family and, theoretically, reduce our expenses. I had to reinvent myself, again. Initially, I thought I would apply my experience in educational leadership to train other professors on online teaching methods and provide consulting services in this area. But I needed a break. I was heartbroken, and I had my own PTSD from leaving my dream behind.

During this time, my view on education shifted. It was in this tumultuous time that my father also passed away. I began reflecting a lot more on my past to find my path forward. I knew in my soul that I was born to be a teacher. I was not willing to give that up. However, I did not want to teach in the system that I felt betrayed by. I wanted to nurture kids and their learning the way I was. I wanted to be one of those exceptional educators who inspired students. I continued to research education, read, and rediscovered a teaching approach that I had written off years before.

After my experiences in academia and at the teacher's college, my perception of homeschooling underwent a drastic change. I started doing research. I met homeschool families. I was a quick convert! My husband and I decided to start a Great Books homeschool curriculum company. We would develop curricula that integrated literature and history, utilizing classics and primary sources for middle school and high school students. For the upper levels, we also added philosophy.

We developed an incredible curriculum over several years, but ultimately struggled to break into the homeschool curriculum market. Most homeschoolers do not want to be sold to. Many are religious and want that integrated into their curriculum. Those who are not spiritual tend to be ideologically aligned with the system I left behind. We lacked a paying audience for our curriculum, but we continued to create amazing units for tweens and teens for a few years.

It was also during this time that I began teaching independently. I taught homeschool kids and tutored children in public and private schools. I used our materials as the curriculum, augmented regular school lessons with additional instruction, and taught executive functioning skills. I still use all those things with the students I work with now.

During lockdowns, we relocated again. This time, we moved to Florida, where I tutored and consulted with small businesses to develop online courses. I also taught for one semester at a community college. I knew what I was getting myself into when I returned to teaching at a college. Yet I needed financial security more than I needed to stay away from academia. I also knew I could work part-time without getting too involved on the campus.

It was during this time that I became curious about money for the first time in my life. I will write more about this in a later chapter, but it led me to consider a move to El Salvador. Which is where I am writing this book. I am still teaching online, writing curriculum and grammar books, and authoring children's books to explain financial sovereignty in a way that children can understand.

This has been my journey, both in terms of education and finances until recently. This is the story that led me to write this book. My goal is to help people find their individual path to ownschooling. Whether it is for your own children, your relatives' children, your friends' kids, or even your educational pursuits, this book is designed to help you lead a sovereign life. How to put in the work and not outsource one's mind or money. To encourage everyone to put in the time and effort. To live with more intentionality. To have **proof of work**. To not live a complacent life. Rather, to be the leading actor in your own life story.

I grew up in amazing public schools. Private school was never even an option for me. I barely knew anyone growing up who attended private school. I lived in a different world. I did not have access to anything but public education, but thanks to my mom, I was able to get a good, solid education. I remained curious. Even when struggling financially and working as much as she could, she was still invested in my schooling. She asked questions, showed interest, and vetted schools to the best of her ability. By the way, this was the 1970s and 1980s, before the internet. She found ways to research by asking questions to the people she knew in the area. I think she even wrote to the Chamber of Commerce at one point. She was present. She was ownschooling.

For the past eight years, I have been a staunch homeschool advocate, telling everyone I could that they should homeschool in some form or another. I was inflexible on this message. I believe it is still the best education. However, after speaking with people and hearing their stories, realities, and reservations, I realized that it is not possible for everyone. Recently, I decided that I do not want to put pressure on parents to do something that was just not possible due to legalities or logistics.

From studying and teaching history and art history, it is easy to begin to see patterns in ideas. It is like a pendulum swinging in one direction and then swinging completely in the opposite way. You can see this in art quite easily: the Renaissance sought to portray humanity in its ideal state, followed by the Baroque, which was characterized by a dramatic contrast between light and dark. Then came the Rococo, characterized by its light, airy, and frivolous nature. After which came Romanticism, where man battled nature and the ideal was celebrated once again. Realism came next, a sometimes gritty take on the world. In stark contrast, Impressionism emerged, featuring light and breaking the established rules.

This pattern can also be seen in my own journey to creating the concept of ownschooling. I only knew public education. When I learned about homeschooling, I was completely turned off by the idea. I then advocated for both public schools and private schools.

Then, after a time, I became fully committed to homeschooling, and I began to strongly advocate against public and private schooling. It took all those strong ideas, my own experience with education from child to adulthood, as well as my unquenchable curiosity, to finally land in the middle, settled without strongly swinging one way or the other. Rather, to focus on the parents and family unit to determine their own path but with parents who are present, who advocate, and who are making informed decisions about their children's schooling.

I now realize that, similar to what my mom did for her kids, there are other paths to ensuring a child has the best possible education. I know that schooling is much different from what it was when I was in public school. As you read the upcoming chapters, you will learn more about the current state of education and its underlying causes. However, this does not mean that there are no good options for public schools. If you become an ownschooler, like my mom, you will do your due diligence. You will advocate for your child. You will raise them to be curious and to question ideas. You will protect them from the bad ideas prevalent in education and society.

This book gives you some of the tools to do just that. It will equip you with the knowledge of how, by being more informed about money and taking ownership of your financial freedom, you can provide security for your children. It will give you options for educating your children. As an American, I have more information on schooling in the United States, but I also include options for other areas. I provide you with tools to help you make decisions and determine what is best for you and your family.

Chapter 2: Toward Civilization

Man is by nature a social animal.

- Aristotle

It is a paradox as old as civilization itself: the yearning for freedom, and the simultaneous desire for security. Throughout history, societies have wrestled with the question: How much liberty are we willing to surrender in exchange for the promise of safety, order, and the comfort of not having to worry about life's uncertainties?

Consider the citizens of ancient Rome during the transition from the Republic to the Empire. The Roman Republic was a chaotic, vibrant, and often dangerous place. Political intrigue, economic uncertainty, and the constant threat of civil war made daily life unpredictable. When Augustus Caesar rose to power, he offered something new: the *Pax Romana*, a long period of relative peace and **stability**. In exchange, Romans ceded much of their political freedom. The Senate became a shadow of its former self, and the emperor's word was law. Many Romans accepted this bargain willingly, relieved to trade the burdens of civic participation and the anxiety of chaos for the security and predictability of imperial rule.

A similar dynamic played out in twentieth-century Europe. In the wake of World War I, Germany was a nation in crisis. It was economically devastated, politically fractured, and socially unstable. When Adolf Hitler and the Nazi Party promised order, prosperity, and national pride, many Germans embraced the regime. The price was steep: individual freedoms were crushed, dissent was silenced, and the state dictated every aspect of life. For some, the comfort of not having to think or worry about the future outweighed the loss of personal autonomy. At least, until the true cost became horrifyingly clear.

The tradeoff always persists. In the Soviet Union, the government provided cradle-to-grave security, guaranteeing jobs, housing, education, and healthcare. In return, citizens surrendered not only political freedoms but also the freedom to choose their own paths in life. The state decided where you worked, where you lived, even what you could read or say. For many, especially in the early years, this arrangement was attractive. The certainty of state support replaced the fear of unemployment or homelessness. Yet, beneath the surface, a quiet despair grew… a sense that life was safe, but not truly lived.

These examples illustrate the enduring dilemma: when a centralized authority assumes responsibility for our welfare, it often relieves us of the need to make difficult choices or worry about the future. But this relief comes at a cost. The freedom to think, to choose, to err, in essence, what it means to be fully human and what can be diminished or lost.

History teaches us that the comfort of chains is seductive. The promise of security can lull us into complacency, causing us to forget the value of independence. The challenge for every generation is to strike a balance: to build societies that protect the vulnerable without stifling the spirit of freedom that makes life meaningful.

This has always been a dilemma for humans. Even when they lived in small groups and roamed across the landscape, their primary activity was securing enough food to survive. To better understand this conflict, it is helpful to have some knowledge of how humans have organized themselves over time.

Anthropologists traditionally explain how humans structure themselves, going from bands to tribes, then chiefdoms, and finally states as a progression of increasing social complexity, shaped by changes in subsistence, political structures, economics, kinship systems, marriage practices, and mobility patterns. This framework, notably developed by Elman Service and Morton Fried, remains foundational in understanding how human societies have transformed over time. As societies evolved from nomadic groups to complex civilizations, technology and systems of exchange, including what counted as money, advanced in parallel with social, political, and economic systems.

For most of human history, people lived in **bands**, typically consisting of small, mobile groups typically consisting of twenty to one hundred individuals. These bands were composed of closely related families, bound together by kinship and marriage alliances. Their way of life was nomadic, as they moved frequently across the landscape in response to the seasonal availability of resources.

Subsistence in bands was based entirely on foraging, which included both hunting wild animals and gathering edible plants, fruits, nuts, and roots. The technology of bands was simple yet effective, comprising stone blades, wooden spears, digging sticks, and fire. Every member contributed to the group's survival, with tasks often divided by age and gender but without rigid specialization.

The political structure was highly egalitarian. There were no formal leaders; decisions were made collectively, often by consensus. Elders or particularly skilled individuals might offer guidance, but there was no permanent authority. Economics was based on direct sharing and **reciprocity**, where food and goods were distributed according to need, and there was little concept of personal wealth or property.

Kinship and marriage were central, serving as the main social glue. Marriages were often **exogamous**, meaning they occurred outside the group, thereby linking different bands and fostering cooperation. Because bands were always on the move, mobility was essential, and material possessions were few and portable.

Monetary systems were virtually nonexistent at this stage. Exchange was personal and immediate, with no need for standardized trade goods or proto-money. There was no need for a formal ledger or record of accounts. If a ledger was needed, it was held in the memory of the trading partners. Occasionally, valued items like rare shells or feathers might be exchanged as gifts, but these had more symbolic than economic **value**.

As populations increased and the environment changed, some human groups transitioned into distinct tribal groups. These societies were larger, typically ranging from a few hundred to several thousand people. **Tribes** often became semi-sedentary, establishing permanent or semi-permanent villages but still moving seasonally for farming or herding.

Subsistence strategies diversified. Many tribes practiced **horticulture**, or small-scale gardening, using simple tools such as hoes and digging sticks. Others became **pastoralists**, herding domesticated animals such as sheep, goats, or cattle. Some tribes continued to supplement their diets with hunting and gathering, especially in marginal environments.

Political organization in tribes was more structured than in bands, but still relatively egalitarian. Leadership roles, such as "big men" or headmen, were informal and based on personal qualities like charisma, generosity, or skill in hunting and organizing communal activities and feasts. Authority was persuasive rather than coercive, and councils of elders often played a key role in decision-making.

Economics in tribal societies began to involve the production of surplus food, which leaders could redistribute during feasts or ceremonies. **Barter** became more common, and certain items, including cattle, shells, beads, or salt, began to serve as proto-money, often valued for their rarity or utility. These objects were frequently used in ceremonial exchanges, **bridewealth** or **dowries**, or as symbols of social status.

Kinship and marriage remained the organizing principles of tribal life. Extended families, clans, or lineages provided the framework for social organization, and marriages were often arranged to strengthen alliances between groups. Mobility was reduced compared to bands, but tribes might still move seasonally, especially if they practiced **pastoralism,** where people would move with their herds of animals.

Technology advanced to include pottery, weaving, and more sophisticated tools for farming and herding. These innovations supported larger, more stable communities and enabled the accumulation of modest surpluses.

With further population growth and technological innovation, some societies developed into chiefdoms. These were much larger than tribes, often encompassing thousands to tens of thousands of people living in multiple villages or towns. **Chiefdoms** were characterized by sedentary lifestyles, with permanent settlements and regional integration under a single authority.

Subsistence was based on intensive horticulture or early agriculture, using plows, irrigation, and food storage facilities to support denser populations. Some chiefdoms also practiced large-scale pastoralism or fishing.

The political structure became centralized and hierarchical. Authority was vested in a hereditary chief, who ruled over ranked lineages and controlled the redistribution of surplus goods. The chief organized labor for large communal projects, managed trade, and sometimes led warfare or diplomacy. Society became ranked, with elite families enjoying higher status and privileges, often reinforced through strategic marriages among the ruling class.

Economics in chiefdoms was marked by the collection of tribute and the redistribution of goods. Surpluses were stored and managed by the chief, who used them to reward followers and maintain loyalty.

Luxury items, such as copper, rare shells, or precious stones, became important as symbols of power and were sometimes used as standardized trade goods. In some regions, items like shell beads (e.g., wampum or roanoke) functioned as currency, facilitating trade and reinforcing the chief's authority.

Kinship and marriage systems became more formalized and hierarchical. Chiefly lineages intermarried to consolidate power and maintain alliances. Inheritance of status and resources was strictly regulated, often passing through the elite families.

Mobility was minimal; people lived in permanent villages or towns, and the chief's authority extended over a defined territory. Technology continued to advance, with developments in metallurgy, pottery, textiles, and monumental architecture.

The most complex level of social organization is the state, which emerged with the advent of intensive agriculture and later, with the development of industry. States supported populations ranging from tens of thousands to millions, concentrated in cities, towns, and villages. These societies were fully sedentary, with urban centers acting as hubs of administration, trade, and culture.

Subsistence was based on highly productive agriculture, often involving irrigation, crop rotation, and animal husbandry. As states industrialized, manufacturing and commerce became increasingly important.

The political structure was highly centralized, featuring a formal government, bureaucracy, codified laws, and a monopoly on legitimate force (military and police). Rulers, including kings, emperors, or elected officials, governed vast territories, delegating authority to administrators and officials. Society was stratified into distinct social classes, with clear divisions between elites, commoners, and, in some cases, slaves.

Economics in state-level societies was complex and diversified. Taxation funded public works and the government. Markets and long-distance trade flourished, and monetary systems became sophisticated. **Commodity money** (metal ingots, standardized weights of grain or salt) gave way to coinage, which was durable, portable, and divisible. In some regions, such as ancient China, paper money was developed, revolutionizing commerce. Banks and financial institutions emerged to regulate currency and facilitate economic growth. The use of money became universal, enabling the accumulation and transfer of wealth across generations and regions.

Kinship and marriage played a less central role in state organization, as class, occupation, and citizenship became more important. Marriage laws were formalized, and social mobility, though possible, was often limited by class structures and legal codes.

Mobility patterns shifted dramatically. While most people lived in permanent settlements, states experienced significant rural-urban migration as people moved to cities in search of work and opportunities. Urbanization gave rise to new forms of social interaction and economic activity.

Technology has advanced rapidly in states. Innovations included writing, metallurgy, advanced tools and weapons, monumental architecture, and eventually, industrial machinery and digital technologies. These advances enabled states to coordinate large-scale projects, maintain armies, and administer complex societies.

In state-level societies, the sheer scale and complexity of social, economic, and political organization created fertile ground for the emergence of occupational specialization. As agriculture and industry became more productive, not everyone needed to focus on food production, freeing individuals to pursue specific crafts, trades, or professions.

The presence of a centralized government, formal bureaucracy, and urban centers necessitated the employment of administrators, scribes, soldiers, builders, merchants, artisans, and religious leaders, each with their own unique skills and roles. This division of labor enabled people to develop in-depth expertise in a single field, resulting in greater efficiency, innovation, and cultural advancement.

Specialization not only supported the functioning of the state by ensuring that trained professionals handled complex tasks, but it also contributed to social stratification, as certain occupations became associated with higher status or wealth. In essence, the complexity of state societies both demanded and enabled individuals to focus on one thing: driving progress and shaping the trajectory of civilization.

From small, mobile bands of foragers to the vast, urbanized states of the modern era, the story of human society is one of increasing complexity. This progression is not linear in terms of time or what is best for humanity. There are still people who live at each stage of complexity, a phenomenon that has been the case for nearly 10,000 years. This distinction is based solely on complexity, which does not equate to the idea that more complex equals a better way of living.

Each stage, from bands, tribes, chiefdoms, and states, brought new forms of subsistence, political organization, economic exchange, kinship, and mobility. At every level, technological innovation and the evolution of monetary systems played crucial roles, enabling larger populations, more intricate social structures, and ever-expanding networks of trade and communication. While the path was not strictly linear or universal, these broad patterns help us understand the remarkable diversity and adaptability of human cultures throughout history. Yet, as illustrated in this chapter, with increased complexity came greater centralization, resulting in a more centralized authority with increased specialization among its people. This, in turn, had an impact on one's earnings, or the compensation for their time and money spent.

Chapter 3: The Origins and Development of Money and Banking

Money is a needful and precious thing, and, when well used, a noble thing...

- Louisa May Alcott, Little Women

As illustrated in the previous chapter, the way humans organize themselves has become increasingly complex over time. And, as society became more entangled, so did the money. It is essential to understand money and its evolution if you want to live a financially independent life. A key element to living sovereignly is taking an active role in how you earn, spend, and save your money. Personally, I wish I had learned this at an early age. However, I am still grateful to have acquired this knowledge now.

As I mentioned in the first chapter, my relationship with money was not healthy for a long time. Although I was curious and loved history, I always gravitated towards cultural history, specifically the humanities, including philosophy, art, literature, and music. I had a gap in my learning, one that I repeatedly hear is common not only in the United States but around the world. That gap is what some might refer to as a lack of financial literacy. However, to be knowledgeable about money, one must learn how humans invented it and how they reinvented it, time and time again, seeking to get it right. Once you study money, you realize that one of the main issues lies in how it has been designed by various people over time, specifically that there is always someone or some entity that can control its value, distribution, and/or creation.

This chapter aims to fill the knowledge gaps for people in terms of understanding where the concept of money originated, how it was created, and how it eventually stopped working for users, only to be reimagined by someone else. (If you are curious to learn more, this chapter provides a summary of a much longer work on money that I, along with my husband, published in 2024, titled *Shells to Satoshi: The Story of Money and the Rise of Bitcoin.*)

The story of money is, at its heart, a story of human ingenuity and adaptation. Across time and cultures, societies have devised countless forms of money to meet the ever-changing demands of trade and cooperation. From seashells and cacao beans to stamped metal coins and electronic ledger entries, the various forms of money reflect the totality of human experience. Yet, despite these different types of currency, all money shares a common purpose: to facilitate exchange and overcome the limitations of barter. Barter, while simple in concept, is inherently inefficient. Money solves this problem by providing a universally accepted medium, enabling trade on a scale and with an efficiency that would otherwise be impossible.

The evolution of money is not merely a tale of economic necessity but also one of philosophical depth. Money's value is not **intrinsic**; it is derived from collective trust and mutual agreement about what constitutes value. This trust is the foundation upon which all monetary systems are based. It is what enables money to serve as a **store of value, a unit of account, and a medium of exchange,** meaning it holds its value over time, is used to measure value, and is accepted in exchange for goods and services between different parties, respectively. The reasons societies have chosen one form of money over another often reveal much about their values, priorities, and technological capabilities. Understanding these choices provides insight into the fundamental needs that money fulfills and the ways in which it shapes—and is, in turn, shaped by—human society.

Money's significance reaches far beyond economics. It is a manifestation of trust, a tool for organizing cooperation, and a symbol of progress. As societies grow more complex, the need for reliable systems of exchange becomes ever more pressing. Money enables the specialization of labor, the accumulation of capital, and the investment in future endeavors, all of which are essential for economic growth and cultural advancement. Through money, individuals and communities can coordinate their efforts, pool resources, and pursue collective goals that would be unattainable in its absence.

Moreover, money is a powerful symbol, embodying ideals of stability, continuity, and shared purpose. It links generations, connecting past achievements with future aspirations. The ways in which money is created, managed, and used reflect the values and priorities of a society, serving as a mirror for its hopes and anxieties. In this sense, money is not just a tool but a thread woven through the fabric of civilization itself.

Barter and the Beginnings of Trade

Trade and barter represent the earliest forms of economic exchange, rooted in the direct swap of goods and services between individuals or groups without the use of money as an intermediary. This system is founded on what economists call a **double coincidence of wants**, meaning that both parties must possess something the other desires and be willing to exchange it. The process is complex, as it requires each participant to clearly identify their own needs, recognize what they can offer, and then seek out someone whose needs and offerings align perfectly with theirs.

The search for a suitable trading partner is often challenging. Each party must first pinpoint what they lack and what surplus they can offer in return. Once a potential exchange partner is found, the negotiation of value begins. Unlike in modern markets, where prices are standardized and widely known, barter relies on direct negotiation. The value of goods is determined by supply and demand, the urgency of each party's needs, and subjective judgments about fairness.

The act of barter is typically a simultaneous exchange, with goods and services changing hands at the exact moment, thereby avoiding disputes over trust and delivery. This immediacy is necessary because, without a standardized medium like money, there is no simple way to record or enforce promises of future payment. The lack of standardization also means that barter is often limited to small, close-knit communities where trust is high, such as among family groups or kin networks. In such settings, social ties and mutual obligations can substitute for formal contracts, but as societies grow larger and more complex, the limitations of barter become increasingly apparent.

Barter's inefficiencies are numerous. The need for a double coincidence of wants makes finding trading partners a time-consuming and uncertain process. The absence of standardized values complicates negotiations and can lead to disputes or dissatisfaction. The perishability of goods and the challenge of storing value over time further restrict the scope of barter. These constraints limit the ability of individuals and communities to specialize, accumulate wealth, or plan for the future, all of which are essential for economic growth and the development of civilization.

Despite its challenges, barter played a foundational role in early human societies. It fostered cooperation, encouraged the development of negotiation skills, and laid the groundwork for more complex economic systems. The act of exchanging goods directly helped build social bonds and trust within communities, reinforcing social cohesion and mutual support. Over time, as populations grew and trade networks expanded, the limitations of barter spurred the search for more efficient means of exchange, ultimately leading to the invention of money.

The transition from barter to money marks a pivotal moment in human history. Money emerged as a solution to the problems inherent in barter, providing a common **standard of value**, a store of wealth, and a medium that could facilitate exchanges between strangers and across distances. This innovation enabled societies to overcome the constraints of direct exchange, paving the way for the rise of markets, the growth of cities, and the flourishing of trade on a global scale.

This era of trade and barter illustrates both the ingenuity and the limitations of early economic life. It reveals how the basic human drive to fulfill needs and cooperate with others catalyzed the creation of systems for exchange, negotiation, and value. These early practices laid the groundwork for the economic complexity and interconnectedness that characterize the modern world, underscoring the enduring significance of exchange, whether through barter, money, or more advanced systems, as the driving force behind human progress.

Mesopotamia and the Origins of Monetary Systems

Mesopotamia, often referred to as "the cradle of civilization," occupies a unique place in the history of civilization and money. Situated in the region that is modern-day Iraq, Syria, Jordan, and neighboring countries, Mesopotamia's fertile lands between the Tigris and Euphrates Rivers became the home of the earliest and most influential societies. These early peoples, seeking reliable sources of fresh water for drinking and farming, settled near rivers and developed sophisticated irrigation systems, which in turn supported larger, more complex communities. Over the centuries, the Sumerians, Babylonians, and Assyrians emerged as dominant cultures in this region, each contributing innovations that would shape the trajectory of the ancient world.

The Sumerians, flourishing from around 4100 to 1750 BC, exemplified the decentralized nature of early Mesopotamian civilization. Their society was composed of independent **city-states** such as Ur, Uruk, and Eridu, each governed by its own rulers and centered around its own religious and administrative life. Despite their shared language and cultural heritage, these city-states maintained a degree of political independence, managing their own economic and financial affairs. This autonomy fostered a climate of innovation, particularly in economic organization, as each city developed systems to facilitate trade and manage resources.

Agriculture formed the backbone of the Sumerian economy. The abundance provided by the Tigris and Euphrates allowed for the cultivation of staple crops, especially barley, which became a cornerstone of both sustenance and commerce. The Sumerians' ingenuity in irrigation technology transformed the landscape, enabling them to support larger populations and produce surplus crops for trade. Barley, in particular, was so integral to daily life and economic activity that it was used not only as food but also as a standard measure of value and a medium of exchange. This early form of commodity money enabled Sumerians to conduct both local and long-distance trade.

Trade networks extended far beyond the boundaries of the city-states, reaching into regions as distant as the Indus Valley, Egypt, and Anatolia. Sumerian merchants exchanged textiles, grains, metals, and other goods for resources not locally available, such as timber, stone, and precious stones. The complexity of these trade networks necessitated the development of **accounting systems**, record-keeping, and even early forms of contracts and receipts, as reflected in legal codes such as those attributed to Hammurabi. These innovations laid the foundation for the emergence of more formalized economic systems and the eventual rise of money as a universal medium of exchange.

The cumulative effect of these developments was the creation of a dynamic and interconnected economic system. By establishing standards of value, developing specialized professions, and expanding trade networks across vast distances, the peoples of Mesopotamia laid the groundwork for the economic revolutions that would follow.

Their achievements in agriculture, trade, and administration not only supported the growth of their own societies but also influenced neighboring cultures and subsequent civilizations.

The innovations of Mesopotamia, such as irrigation, standardized measures, written contracts, and the division of labor, represent some of the earliest steps toward the complex economic systems that define the modern world. These advances enabled the accumulation of surplus wealth, the rise of cities, and the flourishing of culture, science, and technology. In doing so, Mesopotamia earned its reputation as the birthplace of economic complexity, laying the groundwork for the development of money, markets, and the enduring legacy of civilization.

The Development of Coins

The emergence of coinage marked the next transformative moment in the history of money, fundamentally altering the way societies conducted trade and managed economic relationships. Prior to this development, **transactions** often relied on barter or the use of unstandardized **precious metals**, which posed challenges in terms of **portability**, perishability, and the lack of a universally recognized value. The introduction of coins, fashioned from gold and silver and stamped with marks indicating their weight, purity, and the authority of the issuing ruler, provided a solution to these issues. Coins offered a portable, durable, and standardized medium of exchange, enabling more efficient and reliable trade both locally and across long distances.

This innovation did not arise in isolation. The foundation for coinage was laid by earlier economic practices, particularly those of Mesopotamia. The Mesopotamians had already developed systems of weights and measures. They used precious metals for trade, creating a complex infrastructure that influenced neighboring regions. Their banking and financial practices, as well as their use of standardized weights, set important precedents for the concept of money as a medium of exchange. Yet, the purity and quality of the metals were difficult to verify. These practices not only facilitated the exchange of goods but also helped to unify diverse economic activities across vast areas, promoting the sharing of ideas and technologies.

The first true coins are attributed to the Lydians, who lived in what is now western Turkey between 1180 and 547 BCE. The Lydians developed **electrum** coins, made from a naturally occurring alloy of gold and silver, stamped with official symbols to certify their authenticity and value. This marked a significant shift from the earlier use of precious metals by weight to the use of standardized, **state-backed currency**. The combination of inherent material value and official validation made coins a trusted and widely accepted form of money, greatly enhancing the efficiency of trade.

Lydia's geographic position on the western edge of Anatolia placed it at the crossroads of major trade routes connecting the Greek city-states of the Aegean coast with the broader Mediterranean world. Although the Lydians were not Greek, their proximity to Greek communities and their robust commercial activity fostered extensive interactions. These exchanges included not only goods but also cultural practices, language, and political alliances. The Lydians' adoption and development of coinage quickly influenced their neighbors, especially the Greeks, who soon began minting their own coins. This diffusion of coinage technology helped to unify economic practices across the region and contributed to the growth of interconnected markets.

Coinage's impact extended far beyond the boundaries of Lydia and the Greek world. The standardization and official validation of coins facilitated not only the exchange of goods but also the movement of people, ideas, and technologies. Traders, explorers, and colonists carried coins and the practices associated with them across the Mediterranean and into the Black Sea, forging new connections and expanding the reach of ancient economies. The spread of coinage thus played a crucial role in the development of complex societies, enabling the rise of markets, the accumulation of capital, and the flourishing of urban centers.

Advancements of Roman Money and Banking

The next innovation in monetary history came from another soon-to-be powerful Mediterranean civilization: Rome. The origins of Roman civilization can be traced back to a small agrarian society that gradually unified neighboring tribes during the Roman Kingdom (625–510 BCE) and continued to expand under the Roman Republic (510–31 BCE). The unification process was aided by a shared language, governance, and a developing monetary system, which helped consolidate Rome's growing territory. Early Roman money consisted of unwrought bronze lumps and ingots, which eventually gave way to cast and then struck bronze coins. These coins were divided into units, such as the *as*, with twelve *as* units equaling one Roman ounce. The exposure to Greek coinage during the Punic Wars prompted Rome to adopt silver coinage, including the denarius, which would become the backbone of Roman commerce.

The **denarius**, introduced in the late third century BCE, quickly became the standard currency for trade across the empire. Its widespread acceptance unified the Roman economy, allowing merchants and citizens to conduct business efficiently from Britain to Egypt. The state controlled coin production, ensuring consistency in weight, purity, and imagery, typically featuring deities or important leaders, which fostered trust and stability in the currency. Gold *aurei* facilitated large transactions, while bronze and copper coins served the daily needs of the people. The state's ability to mint coins from precious metals, especially silver from Spanish mines acquired after the Punic Wars, ensured a steady supply of currency and underpinned the empire's economic might.

The sophistication of its banking system matched the efficiency and reliability of Roman coinage. Early Roman banking began with simple money-changing and the issuance of receipts, but it rapidly evolved to meet the demands of a sprawling commercial empire. By the third century BCE, professional bankers, known as *argentarii*, emerged, offering deposit, lending, and money-changing services.

These bankers played a critical role in facilitating trade, providing **credit**, and supporting both local and long-distance commerce. The state also appointed public bankers, or *mensarii*, to manage public finances and provide banking services to citizens.

Roman banking practices included many features recognizable today, such as deposit-taking, lending with **interest**, and the use of written contracts and receipts. During this time, bankers lent out a portion of their deposits to earn interest, and systems were implemented to protect depositors who wished to withdraw their funds. Associations of bankers, or *societates argentariae*, pooled resources and bore joint liability for deposits, minimizing fraud and protecting depositors' interests. Roman law required meticulous record-keeping, and bankers' account books could serve as legal evidence in court disputes.

The expansion of trade routes and the integration of diverse economies necessitated further innovation. Merchants could secure loans in one port and repay them in another, facilitating long-distance trade across the Mediterranean. The standardized currency and banking infrastructure enabled efficient tax collection, payment of military wages, and funding of public works, including roads, bridges, and ports. Taxes and tariffs on goods moving through the empire generated revenue that supported these projects and the Roman navy, which in turn protected trade routes and ensured the smooth flow of commerce.

Social dynamics also shaped Roman banking. Initially, senators and their families dominated banking. Still, legislation in 218 BCE (*lex Claudia de senatoribus*) barred them from commercial activities, shifting financial power to the equestrian class (*equites*). The *equites*, through their control of lucrative government contracts and tax collection (*publicani*), amassed significant wealth and influence. Their financial activities sometimes sparked tension with the senatorial elite, prompting the introduction of new laws to regulate their power in the provinces.

Later, during the Empire, political power and financial activities were deeply intertwined. Emperors such as Augustus and Tiberius used financial strategies to stabilize the economy, fund public works, and secure political loyalty. Augustus invested his personal wealth and encouraged elite participation in urban development, strengthening both the city and his own authority. Tiberius, facing a financial crisis in AD 33, intervened directly by lending large sums from the imperial treasury to alleviate credit shortages, illustrating how rulers could use state resources for economic and political objectives. Senators and elites also engaged in money lending and commercial ventures, leveraging their wealth for influence and using patronage networks to maintain support among the populace and other power brokers.

Nevertheless, despite the sophistication of Roman banking and currency, not all transactions in the empire were conducted using money. Barter persisted, especially in rural areas, but the widespread acceptance of coinage and the development of banking services created a highly integrated and monetized economy. The Roman monetary system became a cornerstone of imperial power, supporting economic growth, administrative cohesion, and the stability of the empire for a few centuries.

As the Empire evolved, so did its financial systems and regulations. Late Empire emperors, such as Diocletian and Constantine, introduced currency reforms, most notably the gold solidus, to combat **inflation** and restore stability after periods of rampant **debasement** and economic crisis. The state increasingly regulated banking, lending, and commercial activities, as seen in the Theodosian Code and Justinian's Digest, which set legal standards for interest, property rights, and fiduciary transactions. These legal frameworks not only protected creditors and debtors but also reflected broader efforts to ensure economic stability and fairness. Despite the eventual division and fall of the Western Empire, Roman innovations in monetary policy, legal regulation, and the integration of finance with governance left a lasting legacy that influenced both Byzantine and later European banking systems.

The Invention of Paper Money

A few hundred years later, the Chinese Dynasties further impacted the way people used money. The rise of the Silk Road marked a pivotal moment in the evolution of money and commerce, creating a vast network of overland trade routes that connected the East and West. Emerging around the second century BCE, the Silk Road facilitated the movement of silk from China to Central Asia, the Middle East, Africa, and Europe, but its impact extended far beyond the exchange of a single commodity. The Silk Road served as a conduit for a diverse array of goods, including spices, textiles, precious metals, and jewels, as well as a channel for the exchange of ideas, cultures, religions, and technologies. This network played a critical role in shaping the societies and economies along its routes, fostering a unique blend of cultural exchange with enduring global consequences.

The origins of the Silk Road can be traced to the Han Dynasty (206 BC to AD 220), when Emperor Wu sought to establish diplomatic and commercial ties with Western regions to counter threats from the Xiongnu nomads. The mission of Zhang Qian, a Han envoy, played a crucial role in this process. Although Zhang Qian was initially captured, he eventually returned to China with valuable intelligence about lands beyond the empire's borders. His journey marked the beginning of the Silk Road as a primary conduit for the exchange of goods, knowledge, and culture between the East and the West.

Travel along the Silk Road was fraught with challenges. Merchants and caravans faced daunting terrain, including vast deserts and imposing mountains, as well as the constant threat of bandits. The journey was further complicated by harsh weather conditions and the fragmented political landscape, with different segments of the route controlled by various states and tribes. Political instability and shifting alliances could disrupt trade, while the need for protection against theft and extortion added to the cost and complexity of long-distance commerce. Traders often had to pay tolls or negotiate with local rulers to secure safe passage, and the risk of loss was ever-present.

Despite these obstacles, the Silk Road thrived as a commercial and cultural lifeline. The system of relay trade, in which goods changed hands multiple times along the route, allowed merchants to specialize in shorter segments of the journey, reducing their exposure to risk. This relay system also enabled the movement of goods over great distances, with silk, spices, and other valuable items eventually reaching markets thousands of miles from their origins. The Silk Road's influence was not limited to material goods; it also facilitated the spread of religions such as Buddhism, technological innovations like papermaking and gunpowder, and artistic styles that blended Eastern and Western traditions.

One of the most significant innovations to emerge from China during this era was the invention of paper. The development of paper money in China was a response to the practical challenges faced by merchants along the bustling Silk Road during the Tang (618–907) and Song (960–1279)dynasties. As trade flourished, carrying heavy metal coins over long distances became risky and cumbersome. This prompted the innovation of "flying money" during the Tang Dynasty, which were paper receipts issued by deposit houses that could be exchanged for coins or goods. This early form of currency allowed merchants to transfer value safely and efficiently, laying the groundwork for more sophisticated banking practices.

The Song Dynasty advanced this innovation by officially issuing the world's first government-backed paper currency, known as jiaozi. The Song government introduced anti-counterfeiting measures and established offices to manage the issuance and redemption of paper money, creating a rudimentary **central banking system**. However, the new currency faced challenges such as regional acceptance, **counterfeiting**, and inflation caused by over-issuance.

Despite these issues, the use of paper money spread and evolved, reaching a new level under the Yuan Dynasty(1271–1368), when Kublai Khan unified the currency system across China and ensured its acceptance throughout the empire. Marco Polo's accounts of China's paper money system fascinated Europeans and inspired the later adoption of **fiat money** in the West. Furthermore, the deposit houses influenced banking in Europe, particularly in Italy.

Banking Advancements in Renaissance Italy

The Medici, originally wool traders, leveraged their commercial acumen and extensive connections to establish the Medici Bank in Florence (1397–1494). Their success was rooted in their ability to serve the financial needs of powerful institutions, including the Catholic Church and various ruling entities. By providing services such as managing church finances and facilitating the transfer of funds for powerful clients, the Medici were able to rapidly expand their influence. Their approach signaled a shift from simple money-changing and lending to a more sophisticated model that included the accumulation and lending of capital in forms that would be recognized and trusted across Europe.

Among the Medici's most significant contributions was the creation of a banking network that spanned major European trade centers. This network was made possible by innovations such as **double-entry bookkeeping**, which allowed for more accurate and transparent accounting, and the development of standardized banking contracts. Through their innovative accounting practices, they also established a standard for determining **risk** in lending money. These advances not only improved the efficiency of financial transactions but also laid the groundwork for the emergence of modern credit markets and the international movement of capital.

Giovanni di Bicci de' Medici (c. 1360–1429) founded the Medici Bank in the late fourteenth century, and its relocation to Florence marked the start of a banking empire that would last for nearly a century. One of the Medici's key strategies was the establishment of branches in major commercial cities throughout Italy and beyond. These branches, while operating independently in terms of their day-to-day financial management, remained closely linked through shared ownership and coordinated business practices. The Medici carefully chose locations for their branches, favoring cities that were vibrant centers of commerce, culture, and political power, such as Bruges, London, and Milan. These cities offered access to large and diverse client bases, including merchants, monarchs, and religious institutions.

The Medici's organizational structure was highly advanced for its time. They relied on a network of trusted family members, loyal employees, and agents to manage their far-reaching operations. This structure allowed the Medici to maintain tight control over their business while also adapting to local conditions and regulations. Their approach to risk management was equally innovative. By spreading their assets and liabilities across multiple branches and jurisdictions, they minimized the impact of local economic or political disruptions.

Another hallmark of the Medici's banking model was their ability to offer a wide range of financial services. In addition to traditional lending and deposit-taking, the Medici facilitated international payments, managed currency exchange, and handled the transfer of funds for clients engaged in trade, diplomacy, or religious affairs. Their willingness to serve as financial intermediaries for the Catholic Church and other powerful clients further enhanced their reputation and influence.

Throughout history, the evolution of money, from barter and early commodity exchange to coins, paper currency, and the rise of banking, has mirrored the increasing complexity of human society and our persistent drive to solve the challenges of trust, value, and exchange. Each innovation, whether in Mesopotamia, Rome, China, or Renaissance Italy, not only enabled greater economic growth and interconnectedness but also revealed recurring issues of power, stability, and control over money's creation and distribution. As we move forward, these enduring themes set the stage for the next chapter: the rise of central banking and the foundations of modern economic systems, where the centralization of monetary authority would fundamentally reshape global finance and our understanding of economic sovereignty.

Chapter 4: Money in the Modern Era

This Act [Federal Reserve Act of 1913] establishes the most gigantic trust on earth. When the President signs this bill, the invisible government by the Monetary Power will be legalized. The people may not know it immediately, but the day of reckoning is only a few years removed... The worst legislative crime of the ages.

- Charles Lindburgh Sr. (R-MN, on the Federal Reserve Act)

The Medici's success inspired other banking families and institutions across Europe, leading to the emergence of a more integrated and competitive financial landscape. Cities like Bruges and London became important centers of banking activity, attracting talent and capital from across the continent. Over time, the innovations pioneered by the Medici and their contemporaries, such as double-entry bookkeeping, the use of bills of exchange, and the development of branch banking, became standard practices that shaped the evolution of banking for centuries to come.

The Beginning of Central Banking

The legacy of Renaissance banking culminated in the establishment of national banks, such as Sweden's Riksbank (founded 1668), which was founded in the seventeenth century and is recognized as the world's oldest central bank. The transition from private banking dynasties, such as the Medici, to state-regulated central banking marked a pivotal change in financial history. This shift was driven by the belief that political authorities could provide a more structured and regulated approach to managing a nation's economic and financial affairs. By aligning closely with the Swedish Riksdag, the Riksbank's policies became directly connected to Sweden's governance, creating a strong link between government decision-making and the management of national finances.

A key innovation of the Riksbank was its authority to issue currency, transferring control over the money supply from private hands to a centralized public institution. This allowed the government to finance its activities independently of private lenders and to manage the economy without interference. The Riksbank could also influence economic conditions by managing credit and interest rates, further embedding the bank's role in national economic policy. This model set a precedent for modern central banking by demonstrating how state-backed monetary authority could stabilize and guide a country's financial system.

One key feature of central banking is the **fractional reserve system**. Fractional reserve banking is a financial system in which banks keep only a portion of their depositors' money in reserve, lending out the rest to borrowers. This practice enables banks to expand the money supply and stimulate economic activity, although it can introduce risks if too many depositors demand their funds simultaneously. The origins of fractional reserve banking can be traced back to ancient civilizations, where early forms of banking existed, such as in Mesopotamia and Rome.

However, the system took a more recognizable shape in the early modern period, particularly with goldsmiths in the 17th century who issued receipts for stored gold, using unclaimed reserves to make loans. The formal development of the system continued with the creation of central banks, such as the Riksbank and the Bank of

England in 1694, laying the foundation for the widespread adoption of fractional reserve banking seen today.

Global Trade Begins

The expansion of global trade during this era further transformed the world's economic landscape, ushering in new systems of finance, commerce, and cross-cultural exchange. As banking practices evolved in Europe, the rise of international trade networks demanded even more sophisticated monetary solutions. The emergence of powerful trading companies, most notably the British East India Company, marked a decisive shift.

Founded in 1600 under a royal charter from Queen Elizabeth I (1533–1603), the East India Company pioneered the joint-stock model, allowing investors to pool resources and share both risks and rewards. This innovation allowed individuals to invest in ventures without fear of losing their entire investment if a project failed, as liability was limited to the amount invested. Such a structure not only encouraged broader participation in trade but also made it easier for governments and private financiers to raise the vast sums needed for expansive overseas enterprises.

Competing for dominance in the lucrative spice trade of Southeast Asia, the British sought to outmaneuver established Dutch and Portuguese interests. The East India Company's model quickly proved successful and was emulated by other European powers. By the eighteenth century, trading companies from Britain, Spain, Portugal, France, and the Netherlands had established extensive routes across the Americas, Africa, and Asia. This era of exploration and competition brought a flood of new goods, such as spices, sugar, tobacco, tea, and coffee, into European markets, dramatically reshaping tastes, consumption patterns, and economies on both sides of the globe.

The complexity of these trade networks necessitated the development of new forms of money and financial instruments. Gold and silver emerged as the backbone of international commerce, valued for their portability, durability, and universal acceptance. The dual use of both metals, however, introduced complications. Exchange rates between gold and silver fluctuated, and the value of coins could vary from one country to another, making it difficult to settle accounts and price goods consistently. To address this, merchants and bankers developed bills of sale and other forms of credit, allowing transactions to be conducted without the immediate exchange of physical currency. These instruments enabled trade to flourish even in the absence of a universally accepted coinage.

Although **bills of sale** and credit served as a stopgap, the proliferation of global trade routes led to the need for a single, reliable standard of value. While coins minted from gold and silver circulated widely, their actual content and worth could differ depending on the issuing authority. This lack of standardization created opportunities for arbitrage and fraud, but it also spurred efforts to harmonize currency systems. The challenge of reconciling different coinages and values was not fully resolved until the emergence of national banks and the eventual adoption of paper money and standardized currency systems in the centuries to follow.

The rise of joint-stock companies and the expansion of global trade also had profound social and economic consequences. Wealth accumulated in the hands of investors, merchants, and financiers, fueling the growth of cities and the emergence of new social classes. The flow of goods, people, and ideas across continents fostered unprecedented cultural exchange, but it also intensified competition and conflict as European powers vied for control of trade routes and colonial territories. The fortunes of nations increasingly depended on their ability to finance and protect overseas ventures, leading to the development of powerful navies and the establishment of trading posts and colonies around the world.

At the heart of this transformation was the interplay between risk and reward. The joint-stock model democratized investment, spreading risk across many participants and enabling ventures of previously unimaginable scale. The use of gold and silver as international currency provided a foundation for trust and stability, even as the practical challenges of valuation and exchange persisted. The creation of new financial instruments and institutions reflected the growing complexity of the global economy, as merchants and bankers devised ever more ingenious ways to facilitate trade, manage risk, and move capital across borders.

The legacy of this era endures in the modern global economy. The innovations in finance, commerce, and organizational structure that emerged during the Age of Spices and global trade laid the groundwork for today's multinational corporations, international banking systems, and interconnected markets. This played out in the late nineteenth and early twentieth centuries as central banks assumed an increasingly influential role in shaping national economies and managing monetary policy.

The responsibilities of central banks expanded to include the regulation of national currencies and oversight of the banking sector, particularly as governments sought new ways to finance large-scale endeavors such as wars. The authority of central banks to expand the money supply enabled governments to respond to extraordinary circumstances, providing **liquidity** for both domestic initiatives and military campaigns. This power to regulate money supply became critical in efforts to combat inflation and deflation, as well as to ensure that governments could pursue their policies regardless of whether the nation was at peace or engaged in conflict.

The Importance of Gold

Despite the growing intervention of central banks and the evolving relationship between bankers and politicians, monetary systems of this era continued to rely on gold or silver as a foundation. Bank notes issued by central banks were typically redeemable for precious metals, which provided a sense of security and trust in the currency. The **gold standard**, in particular, became the linchpin of the international monetary system. Under this system, the value of a nation's currency was directly tied to a specific quantity of gold, ensuring stability and predictability in exchange rates and fostering confidence among international traders and investors.

Yet, it is the period from 1900 to 1913 that particularly stands out as a defining era for global monetary policy. During these years, adherence to the gold standard was nearly universal among major economies. This era coincided with rapid industrialization, burgeoning international trade, and the early stages of financial globalization. The gold standard's promise of stability was both its greatest strength and its most significant challenge. While it facilitated economic growth and international cooperation, it also imposed rigid constraints on monetary policy. Central banks could not easily expand the money supply without corresponding increases in gold **reserves**, making it difficult to respond flexibly to economic shocks or the demands of wartime spending.

Gold's unique properties: its **divisibility**, durability, and universal acceptance, made it an ideal medium for supporting the global economy during the industrial age. It served as a portable and immutable store of value, enabling large-scale trade and investment across borders. Yet, the very qualities that made gold so valuable also introduced vulnerabilities. The risk of counterfeiting, though limited by gold's physical properties, was always present. Moreover, the reliance on gold reserves meant that monetary expansion was inherently limited, which could constrain economic growth and complicate responses to crises.

It was during this era, specifically in 1910, that a secret meeting took place on Jekyll Island, Georgia. Here, a group of the most influential bankers and financiers in the United States gathered to draft a plan for a central banking system. Initiated by Senator Nelson Aldrich, the meeting included key figures such as Abraham Piatt Andrew (Assistant Secretary of the U.S. Treasury), Henry P. Davison (J.P. Morgan Company), Charles D. Norton (First National Bank of New York), Benjamin Strong (Bankers Trust Company), Frank A. Vanderlip (National City Bank of New York), and Paul M. Warburg (Kuhn, Loeb & Company). The utmost secrecy surrounded the event: participants traveled under the cover of darkness, used code names, and even the servants were kept unaware of their identities. The group's goal was to address the recurring financial panics and instability in the U.S. by designing a centralized and scientific approach to currency and banking, which would later become the Federal Reserve System.

The secrecy and exclusivity of the Jekyll Island meeting fueled decades of speculation and intrigue, with the story only coming to light years later. The participants believed that a central bank could prevent the cycles of booms and busts by managing the money supply and acting as a **lender of last resort**. Paul Warburg, in particular, was regarded as the intellectual architect who linked American banking reform to European central banking practices. The plan they developed laid the foundation for the **Federal Reserve Act**, fundamentally transforming the U.S. financial system by shifting control over monetary policy from private banking interests to a government-regulated central authority.

The early twentieth century was marked by wars, and the period in between resulted in a global financial crisis. The Great Depression, which began in 1929, quickly spread from the United States to the rest of the world, resulting in a dramatic decline in international trade, industrial production, and employment. Britain initially fared better due to cautious financial practices but eventually abandoned the gold standard to make exports more competitive. France, by holding onto the gold standard longer, suffered a deeper economic contraction.

At the same time, countries like Japan and those in Latin America faced severe recessions as exports plummeted and commodity prices collapsed. The interconnectedness of global economies meant that protectionist measures, such as the U.S. Smoot-Hawley Tariff, only deepened the crisis. Recovery was slow and uneven, and the Depression's economic and social turmoil contributed to the rise of authoritarian regimes, setting the stage for World War II.

World War II fundamentally reshaped the global economic landscape. Wartime production spurred unprecedented industrial growth, especially in the United States, which emerged from the conflict as a leading economic power and creditor nation. The war effort accelerated technological advancements, leading to the destruction and subsequent reconstruction of infrastructure in Europe and Asia. Postwar recovery was financed through a combination of international aid, such as the Marshall Plan, and domestic borrowing.

A New Era

In July 1944, as World War II drew to a close, representatives from forty-four countries convened in Bretton Woods, New Hampshire, to design a new international economic order that would promote stability and prevent the financial turmoil that had contributed to the war. The conference centered on two competing proposals: British economist John Maynard Keynes advocated for a global central bank called the Clearing Union, which would issue an international currency (the "bancor") and allow countries to temporarily overdraw to manage trade imbalances, thus encouraging global economic balance and discouraging protectionism. In contrast, the American plan, led by Harry Dexter White, proposed creating the International Monetary Fund (IMF) and the World Bank, with a focus on providing more limited financial support and stricter rules for member contributions and borrowing.

Ultimately, the delegates compromised by establishing both the IMF and the World Bank. These institutions were designed to provide financial stability, facilitate international monetary cooperation, and support postwar reconstruction and development. However, the final agreement reflected more of the American vision, with the IMF overseeing currency stability and the World Bank providing development loans, rather than adopting Keynes's broader Clearing Union concept or the bancor as a global currency.

The Bretton Woods plan also impacted the international monetary system by pegging the U.S. dollar to gold at a fixed rate of $35 per ounce. Other countries then pegged their currencies to the dollar, making it the anchor of global exchange rates. By linking other currencies to the dollar and making the dollar directly convertible to gold for foreign governments and central banks, the plan elevated the U.S. dollar to the status of the **world's reserve currency**. Previously, the British Pound Sterling had been the dominant reserve currency for the previous two centuries. This change meant that central banks around the world held large reserves of dollars to facilitate international trade and maintain currency stability, reinforcing the dollar's central role in the global financial system. As a result, the U.S. dollar became the main medium for international payments, trade, and finance, a role it continues to play today.

The **Bretton Woods Agreement** thus laid the foundation for the postwar international financial system, emphasizing stable exchange rates and economic cooperation while avoiding the extremes of economic nationalism that had destabilized the prewar world. This continued through the mid-twentieth century. However, during the early 1970s, another shakeup occurred in the global monetary system.

Fiat Money Rules

It was in 1971 that the next watershed moment in the history of money occurred, as the world shifted from a system anchored in gold to one based entirely on fiat currency. Mounting pressures from **Keynesian economic** policies, the Bretton Woods framework, and global imbalances in trade and reserves placed the U.S. dollar, and by extension, the international monetary order, under severe strain. Foreign governments, wary of the dollar's stability, increasingly converted their U.S. dollar reserves into gold, further depleting American gold reserves and eroding global confidence in the dollar's value. The interconnected nature of the postwar monetary system meant that decisions made in Washington reverberated throughout the world, binding the fate of other nations' currencies to the policies of the United States.

Amid this climate of uncertainty, another secretive and pivotal meeting took place. This time it was at the presidential retreat, Camp David. In August 1971, President Richard Nixon, accompanied by key advisors and economic strategists, convened a secret gathering reminiscent of earlier historic financial summits. Among those present were Treasury Secretary John Connally, Federal Reserve Chairman Arthur Burns, and future Fed Chairman Paul Volcker, along with a select group of Nixon's inner circle. After intense deliberations, Nixon emerged to announce a momentous policy shift: the suspension of the dollar's convertibility into gold. This decision, which would become known as the "Nixon Shock," effectively dismantled the Bretton Woods system and ushered in the era of floating exchange rates and fiat money.

The Nixon administration's move had immediate and far-reaching consequences. By severing the link between the dollar and gold, the United States established a new precedent: the value of money would henceforth rest not on precious metals, but on government decree and the collective trust of its users. Other nations, whose currencies were pegged to the dollar, quickly followed suit. The world entered a new monetary era in which exchange rates could fluctuate freely. Governments were also no longer bound by the constraints of gold reserves. This transition granted policymakers greater flexibility to respond to economic crises, but it also introduced new risks, such as inflation, currency speculation, and the potential for competitive devaluations.

The abandonment of the gold standard was not merely a technical adjustment; it signaled a profound transformation in the philosophy and mechanics of global finance. For much of the twentieth century, the gold standard had provided a sense of discipline and predictability, anchoring the value of money to a tangible asset and limiting the ability of governments to expand the money supply at will. The system's collapse, accelerated by the fiscal pressures of the Vietnam War and the costs of maintaining a far-reaching military and social agenda, revealed the limitations of tying economic growth to finite gold reserves.

In the aftermath of the Nixon Shock, the world's major economies adapted to the new reality of fiat currency. Countries that had previously pegged their currencies to the dollar, including the United

Kingdom, France, Germany, Italy, and Japan, shifted to **floating exchange rates**, allowing market forces to determine the value of their currencies. This newfound flexibility enabled governments to pursue more independent monetary policies, but it also required a greater degree of international coordination and oversight to prevent destabilizing swings in currency values.

The era of fiat money fundamentally altered the relationship between governments, central banks, and the public. With the power to create money no longer constrained by gold reserves, central banks assumed a central role in managing inflation, employment, and economic growth. At the same time, the system's reliance on trust and prudent governance became more critical than ever, as the value of money now depended entirely on confidence in the institutions that issued it.

The move to fiat currency marked the culmination of a process that had begun decades earlier, as nations gradually loosened their ties to gold in response to the demands of war, reconstruction, and global trade. Central banking and the widespread adoption of fiat money have fundamentally altered the relationship between governments, markets, and individuals, introducing new vulnerabilities and reshaping the notion of economic freedom.

The intellectual foundation of modern central banking, influenced heavily by Keynesian theory, has provided governments with the rationale to intervene in markets through interest rate manipulation, monetary expansion, and regulatory oversight. While these interventions are often justified as necessary for economic stability or growth, they have also led to significant consequences for individuals, businesses, and entire nations.

The power of central banks to print money and manipulate interest rates gives them an outsized influence over the value of currency and the broader economy. When central authorities alter the money supply, they can inadvertently or deliberately erode the purchasing power of savings and wages, effectively confiscating wealth from those who rely on money as a store of value. This process, described by Milton Friedman as "inflation is taxation without legislation," highlights how monetary policy can serve as a covert means of transferring resources from the public to the state. Historical instances in countries such as the U.S., Australia, Cyprus, Greece, India, Venezuela, Zimbabwe, and Canada reveal how government actions, whether through currency **devaluation**, capital controls, or outright confiscation, can undermine trust in money and destabilize individual lives.

The consequences of these policies are not limited to abstract economic indicators; they touch the daily reality of people who depend on money to measure the value of their labor and secure their future. When money ceases to function as a reliable store of value, its primary role as a medium of exchange for real worth is compromised. Individuals lose the ability to plan, save, and invest with confidence, as their financial destiny becomes subject to the unpredictable decisions of policymakers. This erosion of control strikes hardest at those who have the most to lose: ordinary citizens who have worked, saved, and invested in good faith.

Beyond monetary manipulation, governments frequently impose regulations that restrict the movement and use of money. Laws may limit the amount of currency that can be taken out of a country, require disclosure of foreign investments, or regulate currency exchange. These controls, often justified as measures to prevent money laundering or protect economic stability, can also serve as tools for restricting individual freedom and controlling private wealth. The ability of individuals to move their assets, invest abroad, or even hold foreign currency is circumscribed by a web of legal and regulatory barriers, making financial autonomy increasingly elusive.

The regulatory environment extends to the banking sector, where institutions are compelled to report transactions, comply with anti-money laundering directives, and adhere to capital controls. These requirements, while designed to safeguard the financial system, also create a landscape where personal financial privacy is diminished and the autonomy of individuals is further eroded. The interplay between central banks, regulatory agencies, and governments thus creates a system in which economic power is concentrated at the top, and the freedom of individuals to manage their own resources is persistently challenged.

At its core, the modern system of fiat money and centralized monetary control raises fundamental questions about freedom, trust, and the government's proper role in the economy. When individuals cannot fully control the value of their own money or the fruits of their labor, the promise of economic liberty is compromised. The precarious path of monetary control, shaped by the decisions of central bankers and policymakers, continues to define the boundaries of financial freedom and the lived experience of people in an interconnected world.

Chapter 5: Bitcoin Fixes This

Bitcoin is the first completely decentralized transnational platform for exchanging value. It has no borders. It does not care whether you like the transaction or not. It is entirely based on mathematical verifiability. It is the Internet, unleashed, unvarnished, unpolished, and uncensorable.

- Andreas Antonopoulos

The complexity of the modern fiat system discourages many of its users from taking the time to understand it. I was one of these people up until relatively recently. However, expanding my curiosity to understand money, its history, and how it can be easily manipulated by those in power has led me to think in terms of a **low time preference**, or being a long-term thinker when it comes to money. (The opposite is having a **high time preference**, where one is more concerned with the present time without concern for the future.) This realization came about as I decided to learn more earnestly about **Bitcoin**.

I first heard of Bitcoin just a few years after its inception. However, it would take over a decade before I developed a curiosity for Bitcoin and did a deep dive into truly understanding money. We all have our own journey when it comes to finding happiness, living a life with intention, and being sovereign. In the modern world, it is incredibly challenging. A few years ago, I was faced with the decision of what I should do in terms of my happiness and safety. I was feeling increasingly unsafe in the United States and also betrayed by the country's political and economic climate. I was spinning my wheels, unable to make financial progress or find my place in education. I examined my professional and geographic options.

This led to my moving to El Salvador in 2023. My investigations into Bitcoin and money prompted me to consider living in Bitcoin Country. After doing much research and talking with expats who had already made the move, I knew I would feel safer in my day-to-day life. I also had some options for my professional life: I considered starting a school for expats or building another curriculum company for homeschoolers. But ultimately, I felt I had to leave the tumultuous United States. I, like many others, was still struggling through post-lockdown when both professionally and personally, I had to reinvent myself once again. Two years later, I am finally feeling like I have a path, and I am optimistic about my future. As Bitcoin's global adoption continues to grow, I am also optimistic about the world's future direction.

There is a saying amongst the Bitcoin community that we get Bitcoin at the price we deserve. I think this is true to some extent. I chose to share my story to encourage others to be curious about money. Understand that even though you earn it, you cannot control the value it holds in the long term. During the lockdowns, more money was printed than had ever been printed before. This automatically devalued the amount in your bank account. If you are not sure how this happens, keep reading. I had to learn it myself. It was not easy. In fact, I am still learning. But, as with my education, I put in the work. I studied, I found my passion, and I seek to share that with others, just as I do with teaching writing, reading, and the humanities.

With fiat money, we say we have money. With Bitcoin, we can say we own our money. This is a case of a centralized versus a decentralized system. You have no say in how the value of your time and energy is rewarded in a centralized system. The value of money can be stripped instantly. If you do not believe that, just look at Venezuela, Cyprus, and Zimbabwe. It is time to understand the fundamental flaws in fiat currency and learn how to protect yourself and your family against them.

This chapter guides you through why we need Bitcoin. There are wonderful books on how to use it and that explain its technical aspects, which can be found in the resource section of this chapter. I feel my role is to answer, "Who cares?" My goal is to spark your curiosity, as I wish I had been back when I first heard about Bitcoin.

Centralized Systems

From the earliest days of human civilization, the way people have organized themselves, whether in tribes, cities, or nations, has oscillated between two powerful forces: centralization and decentralization. This tension is nowhere more evident than in the evolution of money, which has always mirrored the broader patterns of societal organization.

In ancient times, money was not decreed by kings or governments but emerged organically from the choices of ordinary people. Seashells, cacao beans, glass beads, and grains of rice all served as forms of currency at various points in history, not because a central authority mandated them, but because communities found them useful, recognizable, and portable. Cowrie shells, for instance, became a widely accepted currency across vast regions, their value arising from the mutual agreement of countless individuals, farmers, merchants, and rulers alike, rather than the edict of a single power. This was the essence of decentralization: a system where value and trust were built from the ground up, shaped by the needs and preferences of many rather than the will of one.

Yet as societies grew larger and more complex, the limitations of purely decentralized systems became apparent. The need for uniformity, reliability, and scalability pushed communities toward centralized solutions. In medieval China, for example, the Song

Dynasty introduced government-backed paper money, lending the prestige and authority of the state to a new monetary system. Here, money's legitimacy no longer flowed from widespread, organic acceptance but from the top down, enforced by the power of the state. Centralization brought order, standardization, and the ability to coordinate vast resources, but it also concentrated control in the hands of a few.

Centralization offers undeniable benefits. The division of labor and the pooling of expertise allow organizations to operate efficiently and at scale. Factories, research labs, and multinational corporations all owe much of their success to the ability to concentrate knowledge and resources. Yet, this very concentration of power brings significant risks with it. History is replete with examples of corruption flourishing in centralized structures, from the Enron scandal to authoritarian regimes that stifle dissent and innovation. When a small group holds all the levers of control, oversight can falter, and abuses can go unchecked.

Decentralized systems, on the other hand, empower individuals and communities, fostering resilience and adaptability. Ancient Greece, with its network of independent city-states, embodied the spirit of decentralization. Each polis governed itself, experimenting with different forms of rule and cultivating a culture of individual achievement. When faced with the might of the centralized Persian Empire, the Greeks' flexibility and local knowledge enabled them to unite and ultimately prevail in the Greco-Persian Wars. The Persian model, with its rigid hierarchy and divine kingship, could marshal great resources but struggled to adapt to the unpredictable and rapidly changing tactics of the Greeks.

In the modern world, the pendulum has swung heavily toward centralization, especially in finance. Central banks and governments wield immense power over money, setting policies that affect billions of people. The advent of **Central Bank Digital Currencies** (CBDCs) promises even greater efficiency and inclusion, but also raises profound concerns about surveillance and control. With CBDCs, authorities could monitor every transaction in real-time, restrict spending at will, and even utilize financial tools to reward or penalize behavior. Such power, unchecked, threatens to erode privacy and individual freedom, especially in societies lacking strong legal protections.

Another issue with modern economics is that many people remain outside the formal banking system, not just because of poverty or lack of access, but due to a deep mistrust of centralized institutions. Financial crises, a lack of transparency, and the perception that banks prioritize the interests of the wealthy over those of ordinary people have led to widespread disillusionment. Even as technology offers new ways to reach the unbanked, the fundamental issue of trust remains unresolved.

The Beginning of Bitcoin

Against this backdrop, the emergence of Bitcoin, the only decentralized digital money, represents a return to the principles that once governed the earliest forms of money. Bitcoin operates without a central authority, relying instead on a network of participants to validate transactions and maintain trust. For those wary of centralized power, it offers a vision of financial autonomy and transparency.

The ongoing struggle between centralization and decentralization is not merely a technical or economic debate; it is a question of how societies strike a balance between efficiency and control, on the one hand, and freedom and innovation, on the other. Each model has its strengths and weaknesses, and the future will likely be shaped by the ongoing interplay between these two powerful forces. As technology continues to evolve, the decisions made today will determine whether power remains concentrated in the hands of a few or is more widely shared among the many. It is this conflict that led Satoshi Nakamoto to invent Bitcoin, a truly sovereign form of currency for the first time in human history.

On October 31, 2008, a document quietly appeared online that would eventually reshape the world's understanding of money and trust.

Titled "Bitcoin: A Peer-to-Peer Electronic Cash System," it was authored by the mysterious Satoshi Nakamoto, a name that remains synonymous with both anonymity and innovation. The white paper proposed a radical alternative to the established financial order: an electronic currency system that would allow individuals to transact directly, without the need for banks or central authorities. In essence, it offered a blueprint for a form of money that could move freely from person to person, immune to the dictates and oversight of governments or financial institutions.

The timing and intent of this proposal were significant. For centuries, the power to issue and control money had rested with central authorities, kings, governments, and, in modern times, central banks. These entities not only managed the supply of money but also wielded the power to surveil, restrict, or even confiscate wealth. By contrast, the system Nakamoto envisioned was decentralized and trustless: transactions would be validated not by a single authority, but by a distributed network of participants, each with an equal stake in the system's integrity.

This was not the first attempt to create a form of digital money. Throughout the 1990s, innovators had experimented with various forms of computer-based currency. DigiCash, created by David Chaum, and E-Gold, founded by Douglas Jackson and Barry Downey, were among the earliest efforts. DigiCash used cryptography to ensure privacy and security, while E-Gold allowed users to transact with digital certificates backed by physical gold. Both projects, however, ultimately failed. DigiCash succumbed to a lack of adoption, while E-Gold was shut down by authorities over concerns about money laundering.

Despite these setbacks, the dream of digital currency persisted, fueled by the rise of the internet and the growing desire for privacy and autonomy in financial transactions. Early pioneers, including Adam Back, Wei Dai, and Nick Szabo, developed concepts and technologies such as Hashcash, B-Money, and Bit Gold, which would later influence Bitcoin's design. These projects explored ideas such as proof-of-work, decentralized **consensus**, and digital **scarcity**. Still, none managed to achieve widespread adoption or solve the problem of trust in a fully decentralized manner.

Nakamoto's innovation lay in synthesizing these earlier ideas into a coherent and practical system. By combining cryptographic proof-of-work with a public, **distributed ledger** known as the **blockchain**, Bitcoin made it possible for a global network of strangers to agree on the state of the system without relying on any single trusted party. Transactions were grouped into **blocks**, each cryptographically linked to the previous one, creating an immutable chain of history. This structure ensured that no one could alter past transactions or double-spend coins, and it distributed the power to validate and record transactions across the entire network. Each computer in the network is referred to as a **node**, and anyone can run a node to verify the distributed ledger at any time.

The launch of Bitcoin in 2009 marked the beginning of a new era. For the first time, anyone with an internet connection could participate in a financial system that was open, borderless, and resistant to censorship. Early adopters were drawn by the promise of autonomy and the thrill of participating in an experiment that challenged the very foundations of the monetary order. Over time, as the network grew and the value of bitcoin increased, it attracted a broader community of users, developers, and entrepreneurs, each contributing to its evolution and resilience.

Bitcoin's emergence must be understood not just as a technical achievement but as a response to the deep-seated mistrust of centralized power that had been building for decades. The financial crises of the late twentieth and early twenty-first centuries exposed the vulnerabilities of the traditional banking system and the dangers of unchecked authority. By offering an alternative rooted in transparency, mathematical certainty, and voluntary participation, Bitcoin tapped into a widespread yearning for a more equitable and accountable form of money.

As the years passed, Bitcoin inspired a wave of innovation and debate. Some saw it as a tool for financial liberation, a way to bypass corrupt or oppressive regimes and empower individuals. Others viewed it with suspicion, warning of its potential for misuse and instability. Whatever one's perspective, the impact of Bitcoin was undeniable: it forced a global reckoning with the nature of money, trust, and the role of technology in shaping human relationships.

Today, Bitcoin stands as both a symbol and a reality; a living experiment in decentralized self-governance and a challenge to the established order. Its story is still being written, but its genesis marks a turning point in the ongoing struggle between centralization and decentralization, between the old world of trusted intermediaries and the new world of trustless networks. Ultimately, Bitcoin's true legacy may lie not just in its code or market value, but in the questions it raises about who controls the future of money and, by extension, the future of freedom itself.

Bitcoin's journey from a niche experiment to a global financial phenomenon is a story of rapid evolution, technical ingenuity, and shifting social dynamics. In the early days, acquiring bitcoin was a pursuit for the technically curious and the adventurous. When the network first launched in 2009, anyone with a personal computer could participate in **mining**, using their machines to solve computational puzzles and, in return, earn new bitcoins. The process was accessible and straightforward, open to anyone willing to download the software and join the network.

As interest in bitcoin grew and more people joined the network, the mining process became more competitive. The puzzles became harder, and the computational power required to solve them quickly outpaced what ordinary home computers could provide. This shift led to the development and adoption of specialized mining hardware, known as Application Specific Integrated Circuits (ASICs). These machines were designed solely for mining Bitcoin, making the process far more efficient but also raising the barrier to entry for newcomers. The days when a hobbyist could mine significant amounts of Bitcoin from a laptop have given way to a landscape dominated by those who can invest in powerful, dedicated hardware.

During this period, early adopters also discovered alternative methods to acquire Bitcoin. Online platforms known as "faucets" distribute small amounts of bitcoin for free, aiming to promote adoption and familiarize people with the technology. One notable example was the Gavin Andresen faucet, which gave away five bitcoins per visit, a sum that would later become incredibly valuable. Enthusiasts could also trade bitcoin directly with one another, arranging peer-to-peer exchanges in online forums and chat rooms.

Bitcoin Transforms

A major transformation began around 2013. As mining became less accessible to individuals, the ecosystem responded with new methods for buying and selling bitcoin. Online exchanges emerged, providing marketplaces where users could purchase bitcoin with traditional currency. These platforms made the process more user-friendly and opened the door for a broader audience. The growth of exchanges also coincided with a wave of merchants and small businesses beginning to accept bitcoin as payment, further cementing its place in the digital economy. For the first time, it became possible for people to acquire bitcoin not just through mining or informal trades, but by purchasing it directly from established services.

There is, however, a problem for some people worldwide. Even though Bitcoin itself cannot be managed by a central authority, its on-ramps can be. Countries can shut down access to websites and arrest people who are mining Bitcoin. So, although they cannot shut down Bitcoin as a whole, in some places, authorities and centralized agencies are making it difficult, and in some cases, illegal, to interact with Bitcoin. The reason is that Bitcoin challenges the control that authorities have over their citizens. It is a form of money that, in and of itself, cannot be controlled by a single entity. This was deliberate when Nakamoto created it.

More recently, the expanding ecosystem soon attracted the attention of institutional investors. Financial products, such as **exchange-traded funds** (ETFs), futures, and options markets, began to emerge, offering new ways for individuals and organizations to gain exposure to bitcoin without needing to hold or manage the digital asset themselves. This influx of institutional interest brought legitimacy and liquidity, but it also drew the gaze of regulators. Governments and financial authorities around the world began to scrutinize the exchanges and platforms that facilitated bitcoin trading. In major markets such as the United States and Europe, new regulations were introduced to combat money laundering and ensure compliance with financial laws. Exchanges were required to implement "**Know Your Customer**" (KYC) procedures, collecting identification and personal information from users before allowing them to trade.

These regulatory changes marked a new phase in the evolution of Bitcoin. The process of buying and selling bitcoin became more formalized and secure, but also less anonymous and more tightly controlled. For many, the added oversight was a necessary step toward mainstream acceptance. For others, it represented a departure from the original ethos of privacy and autonomy that had inspired the creation of Bitcoin. Despite these changes, the ecosystem continued to grow and diversify.

Using Bitcoin

Today, individuals can acquire bitcoin through various channels, including mining, purchasing on exchanges, peer-to-peer trades, or earning it as payment for goods and services. The infrastructure supporting Bitcoin is more robust and user-friendly than ever, with wallets, payment processors, and educational resources available to help newcomers navigate the digital landscape.

To use Bitcoin, you need a **wallet**, which is a digital tool for storing, managing, and transacting with your bitcoins. The term "wallet" is a metaphor. Unlike a physical wallet, a Bitcoin wallet does not hold physical money but instead stores the cryptographic keys needed to access and transfer your bitcoins on the blockchain. A wallet generates and stores both **private keys** (which authorize transactions) and **public keys** (used for receiving bitcoins). If you lose your wallet's private key, you lose access to your bitcoins, as the coins themselves are always recorded on the Bitcoin network.

There are three main types of Bitcoin wallets: software, hardware, and paper.

Software wallets (also called hot wallets or hot storage) are apps or programs that run on your smartphone or computer. They are convenient for frequent use and daily transactions, much like a checking account. Software wallets are easy to access and often free to download, but because they are connected to the internet, they are more vulnerable to hacking and malware. In many regions, using certain software wallets may require identity verification (KYC). Some software wallets also support fast, low-cost transactions through technologies like the Lightning Network.

Hardware wallets (cold wallets) are physical devices designed to store your private keys offline. They are ideal for securely storing large amounts of bitcoin for extended periods, similar to a savings account or a safe deposit box. Because hardware wallets are not connected to the internet, they are much less susceptible to hacking. They are portable, easy to use, and considered one of the most secure storage options.

Paper wallets are simply printouts or written records of your private and public keys. They are also considered **cold storage**, as they are offline and immune to online attacks. However, paper wallets can be lost or damaged and are less convenient for frequent transactions.

When choosing a wallet, consider how often you plan to use your bitcoin and how much security you need. For everyday spending, a software wallet offers convenience. For long-term storage and larger amounts, hardware or paper wallets provide greater security. Regardless of the type, always ensure that you back up your wallet and keep your private keys safe, as losing them means permanently losing access to your bitcoins.

Bitcoin transactions involve **transaction fees**, which users pay to incentivize miners to process and confirm their payments. When you initiate a transaction, it first enters a waiting area called the **mempool**, where it remains until a miner adds it to a new block on the blockchain. Miners usually prioritize transactions with higher fees, which means your transaction will be confirmed more quickly if you pay a higher fee. This process, where a transaction is verified and becomes part of the permanent ledger, is called an on-chain transaction. However, when many people are using the network, the mempool can become full, causing higher fees and longer wait times for on-chain confirmations.

To address these issues, Bitcoin also uses **off-chain** solutions such as the Lightning Network. Off-chain transactions occur away from the main blockchain, so they don't immediately enter the mempool or require direct miner confirmation. These transactions are much faster and often have lower or no fees. After multiple off-chain transactions are completed, only the final result is settled **on-chain**, reducing congestion on the main blockchain. By combining on-chain security with the speed and efficiency of off-chain networks, Bitcoin can handle more transactions while keeping fees manageable and the network decentralized.

The narrative of Bitcoin is not just about technology; it is about values, decentralization, transparency, and individual sovereignty. Unlike traditional money, which can be inflated, confiscated, or censored by governments, Bitcoin's supply is capped, and its ledger is open for all to see. This transparency and predictability have attracted both idealists seeking financial freedom and investors searching for a hedge against inflation and instability. Additionally, Bitcoin requires proof of work. People need to understand how to use it, as well as have informed and dedicated individuals to run nodes and mine Bitcoin.

Bitcoin's journey has not been without setbacks. High-profile exchange hacks, regulatory crackdowns, and wild price swings have tested the resolve of its community. Yet, each crisis has spurred further innovation. Upgrades such as SegWit and the Lightning

Network have enhanced scalability and lowered transaction costs. At the same time, the rise of institutional investment and the development of bitcoin-backed financial products have brought new legitimacy and liquidity to the market.

Perhaps most remarkable are the personal stories that have emerged. Teenagers like Erik Finman became millionaires by investing early in bitcoin's potential, while others found it a tool for survival in economies plagued by **hyperinflation** or capital controls. For some, bitcoin has been a ticket to financial independence; for others, a symbol of rebellion against a system they see as rigged or exclusionary.

Bitcoin's evolution continues, shaped by a global community of developers, miners, investors, and users. Its open-source nature means that anyone can propose changes, but only a broad consensus can alter its rules, reflecting the decentralized ethos at its core. As governments and institutions grapple with how to regulate or integrate this new form of money, the debate over centralization versus decentralization remains as relevant as ever.

The story of Bitcoin's ecosystem is one of constant adaptation. From the early days of home mining and online faucets, through the rise of powerful hardware and global exchanges, to the era of institutional investment and regulatory scrutiny, each phase has brought new challenges and opportunities. What remains unchanged is the underlying vision: a distributed, borderless currency that empowers individuals to transact freely, protected from the whims of centralized authorities and unexpected inflation. As Bitcoin continues to evolve, it stands as a testament to the power of innovation and the enduring human desire for financial sovereignty.

Ultimately, the story of Bitcoin is one of humanity's enduring quest for autonomy, fairness, and trust in a world where these qualities are often in short supply. Whether it will ultimately fulfill its promise as a beacon of freedom or become just another asset in the global marketplace remains to be seen. However, its impact on individuals, economies, and the very idea of what money can be is already undeniable.

Chapter 6: The Evolution of Education

Education is the key to unlock the golden door of freedom.

- George Washington Carver

To truly live with freedom as a family, you must take charge of your finances and your children's education. These are two essential components of living with sovereignty. Like money, education has evolved over a long period. This chapter provides an overview of the history of education. And, much like learning about money and Bitcoin above, this insight allows you to understand the how and why behind the options you have and helps inform the decisions you make. The modern education system did not emerge in a vacuum. Throughout the history of humanity, it has not represented the way children have traditionally learned. Here, you will see that there is no one-size-fits-all system for educating children; this is why I coined the term "ownschooling." You have to find your own path to educate your children best, and that may be a little different for each child.

The history of education is a narrative that mirrors the evolution of human societies and their relationship with money. Across time and continents, education has transformed from informal, family-based knowledge-sharing to complex, institutionalized systems that shape entire civilizations. Understanding this journey provides essential context for any discussion of schooling options today.

Education in Western Civilization

During the earliest civilizations in ancient Mesopotamia, education emerged alongside the development of writing and the establishment of an organized society. The earliest schools, known as *Edubbas*, were attached to temples and run by priests, later transitioning to secular teachers as society evolved. The core curriculum centered on **cuneiform** writing, a complex system of over a thousand pictographic symbols, crucial for administration, law, and commerce. Education was reserved for wealthy boys, who endured long days and strict discipline, often enforced by corporal punishment. Mastery of writing and arithmetic opened doors to prestigious roles as scribes, essential to the infrastructure of Mesopotamian civilization.

Ancient Egypt's educational system was similarly elite-driven, rooted in the country's religious and social hierarchies. Houses of Life and scribal schools, often attached to temples, trained future priests, administrators, and scribes. The curriculum combined literacy in hieroglyphics, mathematics, and religious doctrine, reflecting the belief that knowledge upheld both spiritual and social order. Teachers, usually scribes or priests, were respected figures who emphasized memorization, moral instruction, and practical skills. Access was restricted mainly to the nobility and priestly families, with education serving as a means of preserving culture and maintaining stability.

Education in the Classical World

In ancient Greece, education was not a monolithic system but reflected the unique values and ambitions of each city-state. Nowhere was this more evident than in the contrast between Athens and Sparta, two societies with fundamentally different visions of what it meant to be an educated citizen.

Athens was the intellectual heart of the Greek world, a city that prized knowledge, debate, and artistic achievement. Education in Athens was primarily a private affair, accessible mainly to boys from affluent families. From a young age, Athenian boys were accompanied to school by a *paidagōgos,* a trusted household servant who ensured their safety and discipline. Their early schooling focused on literacy, numeracy, music, and poetry, especially the works of Homer, which were seen as the foundation of Greek identity and virtue. Physical education was also central, as the Greeks believed in the harmony of mind and body, and boys spent much time in the gymnasium training in athletics.

As they grew older, Athenian youths who could afford it sought out higher learning from philosophers and sophists. The city became renowned for its philosophical schools, most famously Plato's Academy (founded 387 BC) and Aristotle's Lyceum (335 BC). These were not schools in the modern sense but intellectual communities where students engaged in dialogue, debate, and the pursuit of wisdom. The curriculum was wide-ranging, encompassing logic, ethics, politics, mathematics, and the natural sciences. The goal was to cultivate well-rounded citizens capable of participating in the democratic life of the city, individuals who could speak persuasively, think critically, and act with virtue.

In stark contrast, Sparta organized its education around the needs of the state, which was perpetually focused on war. At the age of seven, Spartan boys were taken from their families and enrolled in the *agoge,* a rigorous system of public education and training. Here, the emphasis was on physical endurance, obedience, and martial skill. Boys lived communally, enduring harsh discipline, scant rations, and constant competition. Reading and writing were taught, but only to the extent that they served military needs. The highest virtues in Sparta were courage, loyalty, and the ability to endure pain and hardship. Spartan education was designed to produce not philosophers or poets, but warriors, citizens who would sacrifice everything for the survival and glory of their city.

Despite their differences, both Athens and Sparta viewed education as essential to the state's health, although they defined its purpose in radically different ways. Athens sought to nurture the intellect and civic engagement; Sparta, to forge discipline and collective strength.

The Greeks profoundly influenced Roman education. However, as Rome evolved from a Kingdom to a Republic to an Empire, it adapted and systematized these traditions to serve the needs of a vast and diverse empire. Education in the Roman Kingdom was informal and centered within the family. The *pater familias*, or male head of household, was responsible for teaching children essential skills for daily life, such as farming, basic literacy, domestic duties, and military preparedness. Boys learned practical tasks and Roman values like courage and duty, while girls were taught household management. There were no formal schools during this period; knowledge was transmitted orally and by example within the home.

With the advent of the Roman Republic, education began to move outside the household, especially among the wealthy. Private tutors, often enslaved Greeks or freedmen, were employed, and small private schools started to appear. The Roman educational system developed a three-tiered structure: young children attended the *ludus* for basic reading, writing, and arithmetic; older, affluent boys (and rarely girls) studied with a *grammaticus*, focusing on grammar, literature (especially Greek and Latin), history, and mythology; and those aspiring to public life trained with a *rhetor* in rhetoric, oratory, philosophy, and law. Greek influence became central to Roman education, especially after Rome's conquest of Greece. Education at this time was a marker of social status, with the poor rarely advancing beyond basic literacy, and most girls' education remaining home-based.

During the Roman Empire, the tiered educational system became more formalized and widespread, though still largely tuition-based and private. The curriculum emphasized reading, writing, arithmetic, grammar, Greek and Latin literature, rhetoric, and philosophy, with some exposure to sciences and music. Learning was assessed through oral recitation and public declamation, and discipline was strict, often involving corporal punishment.

While most education remained private, the imperial government occasionally supported schools, particularly for higher education in rhetoric, law, and philosophy. Access to advanced education was primarily reserved for boys from wealthy families, though some elite girls also received broader instruction. Despite changes in government and society, the structure and content of Roman education remained remarkably consistent, reflecting the enduring Roman emphasis on rhetoric, public speaking, and preparation for civic life. This influence would echo through Western educational traditions for centuries.

The Roman curriculum became famous for its organization into the Trivium and Quadrivium, a structure that would later underpin medieval and Renaissance education in Europe. The Trivium, comprising grammar, logic (or dialectic), and rhetoric, was the foundation. Grammar involved mastery of Latin (and often Greek) language and literature, enabling students to read, write, and appreciate the classics. Logic taught the principles of reasoning, argument, and debate, while rhetoric was the art of persuasive speaking and writing, essential for public life in the Roman Republic and Empire. Once students had mastered the Trivium, they advanced to the Quadrivium, which included arithmetic, geometry, music (studied as mathematical ratios and harmonies), and astronomy. These subjects were seen as the gateway to higher knowledge, preparing students for philosophy and, eventually, leadership roles in administration, law, or the priesthood.

Roman education was both practical and intellectual. It aimed to produce citizens who could serve the state, whether as orators, lawyers, soldiers, or governors. The Roman ideal was the *vir bonus dicendi peritus*, or the good man skilled in speaking. Education was a means of social mobility for some, while for others a marker of social status.

Scholasticism and Medieval Education

With the fall of the Western Roman Empire in 476 AD, Europe entered a period marked by political fragmentation, social upheaval, and a sharp decline in urban life and intellectual activity. In this vacuum, the Roman Catholic Church emerged as the central institution not only for spiritual guidance but also as the primary guardian of learning and culture. As secular governments weakened or disappeared, the Church became the leading provider of education and literacy, shaping the intellectual life of medieval Europe for centuries.

Monastic communities, particularly those following the Rule of St. Benedict (c. 530), offered stability and continuity during a tumultuous era. Monks dedicated their lives to prayer, manual labor, and scholarly pursuits, and monasteries became sanctuaries for the preservation and production of knowledge. *Scriptoria*, or specialized rooms for copying manuscripts, were established in monasteries such as Monte Cassino and Cluny, where monks painstakingly transcribed religious texts, classical works from antiquity, scientific treatises, and legal documents. This labor-intensive process ensured that much of the knowledge of the ancient world survived the so-called "Dark Ages" and was transmitted to future generations.

During the Carolingian Renaissance (780–900), which unfolded in the late eighth and early ninth centuries, education experienced a significant revival across Western Europe, largely due to the efforts of Charlemagne (c. 742–814) and his court. Charlemagne was deeply concerned by the decline in literacy and learning that had followed the collapse of the Western Roman Empire. He believed that the renewal of education was essential not only for religious reasons but also for the effective administration of his vast empire. To address this, he issued several decrees, such as the *Admonitio Generalis* in 789, which required that every bishopric and monastery establish schools to teach reading, writing, the psalms, chant, calculation, and grammar. These reforms were intended to ensure that clergy could interpret the scriptures accurately and that the standards of Latin, the language of the Church and administration, were maintained at a high level.

The educational system that emerged during this period was centered around cathedral and monastic schools, which became the primary institutions for learning. The curriculum was based on the seven liberal arts, taken from the trivium (grammar, rhetoric, and logic) and the quadrivium (arithmetic, geometry, music, and astronomy), inspired by earlier Roman models. It was designed to produce a learned clergy capable of teaching others and maintaining doctrinal unity. Alcuin of York, a prominent scholar invited to Charlemagne's court, played a crucial role in shaping the curriculum and raising educational standards. He emphasized the importance of correct Latin usage and the study of classical texts, which led to a revival of classical learning and the preservation of many ancient works through careful copying and transmission.

Education during the Carolingian Renaissance was not limited to the clergy. While the primary focus was on training priests and monks, literacy among the lay population also increased, particularly among the nobility and, to a lesser extent, among commoners and women. The court itself became a center of learning, with Charlemagne and his family participating in lessons alongside members of the royal household. This period also saw the establishment of palace schools, most notably at Aachen, where scholars from across Europe were brought together to teach and learn. The influence of these reforms extended beyond the Carolingian Empire, setting a precedent for later developments in European education and laying the groundwork for the rise of medieval universities.

The Carolingian Renaissance also brought about changes in the way texts were written and read. Scribes improved the clarity and legibility of manuscripts by standardizing scripts and introducing new punctuation marks, such as the question mark. The production and preservation of manuscripts flourished, ensuring that a wealth of classical and Christian literature survived for future generations. The legacy of this educational revival was profound, as it not only preserved the intellectual heritage of antiquity but also fostered a culture of learning that would shape education for centuries to come.

By the High Middle Ages (1000–1300), the intellectual movement known as scholasticism arose. This served as the leading intellectual and educational tradition in medieval Europe from about 1100 to 1700. It was not simply a philosophy or theology, but rather a method of learning and inquiry that placed great emphasis on logical analysis, dialectical reasoning, and the reconciliation of Christian theology with classical philosophy, especially that of Aristotle. The movement originated in the monastic and cathedral schools that emerged after the Carolingian Renaissance, where early scholars sought to organize and comprehend the vast body of inherited theological and philosophical knowledge.

The primary goal of scholasticism was to reconcile faith and reason. Medieval scholars believed that religious truths could be explored and clarified through reasoned debate and careful logic. In practice, scholastic education involved a structured curriculum based on the seven liberal arts, with a particular focus on grammar, rhetoric, logic, and later, the works of Aristotle. The method of teaching relied heavily on lectures and formal disputations, where a question would be posed, arguments and counterarguments presented, and contradictions analyzed until a resolution was reached. This dialectical approach became the hallmark of scholastic thought and was applied not only to theology but also to law, philosophy, and the natural sciences.

The rise of universities in the twelfth and thirteenth centuries provided a new institutional home for scholasticism. Universities such as Paris became centers for the training of clergy and scholars, and the scholastic method shaped the intellectual life of Europe for centuries. Figures like Anselm of Canterbury (1033—1109), Peter Abelard (1079–1142), and especially Thomas Aquinas (1225–1274) were central to the development of scholasticism. Aquinas's Summa Theologica is considered a pinnacle of this tradition, synthesizing Aristotelian philosophy with Christian doctrine.

The Church maintained significant control over these universities, dictating what and how subjects were taught. While this control ensured the preservation and transmission of knowledge, it also limited intellectual freedom and reinforced the Church's doctrinal authority. The construction of grand cathedrals and the Church's vast landholdings symbolized its spiritual and temporal dominance during this period. Yet, the Church also preserved classical knowledge and trained clergy, using Latin as the language of instruction.

Although scholasticism was sometimes criticized for being overly rigid or abstract, its emphasis on systematic reasoning and debate laid essential foundations for later developments in Western philosophy, science, and education. The tradition eventually declined with the rise of Renaissance humanism and new scientific methods, but its influence persisted in both Catholic and Protestant educational systems.

Renaissance Education and Humanism

The Renaissance (fourteenth through seventeenth centuries) marked a rebirth of learning in Europe. Humanism shifted focus toward the study of classical texts, individual potential, and civic virtue. Education expanded beyond the clergy and nobility to include the emerging middle class. Critical thinking, the arts, and empirical observation gained importance, laying the foundation for modern science and liberal education.

During the Renaissance, which spanned roughly from the fourteenth to the seventeenth centuries, education in Western Europe underwent a significant transformation. This period marked a departure from the medieval focus on religious orthodoxy and scholasticism, moving instead toward a curriculum inspired by the values of humanism. Humanism was a philosophical and cultural movement that centered on human beings, their capacities, and their achievements, placing them at the heart of intellectual life.

Renaissance education centered on the *studia humanitatis*, a program of studies that included grammar, rhetoric, poetry, moral philosophy, and history. These subjects were drawn from the classical works of ancient Greece and Rome. The aim was to cultivate well-rounded individuals who could think critically, speak eloquently, and participate actively in civic life. Mastery of Latin, and increasingly Greek, was considered essential, as it allowed students to engage directly with classical texts and ideas.

Unlike the rigid and often punitive atmosphere of medieval schools, some Renaissance educators advocated for a more balanced approach that nurtured both mind and body. Physical exercise and moral development were integrated into the curriculum, reflecting the ancient ideal of a "universal man" who was both intellectually and physically accomplished. While Christian teachings remained important, there was a noticeable shift toward preparing students for success in this life, not just the afterlife. This blend of secular and religious instruction was a hallmark of humanist education.

Humanism's influence on schooling was profound. Humanist thinkers believed that education could unlock human potential and foster personal growth, enabling individuals to shape their own destinies. They also emphasized the importance of civic responsibility, drawing inspiration from the traditions of Greek and Roman city-states. Education was seen as a means to create responsible citizens who would contribute to the well-being and governance of their communities.

Renaissance schooling was primarily accessible to the sons of nobility, wealthy merchants, and professionals, though some daughters of elite families also benefited. The humanist approach to education spread from Italy throughout Europe, becoming the foundation for the education of the ruling classes and influencing the development of modern liberal arts education.

Notable educators such as Vittorino da Feltre (1378–1446) established schools that combined intellectual, physical, and moral training in a supportive and joyful environment. Erasmus of Rotterdam (1466–1536) promoted education for all and wrote influential textbooks, while Michel de Montaigne (1533–1592) advocated for independent judgment and a natural, engaging approach to learning.

The legacy of Renaissance schooling and humanism endures in the modern emphasis on the humanities, critical inquiry, and the holistic development of individuals. This educational revolution helped shape Western civilization by fostering creativity, civic engagement, and a lifelong pursuit of knowledge.

Yeshivas and Jewish Education

From the classical period onward, Jewish education developed distinctive characteristics that set it apart from many surrounding cultures. As early as the first century CE, Jewish communities had established compulsory education for boys, with a strong emphasis on early literacy, textual study, and moral instruction. At the same time, the direct influence on Greco-Roman educational systems was limited due to cultural and religious boundaries; the Jewish commitment to universal literacy and community-funded schooling, however, foreshadowed later models of public education. Jewish methods, centered on reading, memorization, and ethical teaching, paralleled certain aspects of early Christian education and indirectly contributed to the structure of religious schooling in the West.

During the medieval period, Jewish communities maintained notably high literacy rates compared to their Christian neighbors, with most boys able to read and write. Jewish educational institutions, such as the *cheder* and *yeshiva*, focused on religious texts but also included instruction in logic, arithmetic, and, in some regions, the sciences. The Jewish tradition of debate, dialectical reasoning, and critical textual analysis had a profound influence on the scholastic methods of medieval Christian universities, particularly as Christian scholars engaged with Jewish and Islamic philosophical works. In places like Spain and Italy, Jewish scholars played a pivotal role in transmitting classical knowledge, acting as bridges between different intellectual traditions.

The Renaissance further expanded Jewish educational influence. As Christian scholars sought to recover classical languages and texts, many turned to Jewish teachers and commentaries to deepen their understanding of the Hebrew Bible. Jewish scholars significantly contributed to the translation and transmission of scientific, medical, and philosophical works from Arabic and Hebrew into Latin, thereby shaping the intellectual landscape of the period. In Italy, Jewish education began to integrate humanistic studies, with students learning Latin and engaging with classical works alongside traditional studies of the Torah and Talmud. The inclusion of Hebrew in university curricula across Europe also reflected the growing respect for Jewish scholarship.

With the onset of the Enlightenment, Jewish education underwent a significant transformation. Inspired by Enlightenment ideals of reason and universal knowledge, Jewish communities, especially in Germany, began to incorporate secular subjects and modern pedagogical approaches into their schools. The Prussian Emancipation Edict of 1812 brought Jewish schools under state supervision, aligning them more closely with the highly structured, compulsory, and standardized Prussian education system. Rather than rejecting this model, Jewish communities adapted to it, integrating secular studies, age-graded classes, and professional teaching standards, while maintaining religious instruction. Jewish families were deeply invested in education, often sending their children to both Jewish and state schools, and Jewish students became overrepresented in higher education relative to their population.

In the modern era, especially following the rise of progressive education, Jewish schooling has continued to evolve. Most Jewish children in Western countries now receive their primary education in public schools, with Jewish studies provided through supplementary schools or private Jewish day schools that often blend secular and religious curricula. Modern *yeshivas* continue to serve as vibrant centers of Jewish learning, blending deep engagement with traditional texts, especially the Talmud and Jewish law, with evolving pedagogical methods. At their core, these institutions emphasize collaborative study, such as the *chavruta* model, where pairs of students debate and analyze texts, fostering critical thinking and autonomy within a framework of respect for tradition and authority. Many modern *yeshivas*, particularly those in the Modern Orthodox community, integrate secular studies alongside religious curricula, preparing students for both higher education and professional life while maintaining a strong Jewish identity. There are also Jewish educational institutions today that employ progressive pedagogical techniques, focusing on identity, community, and relevance to modern life.

In recent years, a resurgence of the classical school model has emerged within Jewish education. Inspired by the Western tradition of the trivium (grammar, logic, and rhetoric), these classical schools prioritize mastery of foundational knowledge, logical reasoning, and persuasive communication. The curriculum often includes the study of great works from both Jewish and Western civilizations, aiming to cultivate moral virtue, intellectual rigor, and a passion for lifelong learning. This movement aims to integrate the best of Jewish textual tradition with the timeless principles of classical education, equipping students to become thoughtful, articulate, and virtuous leaders within both the Jewish community and broader society.

Education in Islamic Society

While Jewish and Christian education spread in Western Europe, from the seventh century onward, the Islamic world developed its own educational system. It was centered on the institution of the *madrasa.* Initially, education in early Islamic society took place in mosques and informal study circles, where students gathered around scholars to learn the Qur'an, hadith (the Prophet Muhammad's sayings), and Islamic law. As the Islamic empire expanded, the need for a more formal and systematic approach to education became apparent, both to train religious scholars and to administer a vast, multicultural realm.

In the early centuries of Islamic civilization, the intellectual landscape was strikingly diverse and dynamic. One of the most influential and controversial currents was the Mu'tazilite movement, which emerged in the eighth century in Basra and Baghdad. The Mu'tazilites were renowned for their commitment to reason, rational inquiry, and the integration of ancient Greek philosophy, particularly the works of Aristotle and Neoplatonists, into Islamic theology. They believed that human reason, guided by revelation, was essential for interpreting the Qur'an and resolving theological disputes, and that individuals possessed free will and moral responsibility for their actions.

The Mu'tazilites' core principles included the unity and justice of God, the createdness of the Qur'an (as opposed to its being eternal and uncreated), the necessity of God's justice and promise, and the idea that humans occupy an intermediate position between belief and unbelief if they commit grave sins. Their rationalist approach allowed for a flourishing of philosophical, scientific, and even ethical debate within Islamic society. They actively engaged with works of Greek, Persian, and Indian philosophy, and their openness to outside intellectual traditions contributed to making the Abbasid period a golden age of learning and translation.

Women and other marginalized voices also found greater opportunities in this pluralistic environment. Historical records and biographical works demonstrate that women have participated as scholars, transmitters of hadith, jurists, and teachers, sometimes instructing both men and women, and even issuing fatwas, or legal opinions. The intellectual openness of the era allowed for a broader spectrum of interpretations, including those that advocated for more equitable treatment of women and the use of reason in matters of law and ethics. This period witnessed the emergence of female scholars whose expertise was highly respected by their contemporaries and whose contributions to religious and philosophical debates were substantial.

However, the Mu'tazilite ascendancy was not to last. Their rationalist theology, especially their claim that the Qur'an was created and their use of Greek philosophy, provoked fierce opposition from more traditionalist scholars and movements, such as the Hanbalis (780–855) and later the Ash'arites (tenth century). The backlash culminated in the ninth century when the Abbasid caliph al-Mutawakkil reversed the official patronage of Mu'tazilism and restored traditionalist Sunni orthodoxy. The Ash'arite school, which sought a middle path between rationalism and strict textualism, gradually became dominant, and the space for philosophical pluralism and rational inquiry narrowed.

This shift had profound effects on the intellectual and social fabric of the Islamic world. The suppression of the Mu'tazilites marked a shift away from open engagement with ancient philosophy and reasoned debate. They were centered toward a more cautious and sometimes rigid approach to theology and interpretation. The narrowing of acceptable viewpoints also had implications for women and other marginalized groups, as the space for alternative readings and progressive voices diminished.

By the tenth and eleventh centuries, madrasas had emerged as independent centers of learning, distinct from mosques, and often supported by wealthy patrons through religious endowments (*waqf*). Madrasas were universal centers of education and culture where the curriculum typically included Arabic grammar, logic (*mantiq*), rhetoric, history, and the teaching of *adab*, or polite culture and ethical conduct. In the Ottoman Empire and other regions, madrasas offered advanced courses in sciences and political studies, reflecting a recognition among leading scholars that secular knowledge was vital for the dynamic development of society.

Over the centuries, madrasas became not only centers of learning but also symbols of cultural prestige and social mobility. Rulers and elites founded madrasas to legitimize their authority, transmit their values, and ensure a steady supply of educated officials and judges. In some cases, madrasas were architecturally integrated with mosques, mausoleums, and public baths, forming the heart of urban life and intercultural exchange.

Modern Islamic education continues to emphasize the integration of religious teachings with general academic subjects. In Muslim-majority countries, Islamic schools and universities typically offer instruction in Qur'anic studies, Hadith, Islamic law (*fiqh*), and the Arabic language, alongside subjects such as mathematics, science, and social studies. The educational approach aims to develop students' intellectual and moral character, with a strong focus on memorization, recitation, and adherence to traditional values. However, there is also a growing trend toward incorporating critical thinking, discussion, and practical application of knowledge, reflecting broader educational reforms and the need to prepare students for participation in modern society.

In Western countries, Islamic education is often provided in private Islamic schools or through supplementary weekend programs. These schools generally follow the national curriculum for secular subjects while maintaining a robust program of Islamic studies. The primary objective is to equip students with a solid foundation in their faith and religious practices, thereby ensuring the continuity of tradition and community values. Islamic schools in these settings may face challenges such as limited resources and regulatory requirements, but they remain committed to fostering a strong sense of religious identity and academic achievement. The focus is primarily on transmitting Islamic teachings and preparing students to live according to their faith, regardless of the surrounding cultural environment.

Non-Western Education

Outside of the West, schooling in Asia and Africa shared similar yet unique aspects. Like other early societies, education in ancient China began as a privilege for the aristocracy, focused on the fifth-century BC Confucian classics, moral values, and preparation for government service. The Zhou Dynasty (551–479 BC) established the first formal schools, while the Han Dynasty (206 BC–AD 220) expanded access and standardized curricula. Over centuries, the imperial examination system allowed for some social mobility, selecting officials based on merit rather than birth. Confucianism's emphasis on virtue, social harmony, and respect for authority shaped Chinese education for millennia. By the Tang Dynasty, schools taught a broad range of subjects, including mathematics, astronomy, and geography, gradually opening opportunities for women and lower classes.

In ancient India, education was deeply intertwined with religious and philosophical traditions. Vedic and later Buddhist systems centered on oral transmission of sacred texts, logic, and debate. *Gurukuls* (teacher's homes) and monasteries served as centers for learning, where students lived and studied under the guidance of gurus. The curriculum included language, ritual, mathematics, and philosophy, with a strong emphasis on discipline and spiritual development.

Education in pre-colonial Africa was as varied and vibrant as the continent itself, reflecting the diversity of its peoples, environments, and cultures. Unlike the formal, institutionalized systems that would later be introduced by colonial powers, African education before colonization was primarily community-based, informal, and deeply integrated into the rhythms of daily life. Its purpose was not only to impart practical skills but also to transmit cultural values, social norms, and collective memory from one generation to the next.

For most African societies, education began in the home and extended into the wider community. Children learned by observing adults and participating in communal activities. Through apprenticeship and imitation, boys and girls acquired the skills necessary for survival and prosperity in their specific environment, including farming, animal husbandry, fishing, hunting, weaving, pottery, blacksmithing, and other crafts. Elders, parents, and master artisans served as teachers, guiding children through hands-on experience and correcting mistakes as they occurred. This system ensured that knowledge was tailored to local needs and that each child's education was relevant and immediately applicable.

Beyond practical skills, African education placed a strong emphasis on socialization and moral development. Children were taught the customs, taboos, and expectations of their community, learning to respect elders, cooperate, be hospitable, and appreciate the importance of kinship ties. Initiation rites or rites of passage, often elaborate ceremonies marking the transition from childhood to adulthood, were central to this process. These rites included instruction in history, ethics, sexuality, and the responsibilities of adulthood, often accompanied by symbolic acts, songs, and dances that reinforced communal identity.

In many regions, especially among the kingdoms of West Africa's Sahelian belt (such as Mali, Songhai, and Ghana), formal schools and centers of learning also existed. These schools, often attached to royal courts or Islamic mosques, trained scribes, administrators, and religious scholars. The city of Timbuktu in Mali, for example, was renowned for its universities and libraries, attracting students and scholars from across the Islamic world. Here, instruction covered not only Islamic jurisprudence and theology, but also astronomy, mathematics, medicine, and literature. Scribes played a vital role in administration, trade, and diplomacy, and their training was rigorous and highly respected.

Yet even in societies with formal schooling, education remained holistic and collective. Storytelling, music, and ritual were essential tools for teaching and preserving knowledge. Griots, hereditary storytellers, musicians, and historians, held a revered place in West African societies, memorizing genealogies, epic tales, and proverbs that conveyed lessons about leadership, justice, and the human condition. Through oral tradition, communities maintained a living record of their past and a shared sense of purpose.

As we have seen, the evolution of education from ancient civilizations through the Renaissance and into the modern era has been shaped by shifting philosophies, social priorities, and cultural ideals. Each period brought new approaches to learning, from the rigorous study of classical knowledge to the more experimental and student-centered models of recent centuries. Yet, despite these transformations, the fundamental question remains: how can education best serve the intellectual and moral development of each generation? As we turn to the next chapter, we will examine the pressing challenges facing today's educational systems: challenges that stem from both the legacies of past reforms and the unique demands of our contemporary world. Understanding these problems is essential for anyone seeking meaningful solutions and a path forward for educating children today.

Chapter 7: The Broken System

The system isn't broken. It's working exactly as it was designed. Rather than encouraging critical thinking and independence, public schools produce obedient workers and passive citizens.

- John Taylor Gatto, *Dumbing Us Down: The Hidden Curriculum of Compulsory Schooling*

Like money, education became more complex, more centralized, and took agency away from the individual. This began in the nineteenth century with the adoption of the Prussian system in the West, but it really started to decline in the U.S. in the early twentieth century. Although this movement originated in the U.S., its educational philosophies and practices have spread throughout the West and globally in the modern world.

In the first chapter, I briefly outlined my experience working in academia. This chapter explains how education got to that point.

The Enlightenment and the Prussian System

The Enlightenment, spanning the seventeenth and eighteenth centuries, was a transformative period that fundamentally reshaped the concept and purpose of education in the Western world and beyond. Enlightenment thinkers, such as John Locke (1632–1704) and Jean-Jacques Rousseau (1712–1778), among others, challenged the longstanding dominance of religious dogma and traditional authority in education, advocating instead for systems grounded in reason, empirical evidence, and the cultivation of individual autonomy. They believed that education should nurture both intellect and character, preparing individuals not only for personal fulfillment but also for meaningful participation in society.

This era witnessed a decisive shift away from education as a privilege reserved for the clergy and elites, often administered by religious institutions, toward the concept of universal, secular, and state-supported schooling. The separation of church and state in education became a central Enlightenment principle, with curricula increasingly emphasizing science, mathematics, philosophy, and the humanities over religious doctrine. Education was reimagined as a public good and a civic responsibility, essential for the creation of rational, informed citizens capable of self-governance and critical thought.

One of the most influential practical outcomes of Enlightenment educational philosophy was the development of the Prussian education system in the late eighteenth and early nineteenth centuries. After military defeats by Napoleon (1769–1821), Prussian leaders concluded that independent thinking among citizens was a liability; they sought to create a population of obedient, loyal, and productive subjects. The system introduced universal education, structured curricula, teacher training, and vocational instruction, all under strict government oversight.

Prussia pioneered the concept of compulsory, state-run schooling for all children, regardless of social class, a radical departure from earlier models. The Prussian system was characterized by its high degree of centralization: the state prescribed curricula, appointed and rigorously trained teachers, and enforced strict discipline and hierarchy within schools. The curriculum balanced classical studies with practical and vocational subjects, aiming to produce not only knowledgeable individuals but also disciplined, obedient, and productive citizens.

Discipline and authority were core tenets of the Prussian model. Schools operated under a rigid, hierarchical structure, with students progressing through levels based on ability and social status. Regular assessments and standardized national examinations, such as the Abitur, determined access to higher education and professional careers. Teacher training was professionalized, with seminaries and certification requirements ensuring a consistent standard of instruction across the system.

The Prussian system's emphasis on universal access, structured curriculum, and state control was driven by both civic and military motivations. Prussian leaders viewed education as crucial for economic development, technological advancement, and the cultivation of a loyal and efficient workforce and army. This model's success in producing a disciplined, literate population inspired widespread imitation: countries across Europe, North America, and eventually the world adopted key elements, including compulsory attendance, standardized curricula, and centralized administration.

While the Prussian model succeeded in reducing illiteracy and fostering national unity, it did so by emphasizing discipline, order, and conformity, often at the expense of creativity, critical thinking, and individual freedom. The model was explicitly designed to produce citizens who would not question authority, a legacy that critics argue persists in many modern educational systems. This centralization of authority in education, first envisioned during the Enlightenment and operationalized in Prussia, remains a defining feature of contemporary public education systems, shaping debates about the balance between state control, individual freedom, and community involvement to this day.

The eighteenth and nineteenth centuries marked a profound transformation in the nature and purpose of education, as societies across Europe and North America responded to the sweeping changes brought by industrialization, urbanization, and the rise of the modern nation-state. What began as a privilege reserved for the elite gradually evolved into a system of universal, compulsory public schooling. This evolution would fundamentally reshape the lives of children, families, and entire societies.

The Industrial Revolution (1760–1840) created a new economic and social order that demanded a literate, numerate, and disciplined workforce. Factories, offices, and bureaucracies required workers who could read instructions, keep records, and perform basic calculations. As mechanization and urbanization accelerated, the traditional systems of apprenticeship and home-based learning were no longer used to meet the needs of rapidly growing cities and industries.

Towards Centralized Education

The shift toward a centralized, state-controlled system began in the nineteenth century, led by reformer Horace Mann (1796–1859). As Secretary of the Massachusetts Board of Education, he championed the idea of the common school, a free, universal, nonsectarian public institution meant to mold virtuous citizens and promote social order. Mann's reforms were inspired by his belief that a democratic society could not survive if its citizens remained ignorant, and that education should be funded, managed, and maintained by a concerned public. He advocated for well-trained, professional teachers and a curriculum that would be moral but not sectarian, aiming to unify diverse populations and prevent social unrest.

However, Mann's vision also reflected a deep skepticism of parental competence and local control. He believed that society, not families, should shape the minds and morals of children, arguing that society must take action early in educating its youngest members, or it will face serious consequences in the future. This shift placed the state, rather than parents, at the center of educational authority, diminishing the role of families in determining what and how their children learned.

Mann's reforms were heavily influenced by the Prussian education system, which he studied during a trip to Europe in 1843. Mann admired the efficiency and order of the Prussian schools and imported many of their features to the United States, believing they could be used for the public good despite their origins in social control. Over time, this model became the foundation for American public education, shifting the focus from cultivating individual potential to producing compliant, predictable citizens.

The efficiency and order of the Prussian system also attracted the attention of reformers and governments across Europe, where Austria, Scandinavia, and eventually France and the United Kingdom adopted versions of the model, introducing compulsory primary education and standardized curricula. In the UK, local church-controlled schools were gradually replaced by a state system in the late nineteenth century. However, private and alternative forms of education remained legal.

Today, the legacy of the Prussian model is visible in the factory-like structure of schools, the emphasis on standardized testing, and the prioritization of obedience and uniformity over innovation and autonomy. Critics from a sovereignty perspective argue that this system suppresses individuality, creativity, and the natural love of learning, replacing them with rote memorization and compliance. Alternatives such as Montessori, democratic schools, and unschooling have emerged in response, seeking to restore freedom and self-direction to education.

Compulsory and Progressive Education

By the nineteenth and into the twentieth centuries, governments recognized that national prosperity and competitiveness depended on an educated populace. In Britain, the Elementary Education Act of 1870 laid the groundwork for compulsory schooling, mandating that children between the ages of five and thirteen attend school, with subsequent acts expanding both the age range and the scope of instruction. Similar reforms swept across continental Europe: France and Germany, motivated by national aspirations and the need for social cohesion, established state-run education systems early in the nineteenth century. In the United States, the Massachusetts Bay

Colony had instituted compulsory education laws as early as the seventeenth century; however, it was not until the nineteenth century that the idea of free, universal public education began to gain nationwide traction.

The spread of compulsory education laws was both a response to and a driver of social change. In the United States, Massachusetts enacted the first statewide compulsory attendance law in 1852, requiring children ages eight to fourteen to attend school for at least three months per year. By 1885, sixteen states had enacted similar laws, and by 1918, all states had mandated school attendance. These laws were often coupled with child labor reforms, as policymakers sought to remove children from factories and put them in classrooms, both to protect their welfare and to prepare them for more skilled forms of work.

As public education expanded, there was a push for standardization. The curriculum shifted away from classical and religious instruction toward subjects deemed essential for industrial society: reading, writing, arithmetic, science, and practical skills. Schools adopted a factory model of organization, with rigid schedules, age-graded classrooms, bells, and a focus on punctuality and obedience. The goal was not only to impart knowledge but to instill habits of discipline, time management, and deference to authority, traits valued in both factories and offices.

The monitorial system (Lancastrian system), which used older students to help instruct younger ones under the supervision of a single teacher, was widely adopted to cope with rapid increases in enrollment and shortages of trained teachers. The practice of dividing students into grades based on age, which originated in nineteenth-century Germany, spread worldwide as schools expanded and became more bureaucratic.

The nineteenth century also saw the professionalization of teaching. Reformers like Horace Mann in the United States advocated for the creation of normal schools, institutions dedicated to training teachers in both subject matter and pedagogy. Mann and his contemporaries pushed for a longer school year, a secular curriculum, and free public education accessible to all, regardless of background. The formation of professional organizations, such as the National Teachers Association (now the National Education Association) in 1857, further advanced the cause of teacher training and educational reform.

While the expansion of public education was a significant achievement, it was not without its limitations and controversies. Access to quality education remained uneven, with girls, children from low-income families, and minorities often excluded or segregated. Reformers like Susan B. Anthony (1820–1906) and Elizabeth Cady Stanton (1815–1902) fought for coeducation and equal subject access for girls, while others worked to establish specialized schools for students with disabilities.

The rapid growth of public education systems brought both progress and new challenges. Overcrowded classrooms, underqualified teachers, and inadequate facilities were common criticisms. Some observers lamented the loss of local control and the increasing bureaucratization of schooling, warning that this Prussian model of education risked stifling individuality and creativity. Nonetheless, by the end of the nineteenth century, universal, compulsory schooling had become the norm in much of Europe and North America, setting the stage for the further expansion and reform of education in the twentieth century.

In the early twentieth century, John Dewey (1859–1952) reshaped American education. Dewey is often referred to as the father of progressive education. His educational philosophy, which centered on student experience, curiosity, and real-life problem solving, represented a significant departure from traditional approaches that prioritized the systematic transmission of knowledge. By shifting the focus away from the mastery of foundational content and intellectual discipline, Dewey's model introduced classrooms where lessons were often shaped by the interests and immediate experiences of students, rather than a carefully sequenced curriculum grounded in established academic subjects.

This move away from a knowledge-based curriculum had profound consequences for educational standards. The deemphasis on memorization, recitation, and the rigorous study of core disciplines led to classrooms that were less structured and often lacked clear academic expectations. Teachers, recast as facilitators rather than authorities, were encouraged to support exploration and group work, but this usually came at the expense of ensuring that all students acquired essential skills in reading, writing, mathematics, and the sciences. As a result, many students were left without the intellectual tools necessary to engage deeply with complex ideas or to build upon the cultural and intellectual heritage that had long been the foundation of Western education.

The flexible, interdisciplinary curriculum promoted by Dewey and his followers sometimes resulted in a dilution of academic rigor. With projects and thematic units taking precedence over systematic instruction in grammar, logic, and rhetoric, students were less likely to develop the habits of attention, perseverance, and analytical thinking that are cultivated through disciplined study. Over time, this approach contributed to a decline in educational standards, as the pursuit of creativity and self-expression was prioritized over the mastery of foundational knowledge. The legacy of this shift is evident in ongoing concerns about declining literacy, numeracy, and general academic achievement, raising questions about whether Dewey's progressive ideals ultimately served the best interests of children's intellectual development.

Dewey's vision was not to foster independent thinkers, but to use schools as instruments for the reconstruction of society, aligning individual interests with the social consciousness and preparing students to function in an interdependent, collective world.

Consequences of Dewey

The twentieth century is often remembered as an era of educational reform, but John Dewey's influence arguably did more harm than good. Rather than equipping students with essential academic skills and a strong moral foundation, Dewey's progressive ideals undermined traditional standards and teacher authority. His emphasis on experiential learning and student-directed activities led to the erosion of disciplined study, the devaluation of core subjects, and the replacement of rigorous instruction with vague notions of life adjustment and socialization. As a result, American classrooms became less focused on transmitting knowledge and more preoccupied with fostering self-esteem and group conformity, leaving generations of students ill-prepared in basic literacy, mathematics, and critical thinking.

Critics argue that Dewey's legacy is a system where teachers are trained more in classroom management than subject mastery, and where the curriculum is diluted by fads and ideological agendas rather than anchored in the liberal arts or cultural heritage. The abandonment of traditional academic standards in favor of progressive experimentation has produced a populace lacking in both intellectual rigor and historical awareness, with many students unable to meet even basic educational benchmarks. Dewey's reforms, intended to liberate, instead left many students behind in watered-down tracks, deprived of the tools needed for true democratic participation or personal achievement.

This led to the emergence of alternative models, such as those initiated by Maria Montessori (1870–1952) and Rudolf Steiner (1861–1925; Waldorf school founder), as a way to advocate for holistic development and honor the individuality of each child. However, these approaches remained on the margins, accessible mainly to those with the means or knowledge to seek them out. For most families, the promise of progressive reform translated into a different, yet still centralized, system, where the state and its appointed experts defined what constituted "good" education. The sovereignty of families and local communities was, in many cases, further eroded under the guise of progress.

The late twentieth and early twenty-first centuries have witnessed an unprecedented surge in technology's influence over education. While calculators, computers, and digital classrooms promise efficiency and access, they also introduce new layers of dependency on corporate platforms, standardized software, and remote algorithms. The rise of online learning, artificial intelligence, and global data networks has made education more convenient in some ways, but it has also distanced students and families from direct, personal engagement with teachers and local communities. The classroom, once a space for human connection and mentorship, risks becoming a node in a vast, impersonal digital system.

Globalization, too, has brought both opportunities and profound challenges. International curricula, student exchanges, and the dominance of English as a global language have opened doors for some, but they have also contributed to the erosion of local cultures, languages, and values. The push for global citizenship often comes at the expense of a sense of rootedness in one's own history and traditions. As educational systems race to align with international benchmarks and corporate standards, families and communities find themselves with less control over what their children learn and how they are taught. The tension between tradition and innovation, local identity and global uniformity, is no longer a theoretical debate; it has become a daily reality for parents seeking to preserve control over their children's education.

Today's educational landscape is often celebrated for its diversity, featuring a range of options, including public, private, charter, and independent schools, as well as international and bilingual programs. On the surface, families have more choices than ever before. Yet, true educational sovereignty remains elusive for many. The expansion of access has not resolved deep-seated modern educational issues; if anything, it has sometimes masked them behind a veneer of choice. Wealth, geography, and political influence continue to determine whose voices are heard and whose values are reflected in the curriculum, largely due to the regulatory environment surrounding education.

Debates rage over what education should be: a means of transmitting culture, a tool for critical thinking, a pipeline to employment, or a vehicle for social engineering and justice. As politicians, school boards, and accrediting agencies debate standards, testing, and the latest educational innovations, a fundamental question is often overlooked: Who decides what is best for children? Should it be the state, administrators, educators, or families themselves?

For those who value sovereignty, the challenge is clear. True educational freedom means empowering families and communities to shape their own educational destinies, resisting the pressures of homogenization, and reclaiming the right to pass on their unique values, histories, and ways of knowing. It is a path to a decentralized way of educating families, with decision-making at the family level.

A More Centralized System

In the early history of the United States, education was a local affair, organized by towns, churches, and families, with curricula reflecting local values and needs. This debate over education in America traces back to the founding fathers, who viewed education as essential for the survival of the republic and the preservation of liberty. Leaders like Thomas Jefferson (1743–1826) and John Adams (1735–1826) believed that an informed and virtuous citizenry was necessary to prevent tyranny and ensure self-government. Jefferson, for example, advocated for public education in Virginia and saw it as a bulwark against ignorance and oppression, while Adams enshrined the importance of education in the Massachusetts Constitution.

Despite this consensus on the value of education, the U.S. Constitution does not explicitly mention education. This omission was intentional: the framers left the responsibility for education to the states, reflecting their commitment to federalism and the decentralized nature of American governance. As a result, education policy and funding became predominantly state and local matters, with each state developing its own system. Over time, this arrangement has fueled ongoing debates about educational access and the appropriate role of federal versus state versus local authority in shaping American schools. The Founding Fathers' ideals continue to influence these debates, even as the Constitution itself remains silent on the issue of education.

By the late nineteenth century, however, state legislatures began consolidating school districts and creating statewide superintendents and boards of education. These bureaucratic structures emphasized uniformity, tight control of students and teachers, and the elimination of local variation in the name of efficiency and economic growth. Critics at the time likened school superintendents to drill sergeants and schools to cotton mills, warning that over-centralization would suppress the aspirations of working-class families and stifle educational innovation.

The twentieth century saw this trend accelerate, especially as industrialization and urbanization demanded more standardized schooling. Progressive reformers argued that centralization would ensure a high-quality, uniform education for all students, regardless of background. The federal government's role expanded dramatically during the 1960s, most notably through President Lyndon B. Johnson's (1908–1973) Great Society programs. The Elementary and Secondary Education Act (ESEA) of 1965 marked the first major federal intervention, directing funding and policy mandates to schools serving low-income students and requiring states to demonstrate accountability for federal funds. Johnson's reforms aimed to address educational inequality and promote integration, but they also set the precedent for ongoing federal involvement in local schools.

The move toward centralization intensified with the No Child Left Behind Act (NCLB) of 2001, which imposed national testing and accountability standards on all public schools. While NCLB was intended to close achievement gaps, it also reduced local and state autonomy, tying funding to compliance with federally mandated assessments and curricula. Critics argued that this overreliance on standardized testing narrowed the curriculum and stifled teacher creativity.

The Common Core State Standards Initiative in the 2010s represented another major step toward nationalization, as states were pressured to adopt uniform standards in exchange for federal grants. This movement further surrendered local control to national organizations and Washington bureaucrats, raising concerns about the loss of educational freedom and the imposition of a one-size-fits-all model for teaching children. While some recent reforms, such as the Every Student Succeeds Act (ESSA) of 2015, have nominally returned some authority to states, the overall trajectory remains one of increased central oversight and diminished local sovereignty.

This American experience is mirrored in many other countries. In Europe, the nineteenth and twentieth centuries saw the rise of national education systems, with central governments designing curricula, setting standards, and controlling funding. France is often cited as the archetype of centralized education, but even countries with traditions of local control, like the UK and Sweden, have seen increasing national regulation, especially through standardized testing and school inspections. In the twentieth century, authoritarian regimes in Germany, Spain, and the Soviet Union used education as a tool for social engineering and political control, eliminating regional autonomy and enforcing strict uniformity.

In China, education has long been a tool of the central state, used to promote official ideology and economic goals. While the 1980s brought some decentralization, allowing local governments more say in administration and curriculum, the central government has retained tight control through national standards, high-stakes exams like the Gaokao, and a unified curriculum. Recent reforms have actually re-centralized many aspects of the system, using national assessment and curriculum as levers of control.

In Latin America, countries like Chile and Colombia have oscillated between centralization and decentralization. Chile's system, for example, was highly centralized under both colonial and later German influence, with the Ministry of Education controlling curriculum, textbooks, and funding. Later reforms devolved some authority to municipalities, but this often led to increased inequality, prompting new waves of centralization to ensure minimum standards and equity.

Centralization has brought some benefits: it can help ensure a minimum standard of education, promote national cohesion, and address glaring inequalities. However, it comes at a significant cost to local autonomy, parental involvement, and educational diversity. Decisions about what children learn, how they are taught, and which values are prioritized have increasingly been made by distant bureaucrats rather than families or local communities. The result is often a system that is less responsive to local needs and less reflective of the unique identities and aspirations of the people it serves.

As debates over education continue, the central question remains: who should decide what is best for children: the state, or the families and communities closest to them? The history of centralization is a reminder that educational sovereignty, once lost, is difficult to reclaim. The ongoing challenge for societies around the world is to find a balance between the benefits of national standards and the fundamental right of families and communities to shape their own educational destinies.

Whose Children?

In the United States, the structure of public education and related services allows parents to outsource significant portions of their children's daily lives, sometimes for more than 40 hours a week. Many schools now offer not only the traditional school day, but also a range of wraparound services that cover early mornings through late afternoons. In some districts, children can arrive as early as 7 a.m. for before-school programs, receive breakfast at school, attend classes, have lunch provided, and then participate in afterschool programs or care that often extends until 6 p.m. or later. For example, the National School Lunch Program and the School Breakfast Program ensure that millions of children receive two meals a day at school, with some districts offering grab-and-go or second-chance breakfasts to accommodate different schedules and appetites.

Afterschool programs are now a standard offering in 85 percent of U.S. public K–12 schools, with many providing academic support, snacks, and enrichment activities well into the evening. In places like the Hatboro-Horsham School District in Pennsylvania, even childcare before and after school has been outsourced to third-party providers, who run pre-kindergarten, before- and after-school care, and summer camps on school premises. This trend is not isolated; it reflects a nationwide shift toward schools and external providers assuming roles that once belonged exclusively to families.

The cumulative effect is that some parents can, in practice, check out of daily parenting responsibilities for the majority of the workweek. As one educator observed, there is a growing expectation that schools not only educate but also provide food, supervision, and even manage basic care and discipline for children. Anecdotes from teachers and school staff highlight how some parents rely on schools for everything from toilet training to providing supplies, with the school day and its associated programs acting as a form of comprehensive childcare. One teacher recounted parents expecting staff to handle not just academics but also personal care tasks, reflecting how deeply the outsourcing trend has taken root.

While after-school and extended-day programs can provide valuable support, especially for working families and those facing economic challenges, they also raise questions about the dilution of parental involvement and the shifting of core responsibilities from families to institutions. Some parents express relief at being able to meet work obligations, while others worry about losing control over their children's upbringing and the quality of care provided by third-party vendors.

This system, for better or worse, allows parents to be largely absent from their children's daily lives for forty or more hours each week, with schools providing meals, supervision, academic support, and even emotional and behavioral guidance. The implications for family connection, child development, and the role of schools in society continue to be debated by educators, policymakers, and parents alike.

Social Emotional Learning and Programming Morality

Social Emotional Learning (SEL) has become a central feature of American education, shifting not only how children are taught to manage their feelings and relationships, but also who shapes their moral and social development. Originally formalized in the late twentieth century, SEL was designed to address the whole child, equipping students with skills such as self-awareness, empathy, and responsible decision-making, alongside academic content. The Collaborative for Academic, Social, and Emotional Learning (CASEL), founded in 1994, played a pivotal role in establishing SEL as a field, building on earlier work by Yale's Child Study Center and other educational theorists.

While the intent of SEL is to foster well-rounded, emotionally intelligent citizens, its implementation has sparked significant debate, particularly around the question of who should control a child's moral upbringing. Traditionally, families have been the primary source of moral and ethical guidance, shaping children's values, beliefs, and sense of right and wrong. However, as SEL programs become more comprehensive and standardized, schools increasingly assume this formative role, teaching children not just how to behave, but also what to value and how to interpret their own experiences.

This shift is not without controversy. Critics argue that SEL laws and curricula represent a qualitative change in the balance of power between the state, the school, and the family. By codifying specific social and emotional competencies, SEL can diminish parental autonomy and override family norms, values, and beliefs. In effect, the state is not only dictating what children learn academically, but also who they should become as people, a move that raises constitutional and ethical concerns about the limits of state power in education. For example, some SEL programs encourage children to look to their own feelings and experiences as the ultimate authority on what is right or wrong, which can conflict with family or religious teachings that emphasize external or transcendent sources of morality.

The postmodern roots of SEL further complicate this dynamic. Postmodernism, as a philosophical movement, questions the existence of absolute truths and emphasizes the fragmentation of identity and morality. SEL's focus on self-constructed meaning, emotional literacy, and critical examination of social norms reflects this postmodern influence. In practice, this can mean that children are taught to question traditional structures, including family authority and long-standing moral frameworks, in favor of constructing their own values based on personal and social experiences. The introduction of Transformative SEL, which explicitly aims to guide students to critically examine root causes of inequity and develop collaborative solutions, underscores this shift toward a more activist and subjective approach to moral and identity-politics-based curriculum.

As SEL becomes more deeply embedded in school policy and practice, parents may find that their role as the primary moral educators of their children is increasingly challenged. The one-size-fits-all approach of SEL can override the diverse values and beliefs found in families and communities, replacing them with a standardized set of attitudes and behaviors deemed desirable by educational authorities. This can leave families feeling disenfranchised, especially when SEL content conflicts with their own convictions about what constitutes the good life or proper conduct.

Topics such as ethnicity, gender, sexuality, and the environment are all under the guise of SEL. Students as young as six years old are exposed to concepts that exceed their cognitive development, thereby serving to indoctrinate rather than educate them. Furthermore, many of these lessons serve to deprive childhood innocence and teach children that they are either a victim or an oppressor. This can ultimately cause anxiety, fear, or even have far more detrimental consequences on a child's mental and physical well-being.

An additional reason why modern education has suffered so much is that the purpose of education has shifted, particularly over the last twenty years. This is because Paulo Freire (1921–1997), the influential Brazilian educator and philosopher, fundamentally reshaped modern education with his concept of "critical pedagogy." Freire rejected what he called the banking model of education, where students are treated as passive vessels to be filled with knowledge by the teacher. Instead, he advocated for a dialogical, problem-posing approach, where students and teachers learn from one another, and education becomes an act of liberation and social transformation. Freire's method, originally developed for adult literacy among the oppressed, is rooted in Marxist and existentialist thought, emphasizing that education is never neutral; its purpose is either to maintain the status quo or to empower individuals to challenge and change systems of oppression.

In the United States and elsewhere, Freire's ideas have been widely adopted, not just in higher education but increasingly in K–12 schooling. His influence is evident in the proliferation of curricula and teaching methods that explicitly aim to foster critical consciousness and social activism, even among young children. The goal is no longer simply to raise curious, independent thinkers, but to guide students, sometimes as early as elementary school, toward identifying and acting against perceived social injustices. This shift is evident in lesson plans that incorporate activism into subjects such as language arts and social studies, and in educational frameworks that encourage students to view themselves as agents of social change from a young age.

While Freire's original vision emphasized dialogue, love, and the affirmation of each learner's reality, the American adaptation often takes the form of direct instruction in activism and social justice. This shift raises profound questions about agency and sovereignty. When schools adopt activist curricula, they risk undermining parental authority and the family's role as the primary moral guide for children. Instead of parents shaping their children's beliefs and values, the state and its agents increasingly assume this role, often without meaningful input or consent from families. The result is a loss of both parental autonomy and the child's individual agency, as the educational system prescribes not only what to think, but also how to act in the world.

At its core, this is a departure from education as a process of nurturing curiosity, critical thinking, and independent judgment. Instead, it positions children as instruments of social change, sometimes before they have the maturity to understand the complexities of the issues at hand. For many families, this is not education, but a form of ideological imposition that erodes the sovereignty of both the family and the individual child.

Who Decides What is Taught?

The process of choosing curriculum and textbooks in American schools is complex. It varies significantly between public and private institutions, with important implications for parental involvement and the increasing presence of political and activist content in core subjects.

In public schools, curriculum decisions are shaped by multiple layers of authority. At the federal level, broad educational goals are set, but the most direct influence comes from state governments and, crucially, local school boards. State boards of education typically establish curriculum frameworks and select approved textbook lists, especially for grades one through eight. Committees, often composed primarily of classroom teachers and subject specialists, review and recommend textbooks, and local school districts then choose from these state-approved options.

Local school boards, which may include elected parents and community members, play a significant role in tailoring the curriculum to reflect community values and needs. However, while parents can attend school board meetings, participate in PTAs, and vote in board elections, their direct influence over specific curriculum choices is limited; the ultimate authority rests with the boards and state agencies.

In private schools, the process is more centralized within each institution. The curriculum is typically set by the school's leadership, often the principal or head of school, guided by the school's mission, philosophy, or religious affiliation. Private schools have far greater flexibility in designing their own courses, selecting textbooks, and introducing specialized or alternative teaching methods, such as Montessori or Waldorf approaches. While some private schools may actively seek parent input, especially in smaller or independent settings, the degree of parental influence is generally determined by the school's governance structure and culture.

Parental agency in both settings is a point of ongoing debate. In public schools, parents have avenues to express concerns or request changes; however, legal precedent affirms that parents do not have a fundamental right to control every aspect of curriculum content, especially when it comes to information that the school deems educationally appropriate. However, recent legal developments, such as the 2025 Supreme Court ruling requiring schools to offer opt-outs for certain lessons that conflict with religious beliefs, are beginning to shift the landscape in favor of greater parental rights in specific contexts.

The influx of political and activist content in core subjects is a growing phenomenon. For example, a textbook titled Social Justice Math incorporates lessons from critical pedagogy and activism, aiming to empower students to address social inequalities through math instruction. Similarly, curricula addressing gender and sexuality are being introduced in lower grades, sometimes with one to two lessons per month on topics like gender expression, consent, and diverse family structures, even in private, religious, or progressive schools. These lessons encroach on parental authority and do not align with everyone's values.

This leads to an age-old debate about banning books. Today, the debate surrounding the so-called "banning books" often focuses on school libraries and is frequently mischaracterized. While headlines frequently frame these actions as broad censorship, the reality is that most parents and community members advocating for book removals are seeking age-appropriate content for children, not the wholesale suppression of ideas or literature. The core concern is not about shielding students from challenging themes, but about ensuring that young children are not prematurely exposed to material that is sexually explicit, graphically violent, or otherwise too mature or complex for their developmental stage.

Many parents argue that having books with adult topics, such as explicit sexual content, graphic violence, or mature language, available in elementary or middle school libraries undermines their ability to guide their children's exposure to such material. For example, in Hilliard, Ohio, parents have voiced discomfort after discovering books with graphic sexual content in elementary school libraries, emphasizing that they want to partner with schools to ensure content is educational and age-appropriate. Similar concerns have driven calls for warning labels or age classifications for library books, akin to movie ratings, so parents can make informed decisions about what their children access. In Washington state, proposals have been made to require libraries to rate books, restricting explicit content to older students or adults.

National surveys reflect this sentiment: about 60 percent of parents believe school libraries should restrict access to certain books by age or require parental permission before a child can check out a book. The 2025 Supreme Court case, Mahmoud v. Taylor, highlighted these concerns, with parents arguing that children should not be exposed to topics like gender transitions or explicit sexual themes without parental consent. Many parents feel that simply opting out of their child is insufficient, as their children are still surrounded by peers who may have access to the same controversial material.

The reasons cited for challenging or removing books are consistent: sexual content, profanity, violence, and other mature themes are the most common triggers for parental concern. These challenges are not limited to one side of the political spectrum; parents from diverse backgrounds and beliefs have objected to books they consider inappropriate for their children's age group.

Ultimately, the push to remove or restrict certain books is less about banning ideas and more about preserving the innocence of childhood and respecting parents' rights to determine when and how their children encounter complex or explicit topics. The conversation is ongoing, with many advocating for transparent review processes, age ratings, and parental involvement in school library decisions, rather than blanket bans or unrestricted access.

Marxism in Education

Over the past several decades, in America and other parts of the world, education has undergone a profound transformation influenced by Marxist and neo-Marxist thought, shifting away from its traditional focus on fostering curiosity, critical thinking, and individual merit. Instead, schools increasingly promote collectivist ideologies, group identity, and activism, often at the expense of family values, independent reasoning, and a merit-based culture.

Critical Marxist educators, such as Michael Apple, have openly advocated for a "thorough-going reconstruction of what education is for," aiming to replace the traditional American model with one rooted in Marxian-socialist ideals. This approach calls for discarding curricula that do not promote the transformation of America from a free, capitalist republic into a socialist society. The process involves teaching students that America is fundamentally flawed and oppressive, and that social justice activism, not academic mastery or productive citizenship, should be the primary goal of education.

Neo-Marxist theorists extend this vision, arguing that education serves as a mechanism for reproducing social class inequalities and legitimizing the dominance of the ruling class. Through what is termed the "hidden curriculum," schools transmit values and attitudes that sustain capitalist hierarchies, such as competition and acceptance of authority, while also increasingly introducing counter-hegemonic narratives that challenge traditional Western values and promote a politics of redistribution and recognition.

The Marxist critique of the family is explicit and longstanding. As Karl Marx and Friedrich Engels wrote in the Communist Manifesto, the abolition of the bourgeois family is a core objective, to be replaced by social (state-driven) education. This ideological stance sees the family as an instrument of capitalist oppression and seeks to transfer the responsibility for moral and social upbringing from parents to the state and its schools. In practice, this translates into curricula and school policies that often undermine parental authority, diminish the role of the family, and promote values that may directly conflict with those held by students' families.

Education in many American schools now emphasizes "equity" and "social justice" over individual achievement and critical inquiry. Lessons in core subjects, including math and language arts, are increasingly infused with activist content, teaching students to view themselves and society through the lens of systemic oppression, identity politics, and collective grievance. Rather than encouraging students to think for themselves, the prevailing approach often tells them what to think, punishing dissent and rewarding conformity to the dominant ideological narrative.

In addition, teacher preparation programs, commonly known as teachers' colleges, have in recent years placed a significant and growing emphasis on diversity, equity, and inclusion (DEI) throughout their curricula. This shift is evident in both the content of coursework and the underlying philosophy guiding teacher education.

Many leading teacher preparation programs now explicitly prioritize DEI as central to their mission. For example, technical assistance providers and national transformation centers, often supported by major philanthropic organizations, have developed comprehensive guides and companion documents to help teacher colleges deepen their focus on diversity, equity, inclusion, and anti-racism at every stage of teacher training. These materials encourage programs to recruit and retain a more diverse teacher pipeline and to ensure that new teachers are prepared to positively impact all students, regardless of background.

Curriculum mapping in teacher education now often includes a dedicated review of how and where DEI outcomes are addressed, with the goal of embedding inclusive practices and culturally responsive pedagogy throughout all courses. This process involves not only adding specific courses on multicultural education and culturally relevant teaching, but also integrating diverse perspectives and anti-bias frameworks into field experiences, lesson planning, and classroom management strategies. Teacher candidates are expected to engage in critical reflection on their own identities, biases, and beliefs, and to design lessons that reflect and affirm the cultural backgrounds of their future students.

Research and policy guidance urge teacher colleges to move beyond token representation, advocating for the intentional inclusion of marginalized perspectives and the validation of students' lived experiences as legitimate sources of knowledge. This includes selecting instructional materials that reflect the diversity of the classroom and society, and encouraging teacher candidates to foster a sense of belonging and empowerment among all students.

Professional development in DEI is also a major component, with many programs offering or requiring diversity training for both faculty and students. These trainings cover a wide range of topics, including cultural competence, anti-racism, gender and sexuality inclusion, and strategies for addressing systemic inequities in education.

While the degree of emphasis on DEI can vary between institutions, the overall trend is clear: diversity, equity, and inclusion now occupy a central place in the curriculum and ethos of teacher preparation programs. This approach aims to prepare teachers to serve increasingly diverse student populations and address persistent achievement gaps. However, it also reflects a broader philosophical shift in education, from a primary focus on subject mastery and pedagogy to a more holistic, identity-conscious model of teaching and learning.

There is mounting evidence, both in the United States and globally, of a significant decline in student preparedness for high school and college-level reading, writing, and mathematics. This trend is documented across standardized tests, international assessments, and educator observations, raising concerns about the future workforce and the overall health of education systems.

In the U.S., the most recent National Assessment of Educational Progress (NAEP), often referred to as the Nation's Report Card, found that reading comprehension scores for both fourth- and eighth-graders in 2024 reached record lows. The percentage of eighth graders scoring below the "basic" level, the minimum for grade-level proficiency, was the highest in the history of the assessment. Math scores have also declined, with eighth graders dropping eight points between 2019 and 2024, and fourth graders performing below 2019 levels despite a slight uptick since 2022.

This decline is not limited to elementary and middle school. Only one in five high school graduates in 2023 was deemed fully prepared for college-level coursework, according to ACT data. More than 40% of graduates did not meet any of the ACT's college-readiness benchmarks, with readiness in math and science particularly low. The average ACT composite score for the class of 2023 was the lowest in thirty-two years, marking a downward trend that has persisted for over a decade.

Writing and Analytical Skills: A Persistent Weakness

Writing skills are also suffering. Only about a quarter of American high school seniors are proficient in writing, and college instructors report that incoming students often lack the ability to write in complete sentences, structure essays, or support arguments with evidence. Many students have not practiced writing beyond short assignments, rarely engage in extended analytical writing, and struggle with basic grammar and research skills. This lack of preparation leaves students unable to meet the demands of college-level writing and critical thinking.

The decline of meritocracy in education has become a defining feature of recent years, as schools and universities increasingly shift their focus from individual achievement and objective standards to policies grounded in identity politics. This transition is evident across admissions, curriculum, and classroom culture, raising concerns about fairness, academic rigor, and the long-term consequences for both students and society.

Where meritocracy once meant that students were evaluated primarily on their abilities, effort, and accomplishments, often measured through standardized tests and academic performance, many institutions now prioritize diversity, equity, and inclusion (DEI) initiatives. These policies often emphasize group identity, such as race, gender, or socioeconomic background, over individual merit. For example, the removal of standardized tests from college admissions and the adoption of subjective criteria, such as personal essays or recommendations, have made the process less transparent and more susceptible to implicit biases. Critics argue that this undermines the objectivity and fairness that are central to a meritocratic system, potentially lowering educational standards and outcomes.

In the sciences and other traditionally merit-based fields, the pressure to increase representation of certain groups has led to changes in how qualifications are evaluated. Mathematical problem-solving and rigorous coursework are sometimes de-emphasized in favor of group projects or qualitative assessments, with the stated goal of ensuring that no one is left behind. While supporters of these changes argue that they help address historical inequalities, detractors warn that they risk sacrificing excellence and innovation in the name of diversity.

The rise of identity politics in education also affects classroom dynamics. Instead of viewing students as unique individuals with varied talents and aspirations, there is a growing tendency to categorize them by group identity and make assumptions about their needs and abilities based on those categories. This can perpetuate stereotypes and self-fulfilling prophecies, rather than encouraging each student to reach their full potential. The focus on equality of outcome, rather than equality of opportunity, shifts attention away from helping all students excel and toward engineering proportional representation across groups, regardless of individual differences in achievement or interest.

At elite schools, students themselves are aware of the tension between meritocratic ideals and the realities of privilege and exclusion. While many embrace the rhetoric of meritocracy, they also recognize that social class and background continue to play a significant role in shaping opportunities and outcomes. As the meritocracy is questioned and sometimes replaced by identity-based frameworks, the belief in achieving success through hard work and talent is weakened, and the legitimacy of educational institutions as engines of social mobility is called into question.

Similarly, educational standards in the United States have faced growing scrutiny as key measures of academic rigor, such as the SAT, Advanced Placement (AP) exams, and international assessments like PISA, have undergone significant changes, often reflecting a broader trend of declining expectations.

One of the most notable shifts is the elimination of the SAT essay and subject tests. The College Board announced in 2021 that it would discontinue the essay section and all subject tests, citing the existence of other ways for students to demonstrate their writing skills and the expanded reach of AP coursework. This move means the SAT is now entirely multiple-choice, removing a component that once required students to construct and defend an argument in writing, a critical skill for college and beyond. The rationale was partly to reduce student stress and streamline the admissions process, but critics argue that this also lowers the bar for assessing college readiness and academic depth.

AP exams have also come under scrutiny. While some AP courses, such as AP Physics C and AP Chemistry, remain challenging, as rated by students, there is a perception that many AP exams are becoming easier, with higher pass rates and less rigorous content in some subjects. For example, new AP courses, such as Precalculus and

African American Studies, have seen high pass rates in their first years, and the overall expansion of AP offerings is sometimes viewed as prioritizing broad access over maintaining high standards of mastery.

For over ten years, I served as a grader for college-credit history exams administered to high school students. Year after year, I would see the grading standards lowered and was told to overlook answers that had historically inaccurate information. We were told to only count what students got correct and overlook anything else. In addition, the writing standards were increasingly relaxed, allowing a thesis statement to be found anywhere in the beginning or ending of a paragraph. When the grading did not meet what I assumed was the passing quota, we were given updates on what to accept for credit, even though some exams had already been graded. Furthermore, the actual classes and tests have become increasingly easier year after year. I finally stopped grading the exams because my ethical principles no longer allowed me to participate.

On the international stage, the United States has struggled to keep pace with global peers. Results from the Program for International Student Assessment (PISA) show a long-term decline in U.S. student performance, particularly in mathematics and science. American 15-year-olds consistently score below many other industrialized nations, with policymakers expressing concern that this trend threatens the nation's competitiveness and economic future. The issue is not unique to the U.S.; countries like New Zealand have also recorded their worst-ever PISA results, reflecting a global decline in educational outcomes. However, the persistent achievement gaps and lack of improvement in U.S. scores underscore the urgency of addressing declining standards.

The cumulative effect of these changes is a system where objective measures of academic achievement are being de-emphasized or simplified, raising concerns about college preparedness and students' ability to compete in a global knowledge economy. The removal of rigorous assessments and the trend toward making advanced coursework more accessible, while well-intentioned, risk diluting the value of these credentials and masking underlying weaknesses in the education system.

The decline in educational standards is a global phenomenon, not limited to the United States. International assessments and historical comparisons of curriculum and textbooks reveal a marked drop in both academic rigor and student performance worldwide.

Recent results from international benchmarks, such as the PISA and the Trends in International Mathematics and Science Study (TIMSS), show that student performance in core subjects, including mathematics, reading, and science, has declined significantly across many countries. The 2022 PISA survey recorded an unprecedented drop in performance globally, with reading abilities declining by an average of 10 points and mathematics by 15 points since 2018, equivalent to nearly a year of learning loss. While some Asian education systems (Singapore, Macao, Taiwan, Hong Kong, Japan, South Korea) continue to excel, students in Europe, North America, and many other regions are falling further behind. In the U.S., TIMSS 2023 results highlight a further decline in science and math, with the country slipping relative to its peers.

Lockdowns exacerbated these trends, but experts note that the decline predates the pandemic, pointing to deeper, systemic issues in education policy and practice. The consequences are profound: millions of students globally are not meeting even basic academic standards, and the gap between high- and low-performing countries is widening.

This is no more evident than when comparing textbooks and reading lists from 100 years ago to today, starkly illustrating the shift in educational expectations. Early twentieth-century textbooks and recommended reading for middle schoolers often included classic literature, works with complex language, historical references, and challenging thematic content. For example, a 1908 curriculum manual from Minnesota listed texts such as *The Odyssey*, *Ivanhoe*, and *The Last of the Mohicans* for seventh- and eighth-graders, books that demand advanced comprehension, critical thinking, and engagement with historical and moral questions.

In contrast, today's middle school reading lists tend to feature more contemporary works, often written in simpler language and focused on themes considered more relatable or accessible to modern students. Thematic complexity and historical scope have often been replaced by more immediate, personal, or socially relevant narratives. While this can make literature more approachable, it also means students are less likely to be challenged by the depth and breadth of material that was once standard.

This shift is not limited to literature. Across subjects, historical textbooks emphasized memorization, mastery of foundational knowledge, and the development of reasoning through rigorous questioning. As educational theory shifted toward student-centered and experiential learning, textbooks became less about conveying a body of knowledge and more about engaging students' interests and experiences. While this has benefits, it also risks lowering the bar for what is expected and achieved in the classroom.

The decline in standards has far-reaching implications. In the West, especially, students are falling behind their Asian peers, with PISA 2022 results showing that U.S. and European students are performing significantly worse than in previous decades, particularly in mathematics and reading. The weakening of academic rigor is also evident in the removal of challenging components from standardized tests (such as the SAT essay), the simplification of AP exams, and the broader trend toward grade inflation and degree devaluation in higher education.

Globally, the learning crisis poses a threat not only to individual opportunities but also to national competitiveness, economic growth, and social stability. According to a joint report by UNESCO, UNICEF, and the World Bank, the current generation of students risks losing $17 trillion in lifetime earnings due to learning losses, with the most vulnerable children suffering the greatest setbacks.

The decline in academic preparedness is not just an American problem. The 2022 PISA revealed an unprecedented drop in mathematics and reading scores across dozens of countries. On average, OECD countries experienced a 10-point decline in reading and a 15-point decline in mathematics since 2018, equivalent to nearly a year's worth of lost learning. Countries such as Germany, Iceland, the Netherlands, Norway, and Poland also experienced particularly sharp declines. Globally, one in four 15-year-olds now fails to meet basic proficiency in math, reading, and science.

While the lockdowns exacerbated learning losses, experts emphasize that the downward trajectory began well before 2020, highlighting deeper, structural issues within education systems. Factors such as over-reliance on technology, teacher shortages, and a shift away from foundational skills have contributed to this crisis.

The consequences of this decline are far-reaching. Students entering high school and college often lack the fundamental skills necessary for academic and career success. In the U.S., the gap between high- and low-achieving students is widening, and many students are unaware of their own lack of preparedness, leading to a "nasty wake-up call" in their first year of college.

Globally, the learning crisis poses a threat to economic competitiveness and social mobility. Countries that have maintained rigorous standards and provided targeted support, such as Singapore, continue to outperform their peers, highlighting the importance of sustained investment in foundational skills and teacher quality.

This shift is also reflected in the decline of meritocracy. The erosion of objective standards, such as standardized testing, and the prioritization of diversity, equity, and inclusion (DEI) policies have led to a system where subjective criteria and group identity take precedence over individual merit and accomplishment. Critics argue that this not only undermines educational quality but also discourages excellence and personal responsibility.

The result of these ideological changes is a generation of students who, upon leaving the K-12 system, often possess an anti-American worldview, lack a balanced understanding of history and civics, and are less prepared for the demands of civic and professional life. The focus on activism and group identity, especially at an early age, can be seen as a form of indoctrination, depriving children of the opportunity to develop their own beliefs and undermining both family sovereignty and individual agency.

Lack of Intellectual Diversity

Due to these issues in education today, there has been a notable decline in intellectual diversity within American education, affecting both K–12 schools and higher education. This trend is evident in the narrowing of acceptable viewpoints among educators and students, the marginalization of dissenting perspectives, and the increasing prevalence of ideological conformity in many academic environments.

In colleges and universities, the commitment to free expression and open inquiry has eroded. While diversity, equity, and inclusion (DEI) initiatives are promoted, they often coincide with a stifling of genuine diversity of thought. Surveys and campus observations reveal that students frequently hesitate to express views that diverge from prevailing campus norms, fearing backlash or social ostracism. This environment discourages robust debate and critical thinking, as only certain viewpoints are considered acceptable, while others are suppressed or excluded from the discourse.

The ideological imbalance among faculty is a significant driver of this phenomenon. Over the past twenty-five years, the proportion of conservative professors has shrunk dramatically, leading to a campus culture where certain academic fields and research topics, such as military history or family breakdown, are neglected or dismissed. Job postings and hiring practices in academia often implicitly, or even explicitly, discourage applicants with dissenting or non-mainstream views, further deepening the homogeneity of thought. The result is an echo chamber in which students are less likely to encounter or engage with ideas that challenge their assumptions, undermining the very mission of higher education to foster critical inquiry.

This decline in viewpoint diversity is not limited to higher education. In K–12 schools, teachers and administrators often display open hostility toward students or colleagues who express politically unpopular opinions. For example, a teacher recounted how faculty reacted with visible disgust to a student wearing a Trump T-shirt, discussing whether the student should be "re-educated" for his political expression. Such incidents reflect a broader climate in which progressive ideas are valorized and conservative or dissenting views are stigmatized, creating a chilling effect on open discussion and learning.

The lack of intellectual diversity among educators is exacerbated by the credentialing process, which often favors candidates who align with dominant ideological perspectives. This further narrows the pool of teachers and professors, making it difficult for students to encounter a broad spectrum of viewpoints throughout their education. Economic barriers also play a role, as the cost and structure of academic careers often exclude those from diverse socioeconomic backgrounds, leading to a more homogenous faculty and a diminished range of life experiences and perspectives represented in the classroom.

Ultimately, the decline of intellectual diversity in education deprives students of the opportunity to develop critical and independent thinking skills. Instead, they are often taught what to think, as professors and teachers promote their own agendas rather than encouraging open exploration of ideas. This trend has significant consequences not only for academic rigor but also for the health of a democratic society, which depends on citizens who are able to engage with a wide range of perspectives and reason for themselves.

The evolution of modern education, as traced from the Enlightenment through the adoption of the Prussian system, reveals a steady shift away from individual autonomy toward centralized, state-controlled schooling. This transformation, while intended to produce rational, civic-minded citizens, has also resulted in a system where education is often treated as a public commodity, managed, regulated, and standardized for the masses.

However, just as with money, the centralization of education can undermine personal freedom and sovereignty. When parents relinquish control over their child's learning to external authorities, they risk losing the ability to shape not only the content but also the values and critical thinking skills their children develop. The issues highlighted in this chapter, loss of individual agency, overemphasis on uniformity, and the detachment of education from family and community values, underscore why passive outsourcing of education is problematic.

True ownership of a child's education is an extension of both parental freedom and responsibility. It means actively engaging in educational choices, questioning prevailing systems, and ensuring that learning aligns with the family's values and the child's unique needs. Just as financial sovereignty empowers individuals to make choices about their own resources, educational sovereignty empowers parents and children to pursue knowledge that is meaningful, relevant, and liberating.

In an era where the default is to outsource and standardize, reclaiming involvement in a child's education is an act of both freedom and stewardship. Parents must resist the urge to blindly trust systems that may not serve their child's best interests. Instead, by remaining informed, involved, and intentional, families can foster not only academic achievement but also the development of independent, thoughtful, and free individuals.

Part 2: Schooling Options

Chapter 8: Your Path to Ownschooling

Education is not the filling of a pail, but the lighting of a fire.

- William Butler Yeats

Even if circumstances, whether legal, financial, or personal, require your child to attend a government-approved public or private school, your role as an engaged parent remains absolutely vital. True educational sovereignty does not end at the schoolhouse door. In fact, when you cannot choose or customize your child's learning environment, your active participation becomes even more important.

In high school, I realized that my sister and I were so different. She was more reserved, studious, and hesitant to try new things. I was quite the opposite. She took AP classes, and I took what I wanted to learn about. She was a baton twirler with the band and studied. She had twirled a baton since she was three years old. I also twirled a baton growing up, but gave it up to try new things by the time I got to middle school. In fact, in high school, I tried many activities, explored various subjects, and had an incredible core group of friends. She rarely had friends over, and my house was our hangout spot. She left for college after my freshman year of high school, and I continued to flourish with my curiosity.

This is not a judgment on either of our parts; it is simply an observation that two kids brought up in the same house have very different educational needs. This is where ownschooling can help them flourish individually. My mom allowed us to be individuals, although when my parents were still together, I was forced to twirl a baton instead of taking gymnastics, as it made it easier for my parents to take us to one place instead of two. In my dad's traditional worldview, girls twirled, while boys played drums. I had to pick up the baton instead of the snare drum, but I still managed to find my own joy and learn new things.

In order to start ownschooling, you need to actively engage in your child's education. If they are enrolled in a school, whether it is a public school, private school, or even a homeschool co-op, you still need to be asking about their learning, communicating with their teachers, and making sure they are being taught things that align with your values while still being curious and challenged appropriately. You can start by building strong, respectful relationships with your child's teachers and school administrators. Attend parent-teacher conferences, open houses, and school board meetings. Introduce yourself early in the year and make it clear that you are invested in your child's education and well-being. Ask questions about the curriculum, classroom policies, and upcoming units of study. Make it a habit to review your child's assignments, textbooks, and reading lists so you know exactly what they are learning.

If you discover that your child is being taught material that conflicts with your family's values or beliefs, you have the right and responsibility to speak up. Approach the teacher or administrator respectfully and request an alternative assignment, reading, or activity for your child. Many schools have policies in place for such accommodations, particularly in subjects such as health, literature, or social studies. If a particular unit or lesson is non-negotiable, you may choose to keep your child home during that period and provide your own instruction.

If your requests are denied or if the school is unwilling to accommodate your concerns, it is crucial to maintain open communication with your child. Discuss what they are learning, encourage critical thinking, and help them process information that may be at odds with your family's values. This process, sometimes called "deprogramming," is not about shielding your child from every idea you disagree with, but about building trust, teaching discernment, and reinforcing your family's beliefs at home.

Ultimately, the most powerful tool you have is your relationship with your child. Foster an environment where they feel safe sharing their thoughts, questions, and experiences. Encourage them to think critically about what they hear in school, to ask questions, and to seek multiple perspectives. When necessary, provide context or counterpoints to ideas presented in the classroom, helping your child develop a strong sense of self and the ability to navigate a world of diverse viewpoints.

Remember, your proof of work as a parent is not just about monitoring or correcting, but about actively partnering with your child in their educational journey, wherever that journey takes place. Your involvement, advocacy, and trust-building are the foundation of true educational sovereignty, even within the constraints of a traditional school system.

As an educator for a long time, both within the system and working independently, I have had numerous opportunities to observe families and students. I will present some anecdotes to illustrate that parental involvement matters, to inspire others, and to show that there are ways to have a say in your child's education, no matter what modality you choose. I want to remind you that even when your child is enrolled in a school that may not align with your values, you are still the ultimate authority in your child's education.

I know a family whose children were in public school. Homeschooling was not an option. Yet, the mother advocated for her children and made decisions based on what was best for them and their learning. Her oldest was struggling with his English Language Arts class due to some learning challenges he faced. In her state, she was allowed to unenroll him from his ELA class and homeschool him for just that subject. She conducted the research and found a workaround that would ensure her son received the best education possible. She hired a tutor, and he was engaged in his learning, able to work through the obstacles of his dysgraphia while reading and writing about more challenging texts than he would have in school.

Another family I know dealt with their private school, which was advocating values that did not align with theirs. The father had raised his son to be curious, to question things, and to think independently. When faced with indoctrinating ideas on identity politics in class, he was not going to take what was said at face value. As a high school-aged young man, he was confident enough in his thinking and questioning that he pushed back against the teacher. His ideas did not always make him the most popular student or the teacher's pet, yet he stood his ground and chose to be curious, to stand up for his values, to not be railroaded by ideas he knew to be unjust or wrong.

Through his father's efforts to engage with his son's learning, understand what was happening at his school, and offer sound advice and support when his son stood up for his beliefs, his son was able to hold onto his ideas and values without compromising them. To not get sucked in and buy into the oppressor/oppressed propaganda being spread on his campus.

These two families serve as models of how parents, even when enrolling their children in public or private schools, can be ownschooling.

Curiosity is a fundamental driver of both learning and living a rich, robust life for children and adults alike. It is more than just a desire to know; it is an intrinsic motivation that fuels exploration, creativity, and resilience.

For children, curiosity serves as the spark that ignites the flame of learning, fueling their natural desire to explore the world around them. When children feel safe and supported, their curiosity encourages them to try new things, ask questions, and engage deeply with their environment. This process not only builds knowledge but also develops confidence and problem-solving skills. Neuroscience shows that curiosity triggers the release of dopamine, a chemical that makes learning pleasurable and reinforces the pursuit of new information. This positive feedback loop helps children retain what they learn and fosters a lifelong love of discovery.

Adults benefit from curiosity in equally profound ways. In the workplace and beyond, curiosity drives innovation and adaptability. Curious individuals are more engaged, creative, and willing to do their own work, that is, to invest time and effort into understanding problems thoroughly rather than seeking quick answers. This patience and persistence, born from curiosity, lead to more profound mastery and genuine proof of work. It also cultivates psychological flexibility, enabling adults to approach challenges with openness and a growth mindset, viewing obstacles as opportunities rather than threats.

Curiosity is closely linked to resilience. By encouraging us to question assumptions, explore alternative perspectives, and remain open to feedback, curiosity helps us navigate uncertainty and complexity with greater ease. It fosters a mindset that embraces continuous learning and self-improvement, essential qualities for thriving in an ever-changing world.

Moreover, curiosity strengthens relationships and empathy. When we genuinely care about others and the world around us, we form stronger interpersonal connections and develop a deeper understanding of diverse perspectives. This social aspect of curiosity enriches both our personal and professional lives.

Ultimately, curiosity is the engine that propels us toward meaningful work and a fulfilling life. It encourages us to take ownership of our learning journeys, to engage fully with our interests, and to achieve authentic, well-deserved outcomes. Whether in childhood or adulthood, nurturing curiosity is key to unlocking potential, fostering resilience, and living with purpose.

Recognizing and Honoring Each Child's Unique Learning Needs

One of the most compelling reasons for families to seek autonomy over their children's education is the simple truth that no two children are exactly alike. Each child brings a unique blend of interests, talents, learning styles, and developmental timelines. When parents have the freedom to direct their children's education, they can nurture these differences rather than suppress them.

Traditional, centralized schooling systems are designed for efficiency and scale. This often means that standardized curricula treat all children as if they learn the same way and at the same pace. Additionally, uniform assessment methods may not capture a child's true abilities or potential. There is also a tendency for limited flexibility to pursue topics or skills that deeply engage or inspire individual students. In such a system, children who do not fit the "average" mold may feel left behind, bored, or misunderstood. There's little room for nuance, adaptation, or the honoring of a child's innate curiosity.

When families reclaim sovereignty over education, they can tailor learning experiences to each child's strengths, challenges, and interests. They are able to adjust the pacing by allowing a child to move quickly through subjects they master easily, and spend more time on those that require deeper exploration. There is also greater flexibility in learning, from hands-on projects and real-world experiences to creative arts and technology, which matches the child's preferred learning style. All of these things help to foster passion and self-motivation by allowing children to pursue topics that genuinely excite them, leading to deeper, more meaningful learning.

Practical Strategies for Individualizing Learning at Home

1. Observe and Listen: Pay close attention to what excites your child, what frustrates them, and how they naturally approach problems.

2. Offer Choices: Let children have a say in what and how they learn, within reasonable boundaries.
3. Set Individual Goals: Work with each child to set personal learning goals that reflect their unique path, rather than relying on external benchmarks.
4. Mix and Match Resources: Utilize a variety of books, online courses, community programs, and hands-on activities to create a rich and customized learning environment.
5. Regularly Reassess: Children's needs and interests change over time. Revisit your approach regularly to ensure it still fits.

In traditional schools, there is also a problem with the one-size-fits-all model. Children are often grouped by age and expected to progress through the same material at the same pace. The curriculum is standardized, assessments are uniform, and there is little room for deviation. For some children, this works well enough. But for many, it can be stifling.

By honoring their children's individuality, parents can create a culture of lifelong learning. Education is not something that happens only in a classroom or according to a schedule. It is woven into the fabric of daily life, sparked by curiosity and nurtured by love.

For many parents stepping into a more autonomous role in their children's education, one of the biggest worries is not having all the answers. It's natural to feel uncertain or even intimidated by the idea of guiding your child's learning, especially if you imagine you need to know everything right from the start.

But here's some reassuring news: You do not have to know it all. In fact, one of the most valuable lessons you can share with your children is that learning is a lifelong journey, one that applies to everyone, including adults.

Children are naturally curious and often ask questions that do not have easy answers. When you encounter something you do not know, it's a powerful opportunity to model curiosity, humility, and resilience. You can say, "I am not sure, but let's find out together." This approach shows your child that it's okay not to have instant answers and that figuring things out is part of the adventure.

Learning alongside your child can deepen your connection and make education more meaningful for both of you. When you research, experiment, and explore together, you're teaching your child how to approach challenges, seek out information, and solve problems, skills that are far more important than memorizing facts.

Time is another concern. Living in a fiat world, where, due to inflation and monetary manipulation beyond our control, many families need both parents' income to survive. However, investing in your child's learning does not have to be that time-consuming. Have conversations about what your children are learning at dinner or during car rides. Be present by keeping in touch with their teachers via email when needed. Look at their homework with them for a few minutes. Encourage your children to ask questions in class. Help them think through the things they are learning by asking questions and guiding them as they engage their minds.

Remember, you do not have to create the perfect educational plan overnight. It's normal to adjust as you go, discovering what works best for your family and each child's unique needs. Permit yourself to grow into this role, just as your children are growing into theirs as learners.

Every step you take, every question you explore, and every challenge you overcome is a victory. Celebrate the progress you and your children make together, and let go of the pressure to be perfect.

Being flexible is one of the most valuable qualities parents can bring to their children's educational journey. Every child is unique, with their own set of strengths, interests, and learning styles, and these can change over time, sometimes even from one day to the next. Flexibility allows parents to adapt to these changes, ensuring that their children's education remains engaging, relevant, and supportive of their growth.

Flexibility is essential because children develop at their own pace. What works well for one child may not be effective for another, and even the same child may need different approaches as they grow and their interests evolve. By remaining open and responsive, parents can tailor learning experiences to fit each child's needs, rather than trying to force everyone into a rigid, one-size-fits-all system. This adaptability helps children feel seen and valued as individuals, which in turn boosts their confidence and motivation to learn.

Life itself is unpredictable, and family circumstances can change unexpectedly. Illness, travel, new opportunities, or simply a shift in a child's interests can all impact your educational plans. When parents are flexible, they can adjust schedules, routines, and expectations without unnecessary stress or guilt. For example, suppose a child becomes fascinated by a new subject. In that case, flexibility allows you to dive deeper into that interest, even if it means setting aside the original plan for a while. If something is not working or is causing frustration, being flexible means you can try a new approach or take a break, rather than pushing through for the sake of sticking to a schedule.

Modeling flexibility also teaches children an important life skill: adaptability. When children see their parents responding to change with creativity and resilience, they learn to do the same. They become more comfortable with uncertainty, better able to handle setbacks, and more willing to try new things. This not only enhances their learning but also prepares them for the inevitable changes and challenges they will face throughout their lives.

Ultimately, embracing flexibility makes the educational journey more joyful and less stressful for both parents and children. It strengthens the bond between you as you navigate learning together, and it empowers your family to thrive no matter what challenges or opportunities arise. By being flexible, you create a nurturing environment where curiosity, growth, and resilience can flourish.

Chapter 9: Teaching Your Own Children

Children learn from anything and everything they see.
They learn wherever they are, not just in special learning places.

- John Holt

As an American educator, my perspective on education is naturally shaped by the landscape, history, and diversity of schooling options available in the United States. In this section, I will provide detailed information about the various educational paths that American families can choose for their children, including public, charter, independent, private, and homeschooling models. However, education is a global phenomenon, and many of the ideas, philosophies, and challenges we encounter in the U.S. have counterparts and unique expressions in countries around the world.

To provide a comprehensive view, I will also examine the history and structure of schooling internationally, highlighting how different societies have addressed the questions of who should educate children, what they should learn, and how learning environments are influenced by culture, law, and tradition. Whether you are considering your options as a parent, educator, or advocate, understanding both the American context and the broader global picture will help you make informed decisions and appreciate the rich tapestry of educational possibilities available today.

Homeschooling in the United States has deep roots, stretching back to colonial times when it was the primary mode of education. In early America, most children learned at home or in small community settings, acquiring reading, writing, arithmetic, and practical skills from their parents or local tutors. Notable historical figures such as Abraham Lincoln, Benjamin Franklin, and Thomas Edison were educated primarily at home. When parents lacked expertise, they would often collaborate with neighbors to hire a teacher, pooling resources to provide instruction for local children.

This landscape began to shift in the mid-nineteenth century with the rise of the common school movement, led by reformers such as Horace Mann. Massachusetts passed the first compulsory attendance law in 1852, with other states following suit over the next several decades. By 1917, all states required children to attend school, making public education the new norm and rendering homeschooling largely illegal. Parents who keep their children out of school could face fines or even lose custody.

Despite these laws, some families, especially in rural or religious communities, continued to educate their children at home, often under the radar. The modern homeschooling movement emerged in the 1970s, driven by dissatisfaction with public schooling and a desire for educational freedom. Educational theorist John Holt (1923–1985), a critic of traditional schooling, emerged as a leading voice, advocating for "unschooling" and publishing the influential newsletter Growing Without Schooling in 1977. Around the same time, Raymond and Dorothy Moore promoted homeschooling as a way to support children's psychological and moral development, particularly in the early years.

Throughout the 1980s and early 1990s, homeschoolers faced significant legal challenges, as many states had strict regulations or outright bans on homeschooling. Grassroots advocacy, court cases (notably Wisconsin v. Yoder in 1972, which protected Amish educational practices), and the founding of organizations like the Home School Legal Defense Association (HSLDA) in 1983 gradually changed the legal landscape. By 1992, homeschooling was officially recognized as a legal educational option in all 50 states, though regulations still vary widely by state.

Since then, homeschooling has grown rapidly, fueled by diverse motivations, including academic, religious, philosophical, and practical ones. By the early 2000s, over a million children were homeschooled in the U.S.; by 2019, the number had risen to nearly two million, with a significant spike during lockdowns. Homeschooling in the U.S. today is a dynamic, diverse movement, shaped by its unique legal history and the enduring belief in parental educational sovereignty.

Globally, homeschooling was once the universal norm. For millennia, children learned at home or within their communities, absorbing skills, values, and knowledge from family members and elders. This tradition persisted until the rise of state-controlled, institutional schooling in the eighteenth and nineteenth centuries, as governments in Europe and beyond began to see education as a public good and a means of shaping citizens. Compulsory schooling laws swept through much of the world by the early twentieth century, relegating home education to the margins in most countries.

Despite this, homeschooling never entirely disappeared. In many indigenous and rural communities, parent-led education remained common. In the late twentieth century, inspired in part by the American resurgence, homeschooling began to re-emerge globally. Countries such as Canada, the United Kingdom, Australia, and New Zealand have seen significant growth in home education, often driven by similar concerns as in the U.S., including dissatisfaction with mainstream education, a desire for religious or cultural preservation, and a belief in parental rights.

Legal acceptance of homeschooling varies widely worldwide. In some countries, such as the UK, Australia, South Africa, and parts of Canada, homeschooling is legal and regulated. In others, such as

Germany, Sweden, and several European and Asian nations, it is tightly restricted or outright banned, reflecting differing philosophies about the role of the state and the rights of parents. In recent years, legal battles and advocacy efforts have continued to shape the global landscape, with some countries liberalizing their laws and others tightening restrictions.

The modern global homeschooling movement is characterized by rapid growth and increasing diversity. Families homeschool for a wide range of reasons: to provide a customized education, to preserve cultural or religious identity, or to escape perceived shortcomings of institutional schools. Research suggests that homeschooled students often perform well academically and socially; however, the practice remains controversial in some regions, with ongoing debates about oversight, socialization, and educational quality.

Educational laws governing homeschooling are shaped by each country's and, in federal systems, each state's unique legal, cultural, and historical context. While some nations view homeschooling as a fundamental parental right and support a diversity of educational approaches, others see compulsory attendance at government-approved schools as essential for social cohesion and oversight. This legal landscape directly impacts the freedom and responsibility parents have in directing their children's education.

In countries where homeschooling is illegal or tightly restricted, parents are required to enroll their children in government-approved public or private schools. The rationale for such policies often centers on concerns about educational quality, socialization, and child welfare. For example, in Germany, compulsory school attendance laws are strictly enforced, with homeschooling permitted only in rare cases, such as those involving severe medical needs. Families who attempt to homeschool outside these exceptions may face severe penalties, including fines, legal action, or even the removal of their children from their homes. Similarly, in the Netherlands, homeschooling is generally not recognized, with only limited exemptions granted for religious or philosophical reasons if no suitable school is available nearby. Greece also prohibits homeschooling except for children with special needs, and Sweden allows it only under extraordinary circumstances.

In contrast, some countries offer legal but highly regulated homeschooling, requiring parents to register with the authorities, follow approved curricula, submit to regular inspections, and hold teaching qualifications. Hungary and Poland are examples where homeschooling is theoretically possible but subject to strict oversight and annual assessments. In Brazil, the situation is evolving: while the Supreme Court has ruled homeschooling constitutional, federal legislation is still pending, and the legality of homeschooling can vary by state.

Even in countries where homeschooling is legal, the level of regulation varies widely. For instance, France allows homeschooling with annual notification and inspections, whereas Ireland requires registration and adherence to minimum education standards. In Italy, parents are required to notify the authorities and submit their children to annual exams. In India and Indonesia, homeschooling is legal and supported by open schooling systems, but families must comply with national testing and certification requirements.

In the United States, homeschooling is legal in all 50 states; however, regulations vary from minimal to highly restrictive. States like Alaska, Texas, Idaho, Oklahoma, and Missouri require little more than notification (or, in some cases, none at all), allowing parents broad autonomy in curriculum and assessment. Conversely, states such as New York, Pennsylvania, Massachusetts, and Rhode Island impose detailed requirements, including submission of instructional plans, quarterly reports, annual standardized testing or evaluations, and mandatory instruction in specified subjects. Some states, such as California and Colorado, have unique requirements, including instruction in English and periodic standardized testing.

The variations in these regulations mean that parents must be diligent in researching and complying with their local laws. Failure to do so can result in truancy charges or other legal consequences. For families living in or moving to countries or states where homeschooling is illegal or severely restricted, the only legal options are government-approved public or private schools. In these cases, parents should focus on being actively involved in their child's education within the available system, including meeting with teachers, monitoring the curriculum, and advocating for their child's needs and values.

Because educational laws can change and enforcement may vary, parents need to consult authoritative, up-to-date resources before making decisions. For U.S. readers, a comprehensive, regularly updated guide to each state's homeschooling laws is included in the appendix of this book. For international readers, the HSLDA provides detailed legal summaries, news, and advocacy updates for homeschooling worldwide. Always verify current requirements with local education authorities or legal counsel, especially if you are relocating or considering homeschooling in a new jurisdiction.

Global Overview: Where Homeschooling Is Legal, Regulated, or Illegal

- Countries Where Homeschooling Is Legal:
  Homeschooling is legal and widely practiced in countries such as the United States, Canada, the United Kingdom, Australia, New Zealand, South Africa, Austria, Italy, Norway, France, Denmark, Belgium, Switzerland, Japan, South Korea, Singapore, India, Ireland, Portugal, Finland, Russia, Brazil, Argentina, Mexico, Chile, Costa Rica, Panama, Honduras, the Philippines, and Thailand. However, even in these countries, the level of regulation varies; some require only notification to authorities, while others demand detailed documentation and periodic assessments.
- Countries Where Homeschooling Is Heavily Regulated or Restricted:
  In countries such as Hungary, Iceland, Poland, and Indonesia, homeschooling is permitted but subject to strict regulations. Requirements may include annual exams, registration with local authorities, or parental qualifications. In Brazil, for

example, homeschooling is in a legal grey area, with some states legalizing it and others awaiting federal legislation.

- Countries Where Homeschooling Is Illegal or Practically Impossible:
  In several nations, homeschooling is illegal or only permitted under very limited circumstances, such as for children with special needs. Families in these countries are required to send their children to government-approved public or private schools. Attempting to homeschool can result in legal penalties, including fines or even the removal of children from the home.

Below is a list of countries where homeschooling is illegal or only allowed under rare exceptions:

- Germany
  Homeschooling is generally illegal, except in rare medical or special circumstances. All children must attend state-approved schools.
- Greece
  Homeschooling is illegal for the general population. Only children with special needs may be homeschooled, and all others must attend formal schools.
- Netherlands
  Homeschooling is generally illegal, with very limited exemptions for specific religious or philosophical reasons, or for children with certain disabilities.
- Spain
  Homeschooling exists in a legal grey area and is not officially recognized. Most regions require children to be enrolled in registered schools, and families who homeschool risk legal action.
- Sweden
  Homeschooling is only permitted under exceptional circumstances, such as for children with medical issues or for families temporarily residing in Sweden.

- China
  Homeschooling is not permitted for Chinese citizens, although foreign residents may have more flexibility.
- Other Countries with Homeschool Bans or Severe Restrictions:
  Albania, Andorra, Armenia, Azerbaijan, Belarus, Bosnia & Herzegovina, Bulgaria (except for some special needs cases), Costa Rica, Croatia, Cyprus, Germany, Greece, Lithuania, Luxembourg, Malta, Montenegro, North Macedonia, San Marino, Serbia, Slovakia, Slovenia, Turkey, and Ukraine.

In the United States, homeschooling is legal in all 50 states, but regulations vary widely:

- States with Minimal Regulation:
  States like Idaho, Alaska, Texas, Oklahoma, Missouri, Iowa, Illinois, Indiana, Michigan, and New Jersey have little to no regulation. Parents may only need to notify authorities or keep basic records.
- States with Moderate to High Regulation:
  States such as New York, Pennsylvania, Massachusetts, and North Dakota require more detailed documentation, regular assessments, or approval of curriculum.
- Unique Requirements:
  - California requires that homeschool subjects be taught in the English language.
  - Colorado mandates standardized testing every other year starting in the third grade.
  - Wisconsin and Nebraska require the primary purpose of homeschooling to be private or religious-based education.

If you live in a country or state where homeschooling is illegal or highly restricted, you must enroll your child in a government-approved public or private school. Attempting to homeschool without approval can result in legal action, fines, or even loss of custody in extreme cases. In these locations, your educational choices are limited to the options recognized by the state, and you may need to work within the system to advocate for your child's needs.

Always check your local laws and consult with legal experts or homeschooling associations before making educational decisions. Laws and regulations can change, and compliance is essential to avoid legal complications.

Types of Homeschooling

Classical Homeschooling

Classical homeschooling is rooted in the ancient tradition of the Trivium, which divides learning into three stages: grammar (foundation of facts and language), logic (critical thinking and reasoning), and rhetoric (articulate expression). This approach emphasizes mastery of language, history, mathematics, and the great works of Western civilization. Children are introduced to classic literature, ancient languages like Latin or Greek, and are encouraged to develop strong reasoning skills through Socratic dialogue and debate. The curriculum is often rigorous and sequential, enabling students to develop a deep, interconnected understanding of the world.

Parents who choose classical homeschooling often appreciate its structured nature and focus on intellectual development. However, it requires a significant commitment to guiding children through increasingly complex material. While some families use formal classical curricula, others blend this approach with other methods to suit their child's needs. Classical education can foster a love of learning, critical thinking, and articulate communication, which serve as essential skills that benefit children throughout their lives.

Benefits:

- Develops strong critical thinking and communication skills

- Emphasizes deep understanding of literature, history, and logic
- Structured, time-tested curriculum

Challenges:

- Requires significant parental guidance and preparation
- Can be rigid or overwhelming for some learners
- It may be less flexible for students with different learning styles

Charlotte Mason

The Charlotte Mason method centers on the belief that education is an atmosphere, a discipline, and a life. It emphasizes living books, well-written and engaging literature, rather than dry textbooks, and incorporates nature study, art, music, and the development of good habits. Lessons are intentionally short to keep children engaged, and narration (retelling what was learned) is a key assessment tool. Children spend ample time outdoors, observing and journaling about the natural world, which acts as their first science curriculum.

This approach is known for its gentle, holistic philosophy, treating children as whole persons and encouraging joyful discovery. Parents act as facilitators, curating resources and experiences, and often integrate Scripture or moral lessons into their approach. The Charlotte Mason method can be especially appealing to families seeking a nurturing, beauty-focused education, but it does require a parent's active involvement in planning and guiding daily activities.

Benefits:

- Nurtures curiosity and love of learning through "living books"
- Short lessons keep children engaged
- Strong emphasis on nature, art, and character development

Challenges:

- Requires parent involvement in resource curation and lesson planning
- Less focus on standardized testing or modern technology
- It may be difficult for parents unfamiliar with the method

Eclectic Homeschooling

Eclectic homeschooling is a flexible, personalized approach that allows families to blend multiple educational philosophies and resources. Rather than adhering to a single method, eclectic homeschoolers select the approaches that work best for each child and subject, often combining traditional textbooks, online courses, hands-on projects, and real-world experiences. This adaptability enables easier addressing of individual learning styles, interests, and family dynamics.

The main strength of eclectic homeschooling is its responsiveness to change parents can adjust methods as their children grow or as new resources become available. However, this approach requires ongoing research, organization, and reflection to ensure a well-rounded education. For families willing to invest the time, eclectic homeschooling can be both liberating and highly effective for creativity and deep engagement.

Benefits:

- Highly flexible and customizable to each child's needs
- Allows adaptation as interests and needs change
- Can blend the best aspects of multiple methods

Challenges:

- Requires ongoing research and organization
- Potential for gaps in learning if not carefully planned
- Less structure may be challenging for some families

Unit Studies

Unit studies organize learning around a central theme, such as oceans, ancient Egypt, or a beloved book, integrating multiple subjects like language arts, science, history, and math into one cohesive study. This approach is highly engaging, as children see connections between disciplines and can dive deeply into topics that interest them. Unit studies are especially effective for families with multiple children, as all ages can learn together, with activities tailored to different skill levels.

Planning unit studies can be time-intensive, as parents must gather resources and design multidisciplinary activities. However, many families enjoy the collaborative, project-based nature of this method, which often includes field trips, experiments, and creative projects. Unit studies foster enthusiasm, critical thinking, and a love of learning by making education relevant and meaningful.

Benefits:

- Integrates multiple subjects for deeper understanding
- Highly engaging, especially for hands-on learners
- Suitable for teaching multiple ages together

Challenges:

- Time-intensive planning for parents
- May not cover all required standards unless supplemented
- It can be difficult to assess progress in traditional ways

Montessori Homeschooling

Montessori homeschooling is based on the philosophy of Maria Montessori, emphasizing independence, self-paced learning, and a carefully prepared environment. Children choose activities from a range of hands-on materials designed to teach specific concepts, developing practical life skills alongside academic knowledge. Multi-age groupings encourage peer learning, and parents act as guides, introducing new materials as children are ready.

This approach values order, beauty, and purposeful activity, with an emphasis on respect for the child's natural curiosity. Montessori homeschooling can be particularly effective for young children, but it is also adaptable for older students. It requires an investment in specialized materials and a commitment to the Montessori philosophy, but many families find it fosters confidence, focus, and a lifelong love of learning.

Benefits:

- Encourages independence and self-motivation
- Hands-on, experiential learning
- Supports multi-age, peer learning

Challenges:

- Requires investment in specialized materials
- Demands commitment to the Montessori philosophy
- It may be challenging to implement at home without training

Waldorf Homeschooling

Waldorf homeschooling, inspired by Rudolf Steiner, emphasizes educating the whole child, body, mind, and spirit. The early years focus on play, nature, and the arts, with formal academics introduced gradually. Storytelling, music, handcrafts, and seasonal rhythms are central, and technology is minimized, especially in the early grades.

Parents who choose Waldorf often value its holistic, imaginative approach and emphasis on creativity and emotional development. Children create their own books instead of using standard textbooks, and assessment is based on observation and portfolios rather than tests. Waldorf homeschooling requires a commitment to hands-on activities. It often benefits from participation in a supportive community or co-op.

Benefits:

- Holistic, arts-integrated curriculum
- Fosters imagination, creativity, and emotional development
- Emphasizes nature and hands-on activities

Challenges:

- Limited use of technology, especially early on
- Requires parent involvement in creative activities
- It may be difficult to find local Waldorf communities

Road Schooling

Road schooling integrates travel and real-world experiences into a child's education. Families take learning on the road, usually via a camper or an RV in their home country. They integrate a structured or semi-structured curriculum, combining traditional subjects (math, language arts, science) with experiential learning at each destination, such as visiting museums, historical sites, national parks, and different communities. This approach offers unparalleled opportunities for hands-on learning, cultural immersion, and adaptability, as children learn directly from the places they visit.

While road schooling can be logistically challenging, requiring flexibility, planning, and sometimes remote work arrangements, it allows families to tailor education to their travels and interests. Children gain a broader perspective, adaptability, and real-world problem-solving skills. This lifestyle may not be feasible for every family, but for those who can embrace it, road schooling can be transformative.

Benefits:

- Real-world, experiential learning
- Exposure to different cultures and educational sites, like museums and national parks
- Flexible, adaptable schedule

Challenges:

- Requires significant family flexibility and resources
- Can disrupt routines and stability
- It may limit access to consistent extracurriculars or peer groups

World Schooling

World schooling uses travel and cultural immersion as the primary curriculum. Families may live abroad or travel extensively, integrating local history, language, and customs into daily learning. This approach emphasizes adaptability, global awareness, and real-world learning, often blending formal academics with experiential education.

World schooling requires significant flexibility and resources, as well as a willingness to embrace non-traditional schedules and environments. It can be deeply enriching, fostering independence, open-mindedness, and cross-cultural understanding. For families seeking a global perspective, world schooling offers a unique and powerful educational experience.

Benefits:

- Global perspective and cultural immersion
- Flexible, personalized learning
- Encourages adaptability and independence

Challenges:

- Requires significant time, resources, and planning
- Less consistency in academic structure
- Social connections may be transient

Relaxed Homeschooling

Relaxed homeschooling is a less structured approach that prioritizes the child's interests and natural learning rhythms. Parents provide gentle guidance and resources, allowing learning to unfold organically through daily life, conversations, and exploration. This method reduces pressure and stress, creating a more harmonious home environment.

While relaxed homeschooling can be highly effective for self-motivated learners, it requires trust in the child's curiosity and a willingness to adapt as needed. Parents must remain attentive to ensure educational goals are met. For families seeking a balance between structure and freedom, relaxed homeschooling can offer a joyful and low-pressure alternative.

Benefits:

- Low-pressure, stress-free learning environment
- Allows learning to follow the child's interests and rhythms
- Adaptable to family needs

Challenges:

- Requires trust in the child's natural curiosity
- Less structure may not suit all learners
- Parents must monitor for academic gaps

Virtual Homeschooling (Cambridge, Stanford, Pearson, etc.)

Virtual homeschooling utilizes accredited online programs, often affiliated with prestigious institutions, to provide structured, high-quality education from the comfort of home. These programs offer rigorous academics, interactive lessons, and access to certified teachers, allowing families to combine the flexibility of homeschooling with the accountability of a formal curriculum.

Parents play a crucial role in supporting their child's engagement, managing schedules, and supplementing with hands-on experiences or local activities. Virtual homeschooling can be ideal for families seeking academic rigor or international accreditation, but it requires reliable internet access and proactive involvement to ensure social and emotional needs are also met.

Benefits:

- Access to accredited, high-quality curricula
- Flexible location and pacing
- Often includes support from certified teachers

Challenges:

- Requires reliable internet and technology
- Less hands-on or experiential learning
- Socialization opportunities may be limited

Unschooling

Unschooling is the most child-directed form of homeschooling, allowing children's interests and life experiences to drive learning. Parents act as facilitators, providing resources, encouragement, and support as needed. There are no set curricula or schedules; instead, learning happens organically through exploration, play, and real-world problem-solving.

This approach fosters independence, creativity, and a deep love of learning, but requires a high degree of trust and active parental engagement to ensure a well-rounded education. Unschooling may look different for every family, reflecting the unique passions and rhythms of each child.

Benefits:

- Highly individualized, interest-driven learning
- Fosters independence and creativity

- Flexible and adaptable to each child

Challenges:

- Requires high parental engagement and trust
- Potential for academic gaps if not monitored
- May be misunderstood or challenged by others

Collaborative & Alternative Models

Homeschool Co-ops

Homeschool co-ops are collaborative groups where families share teaching responsibilities, resources, and social opportunities. Co-ops can be academic, enrichment-focused, or a blend of both, and may meet in homes, churches, or community centers. Classes are often taught by parents or hired instructors, covering subjects like science labs, art, music, or field trips.

The benefits of co-ops include increased socialization for children, shared resources, and support for parents. Co-ops can help reduce isolation, provide a wider range of learning experiences, and foster a sense of community. However, they also require coordination and compromise, as families must agree on curriculum and policies. For many, co-ops are a vital supplement to homeschooling, offering both structure and flexibility.

Benefits:

- Shared teaching responsibilities and resources
- Increased socialization for children
- Community support for families

Challenges:

- Requires coordination and compromise among families
- Less individual control over the curriculum

- Potential for conflicts or inconsistent quality

Microschools

Microschools are small, student-centered learning environments, modern versions of the one-room schoolhouse, typically serving 5–15 students. They combine the personalization of homeschooling with the structure and community of traditional schooling. Microschools often employ a combination of online and hands-on, project-based learning, and can be tailored to meet the needs of local families.

Microschools offer individualized attention, flexible schedules, and innovative curricula, often incorporating subjects not typically found in traditional schools, such as coding or entrepreneurship. Teachers have more freedom, and parents are typically more involved in shaping the educational experience. Microschools are adaptable, can quickly implement new teaching methods, and focus on holistic development, measuring progress through projects and collaboration rather than standardized tests.

Benefits:

- Small class sizes and individualized attention
- Flexible, innovative curriculum
- Strong sense of community

Challenges:

- Limited extracurricular options compared to larger schools
- It may be costly or have limited availability
- Regulatory recognition can vary

Chapter 10: Public Schooling

An investment in knowledge pays the best interest.

- Benjamin Franklin

Public schools are government-funded and serve the vast majority of children in the United States. They provide a standardized curriculum, access to certified teachers, and a wide range of extracurricular activities and support services. Public schools are required to serve all students, regardless of background or ability, and are accountable to elected school boards and state standards.

The story of public education in the United States is deeply intertwined with debates over individual autonomy, state authority, and the purpose of education. In early America, education was largely a family or community affair, localized, diverse, and often rooted in religious or practical instruction. This decentralized approach reflected the nation's founding values of autonomy and self-governance.

From a sovereignty perspective, the evolution of public education in America represents a significant transfer of authority from families and communities to the state. The Prussian-inspired model, adopted and expanded by Mann and Dewey, prioritized social order and collective values over individual development and parental rights. Over time, this has led to a system that often values conformity, compliance, and social engineering above intellectual rigor and personal growth.

Critics argue that this centralization has led to a decline in educational standards, as evidenced by declining literacy rates and academic achievement, and has limited families' freedom to direct their children's education in alignment with their own values and aspirations. The legacy of Mann, the Prussian system, and Dewey is a public education system that, while universal and accessible, often falls short of nurturing the independent, critical thinkers needed for a truly free and sovereign society.

The History of Public Education Around the World

The global history of public education is similarly marked by the tension between state control and individual or community sovereignty. For centuries, education was a local, family-driven affair across much of the world. The rise of state-sponsored, compulsory schooling is a relatively recent phenomenon, largely inspired by the Prussian model.

Overall, the global history of public education reveals a pattern of increasing state control and standardization, often at the expense of parental rights and individual sovereignty. The influence of the Prussian system, amplified by reformers such as Horace Mann and John Dewey, has shaped a world where education is less about cultivating free, independent thinkers and more about producing compliant citizens. This legacy continues to shape debates over the future of schooling today.

For many families, public schools are the most practical or only option. Parental involvement, attending meetings, communicating with teachers, and advocating for your child, remains crucial. By staying informed and engaged, parents can help ensure their child's needs and values are respected and can supplement learning at home as needed. Active participation is key to maximizing the benefits of public education.

Benefits:

- Free and widely accessible
- Certified teachers and broad resources
- Diverse social environment and extracurriculars

Challenges:

- Less flexibility in the curriculum and schedule
- Larger class sizes may limit individual attention
- Potential misalignment with family values or needs

Charter Schools

Charter schools are publicly funded but independently operated, often with a specific educational focus such as STEM, the arts, or college preparation. They have more flexibility in curriculum and teaching methods than traditional public schools, and are held accountable for meeting performance goals outlined in their charter. Admission is typically open to all, and schools that do not meet standards risk closure.

The History of Charter Schools in America

Charter schools are a relatively recent innovation in American education, emerging from a desire to inject autonomy, accountability, and choice into the public school system. The concept traces its roots to the 1970s, when education reformers, such as Ray Budde, a professor at the University of Massachusetts Amherst, proposed the idea of granting teachers a "charter" to operate schools outside the traditional district structure. Budde's 1974 paper laid the theoretical groundwork, envisioning schools that would be publicly funded but independently run, with the freedom to innovate and be held accountable for results rather than adherence to bureaucratic rules.

The idea gained traction in the late 1980s when Albert Shanker, president of the American Federation of Teachers, publicly advocated for charter schools as laboratories for educational experimentation and improvement. Shanker's vision was to empower teachers to try new pedagogical methods and share successful practices with the broader public school system. The first concrete step came in 1991, when Minnesota passed the nation's first charter school law. The following year, City Academy in St. Paul became the first charter school to open its doors, primarily serving students who had dropped out of traditional schools or faced significant challenges.

From there, the charter school movement spread rapidly. By 1995, eighteen more states had enacted charter school legislation, and the number of charter schools grew from just a handful to thousands within two decades. Charter schools are publicly funded, tuition-free, and open to all students, but they operate independently of many district regulations, allowing for greater flexibility in curriculum, staffing, and school culture. They are held accountable through performance contracts (charters) that can be revoked if the school fails to meet agreed-upon outcomes. This model was designed to encourage innovation and competition, with the hope of raising educational standards across the public system.

Today, charter schools serve millions of students across the United States. They are diverse in mission and approach, ranging from STEM-focused academies to arts schools and those serving at-risk youth. While research on their effectiveness is mixed and the movement remains controversial, charter schools have become a permanent and influential part of the American educational landscape.

Charter-Style Schools Around the World

The charter school model, pioneered in the United States, has inspired similar reforms globally, though each country adapts the concept to its own context. At least 14 countries have introduced publicly funded, independently operated schools that share key features with American charter schools, such as increased autonomy, accountability, and parental choice.

- United Kingdom: The most prominent counterpart is the academy system, launched in 2003. Academies are publicly funded but operate independently of local authority control, with the freedom to set their own curricula and management structures. "Free schools," a subset of academies, can be established by parents, teachers, or community groups to meet local needs. As of the 2020s, a significant proportion of UK schools operate under this model, and research suggests that many academies have improved performance compared to their predecessor council-run schools.
- Sweden: The free school (*friskola*) movement began in the 1990s, allowing private entities to run publicly funded schools with significant autonomy. These schools can be operated by for-profit or non-profit organizations and are open to all students. Studies have shown generally positive effects on student achievement and parental satisfaction.
- The Netherlands and Belgium: These countries have a long history of government-subsidized independent schools, including religious and pedagogical alternatives. Schools are free to design their own curricula and hire staff but must meet national standards.
- New Zealand: Partnership schools (*kura hourua*), introduced in the 2010s, were directly modeled on U.S. charter schools, targeting students underserved by the mainstream system. These schools have autonomy over curriculum and staffing but are held to performance contracts.
- Other countries, such as Australia, parts of Canada, Chile, France, Japan, Qatar, and Singapore, among others, have charter-style or independent public schools. In Qatar, for example, a major reform effort has converted a majority of public schools into charter-like entities, granting them substantial autonomy and accountability.

The main differences between U.S. charter schools and their international counterparts often relate to religious affiliation (many countries allow religious charter-style schools), profit status, and the degree of government oversight. Despite these variations, the global spread of charter-style schools reflects a common desire for greater flexibility, innovation, and parental choice within public education systems.

Charter schools promote strong parental involvement and community engagement, which can result in improved academic and personal outcomes for students. They may offer innovative programs, smaller class sizes, and a unique school culture. However, availability and quality can vary widely, so parents should research options carefully and remain actively involved in their child's education.

Benefits:

- Innovative curricula and teaching methods
- Often, smaller class sizes than public schools
- Greater parental involvement and accountability

Challenges:

- Quality and availability vary by location
- Admission may be competitive (lottery-based)
- May lack the resources of traditional public schools

Hybrid Models (Homeschool + Public/Private School)

Hybrid homeschooling combines home education with attendance at a traditional school or learning center for part of the week. Students may attend classes on campus 2–3 days per week and complete assignments at home the remaining days. This model offers structure, socialization, and expert instruction while preserving family time and flexibility.

Hybrid programs can be more affordable than full-time private schools and are adaptable to a variety of family needs. Parents play a key role in co-teaching and monitoring progress, gradually fostering independent learning as children mature. Hybrid models are ideal for families seeking a balance between the benefits of homeschooling and traditional schooling.

Benefits:

- May combine the structure of school with the flexibility of homeschooling
- Opportunities for socialization and expert instruction
- Gradual transition to independent learning

Challenges:

- Requires careful coordination of schedules
- May involve tuition or fees
- Not available in all areas

Chapter 11: Private Schools

Private schools should be a genuine alternative to public schools. They should be free to innovate with calendars and schedules, curriculum, teaching methods, and more. As Milton Friedman argued years ago, parents should have the freedom to choose between various educational models to find the best fit for their child.

- Michael McShane, *Forbes*

Private schools are independently funded educational institutions that operate outside the public school system. They offer families an alternative to public education, often providing distinctive curricula, teaching methods, and educational philosophies that cater to their needs. Private schools may be religious or secular, and they typically have greater flexibility in setting academic standards, hiring teachers, and designing programs. Many families choose private schooling for its smaller class sizes, specialized programs, and the ability to align education with personal values or beliefs. While tuition is generally required, private schools aim to foster academic excellence, personal growth, and a strong sense of community.

History of Private Education in America

Private education in America predates the nation itself. The earliest schools established on what would become U.S. soil were private and religious in nature. In 1606, the Franciscan order opened a Catholic school in St. Augustine, Florida, and mission schools soon followed throughout the Southwest and California. The Pilgrims, arriving in 1620, quickly established their own schools. By 1628, parents from the Dutch Reformed Church had founded Collegiate School in New York City, the oldest continually operating school in the United States.

During the colonial era, the distinction between public and private education was minimal. Towns and parents collectively established schools to impart religious and Enlightenment values, with tuition often covering the cost of instruction. By the late seventeenth century, venture or adventure schools, which were private institutions run by individual teachers, had become common, especially in cities such as New York and Philadelphia. These schools served apprentices and adults, offering flexible schedules and affordable fees.

The nineteenth century saw the rise of universal, free public schools, but private schools remained influential, especially among religious and immigrant communities. Catholic bishops, in particular, established parish schools in response to the Protestant-dominated public system. This parallel system grew rapidly in the late 1800s, offering an alternative for families seeking instruction aligned with their faith.

Legal challenges to private education arose in the early twentieth century, as some states attempted to mandate public school attendance. The landmark 1925 Supreme Court decision in Pierce v. Society of Sisters struck down such laws, affirming the constitutional right of parents to choose private or religious education for their children. Private school enrollment expanded until the mid-twentieth century, peaking during periods of social upheaval, such as the desegregation of public schools in the South. During this era, many "segregation academies" were established to circumvent integration mandates, especially in the Southern states.

Since the 1960s, private school enrollment has fluctuated, with Catholic schools experiencing significant declines due to urban demographic shifts and secularization. Meanwhile, non-Catholic religious schools and nonsectarian private schools have grown, reflecting changing social values and educational preferences. Today, approximately one in ten K-12 students in the U.S. attend a private school, with the sector encompassing a diverse range of institutions, from elite preparatory academies to Montessori, Waldorf, and evangelical Christian schools.

History of Private Education Around the World

Private education has ancient roots globally, often serving as the primary means of instruction for the elite. In ancient Egypt, Greece, and Rome, private tutors educated the children of wealthy families in philosophy, mathematics, and rhetoric. These early forms of private schooling were tailored to the needs of the ruling classes, with an emphasis on leadership and intellectual development.

During the Middle Ages, education in Europe was dominated by monastic and cathedral schools, which, while not private in the modern sense, were selective and religiously oriented. In the Islamic world, madrasas provided both religious and secular education, becoming centers of intellectual activity. The Renaissance witnessed the emergence of private academies in cities such as Florence and Paris, broadening the curricula to include literature, science, and the arts.

In England, the development of "public schools" such as Eton (1440) and Harrow (1572), which are actually private, independent institutions, set the standard for elite education. These schools emphasized classical studies, discipline, and character-building, influencing private education models worldwide.

The expansion of European empires in the seventeenth and eighteenth centuries led to the export of private education to colonies in the Americas, Africa, and Asia. Missionary schools, often blending religious and Western academic traditions, played a significant role in spreading literacy and new curricula. In the nineteenth and twentieth centuries, the Industrial Revolution and the rise of a middle class led to an increased demand for private schooling, as families sought alternatives to public education and specialized curricula.

Today, private schools serve roughly one in four children globally, with especially rapid growth in emerging markets such as India, Malaysia, and Brazil. Drivers of this growth include inadequate public provision, rising household affluence, demand for English-language instruction, and a focus on holistic "twenty-first-century" education. The global private education sector is highly diverse, ranging from small "mom and pop" schools to elite international academies, and from religious institutions to innovative pedagogical models like Montessori and Waldorf.

Types of Private Schools

Secular Private Schools

Secular private schools offer an education that is free from religious instruction, instead focusing on academics, critical thinking, and personal development. These schools have the freedom to design their own curricula, often emphasizing inquiry-based learning, global awareness, and a broad range of extracurricular activities. Families who choose secular private schools often seek a rigorous, values-neutral environment that prepares students for higher education and diverse worldviews.

Secular private schools may be independent or part of larger networks, and often feature small class sizes and personalized instruction. Tuition can be significant, but scholarships and financial aid may be available. Parental involvement in school selection and ongoing engagement is crucial to ensure the school's philosophy aligns with family values and educational goals.

Benefits:

- Academically rigorous, values-neutral environment
- Freedom to design innovative curricula
- Small class sizes and personalized instruction

Challenges:

- Tuition costs can be high
- Admission may be selective
- May lack religious or cultural alignment for some families

STEM-Focused Private Schools

STEM (Science, Technology, Engineering, Math) private schools are designed to immerse students in hands-on, inquiry-driven learning in these critical fields. The curriculum is often project-based, with opportunities for robotics, coding, laboratory research, and collaboration with professionals. These schools aim to prepare students for the demands of a technology-driven future, fostering problem-solving, creativity, and teamwork.

STEM schools may offer advanced placement courses, internships, and partnerships with local universities or businesses. They attract families who value innovation and want their children to develop strong analytical and technical skills. Parental involvement is essential in supporting extracurricular projects and staying engaged with rapidly evolving STEM fields.

Benefits:

- Strong emphasis on science, technology, engineering, and math
- Hands-on, project-based learning
- Access to advanced resources and partnerships

Challenges:

- May underemphasize the arts or humanities
- Tuition and fees can be significant
- Competitive admissions

Arts-Focused Private Schools

Arts-focused private schools integrate music, theater, visual arts, and dance throughout the curriculum. These schools nurture creativity, self-expression, and discipline, often providing specialized facilities and instructors. Students may participate in performances, exhibitions, and competitions, thereby gaining confidence and developing their artistic skills.

Families choose arts schools to foster their child's talent and passion, often with the goal of pursuing advanced study or careers in the arts. These schools balance rigorous academics with intensive arts training, and parental support is key, both in encouraging practice and participating in school events.

Benefits:

- Intensive training in music, theater, visual arts, or dance
- Fosters creativity and self-expression
- Opportunities for performances and exhibitions

Challenges:

- May offer less focus on STEM subjects
- Costs can be high
- Admissions may be talent-based

Religious Private Schools (Including Parochial)

Religious private schools integrate faith-based instruction with academics, aligning curriculum and community life with specific religious values. Parochial schools are a subset, typically affiliated with a local church and supported by its congregation. These schools may include daily prayers, religious studies, and expectations for conduct in line with their faith tradition.

Families choose religious schools to ensure their children receive an education consistent with their own beliefs, often valuing the strong sense of community and the emphasis on moral development. Religious schools vary in their balance between faith and academics, so it's important for parents to visit, ask questions, and ensure the environment aligns with their expectations.

Benefits:

- Integration of faith and academics
- Strong sense of community and shared values
- Moral and character education

Challenges:

- May not be inclusive of all beliefs
- Tuition costs
- The curriculum may be less flexible

College Preparatory Private Schools

College preparatory (prep) schools emphasize rigorous academics, critical thinking, and leadership development to prepare students for higher education. These schools may offer advanced placement courses, college counseling, and a strong record of graduates attending elite universities. The environment is often competitive and intellectually stimulating, with high expectations for achievement.

Prep schools attract families who prioritize academic excellence and want their children to be challenged and supported in reaching their full potential. Parental involvement is important in navigating course selection, extracurricular activities, and the college application process.

Benefits:

- Rigorous academics and college counseling
- High rates of college admission
- Extensive extracurricular and leadership opportunities

Challenges:

- Highly competitive environment
- Significant tuition and fees
- Pressure to perform academically

Montessori Private Schools

Montessori private schools follow the educational philosophy of Maria Montessori, emphasizing independence, self-directed learning, and respect for the child's natural development. Classrooms are multi-age, materials are hands-on and carefully designed, and teachers act as guides rather than lecturers. Montessori schools value order, beauty, and purposeful activity, fostering a nurturing environment that encourages exploration and growth.

Parents are often invited to participate in the classroom and school community, reinforcing the connection between home and school. Montessori education is especially popular for early childhood, but can be adapted for older students as well. Families who value curiosity, autonomy, and holistic development often find Montessori schools a good fit.

Benefits:

- Child-centered, self-directed learning
- Emphasis on independence and practical skills
- Multi-age classrooms and individualized pacing

Challenges:

- Tuition and materials can be expensive

- It may be hard to find at higher grade levels
- Requires buy-in to the Montessori philosophy

Waldorf Private Schools

Waldorf private schools, based on Rudolf Steiner's philosophy, emphasize holistic, arts-integrated education. The curriculum nurtures creativity, critical thinking, and social skills, with a strong focus on storytelling, music, handcrafts, and movement. Technology is minimized, especially in early grades, and assessment is based on observation and portfolios rather than standardized tests.

Waldorf schools foster a sense of wonder and respect for nature, encouraging children to develop at their own pace. The community is often close-knit, with parents involved in festivals, workshops, and school governance. Families who value imagination, emotional intelligence, and a non-traditional approach to academics often find Waldorf schools a good match.

Benefits:

- Holistic, arts-integrated education
- Emphasis on imagination, nature, and emotional growth
- Strong community involvement

Challenges:

- Limited use of technology
- May not align with standardized testing requirements
- Tuition and availability may be limiting

Reggio Emilia

The Reggio Emilia approach is an educational philosophy originating from northern Italy, centered on the belief that children are capable, curious, and full of potential. In Reggio Emilia-inspired schools, learning is viewed as a collaborative process between children, teachers, and families. Classrooms are designed to be welcoming, flexible, and filled with natural light and materials, encouraging exploration and creativity. Teachers observe children closely, document their progress, and design projects based on the interests and questions that emerge from the group, making learning highly individualized and dynamic.

A hallmark of the Reggio Emilia approach is its emphasis on relationships and community building. Children are encouraged to express themselves through various mediums, including art, music, movement, and play, while collaborating on long-term, experiential projects. Parents are considered essential partners in the educational process, contributing to classroom life and school decisions. This approach fosters respect, autonomy, and a strong sense of belonging, making it particularly well-suited for families who value child-led learning and deep community engagement.

Benefits:

- Child-centered, experiential learning
- Strong focus on respect, relationships, and community
- Encourages creativity and collaboration

Challenges:

- A less structured curriculum may not suit all families
- Requires active parental and teacher involvement
- It may be difficult to find outside early childhood settings

Language Immersion

Language immersion programs provide instruction in a foreign language for all or part of the school day, allowing students to acquire fluency through natural, everyday use. These programs can begin as early as preschool or kindergarten. They may continue through high school, offering full or partial immersion in languages such as Spanish, French, Mandarin, or others. Academic subjects, like math, science, and social studies, are taught in the target language, helping students develop both linguistic and cognitive skills simultaneously.

Families choose language immersion for a variety of reasons, including fostering bilingualism, enhancing cultural understanding, and providing a competitive edge in a globalized world. Immersion students often achieve high levels of proficiency and demonstrate greater cognitive flexibility. Parental involvement is crucial, especially if the family does not speak the target language at home. Supporting homework, attending cultural events, and communicating with teachers helps reinforce learning and build confidence.

Benefits:

- Develops bilingualism and cross-cultural understanding
- Enhances cognitive flexibility
- Prepares students for a globalized world

Challenges:

- It may be challenging for families who do not speak the target language
- Academic content can be more difficult initially
- Limited availability in some regions

Special Education Schools

Special education schools are designed specifically to meet the needs of students with learning differences, developmental delays, physical disabilities, or other special needs. These schools offer individualized education plans (IEPs), specialized staff such as speech and occupational therapists, and adaptive technologies to support each child's unique learning profile. Class sizes are typically small, allowing for more personalized attention and tailored instruction.

The curriculum in special education schools is often highly flexible, focusing on both academic and life skills, with an emphasis on building independence, confidence, and social-emotional growth. These schools foster a supportive environment where students can thrive without stigma or isolation. Parental involvement is crucial; families work closely with educators and therapists to set goals, monitor progress, and advocate for their child's needs. For many families, special education schools provide a sense of community and hope, empowering children to reach their fullest potential.

Benefits:

- Tailored instruction and specialized staff
- Small class sizes and individualized plans
- Supportive environment for diverse needs

Challenges:

- It may be costly or have limited spaces
- Can separate students from mainstream peers
- Requires ongoing advocacy and involvement from parents

Independent Schools

Independent schools, often referred to as private schools, are educational institutions that operate independently of government control and funding. They are typically governed by private boards or organizations and funded through tuition fees, donations, and endowments, rather than public tax dollars. This independence grants them significant flexibility in curriculum design, teaching methods, and school culture, allowing them to tailor educational experiences to their students' needs and interests.

Independent schools come in many forms, including secular, religious, single-sex, international, and specialized institutions (such as those focused on the arts or STEM). They often feature smaller class sizes, highly qualified teachers, and a broad range of extracurricular activities and support services. Many independent schools emphasize community involvement and parental engagement, creating environments where families actively participate in their children's education.

Benefits of Independent Schools

- Smaller Class Sizes
- Curricular Flexibility
- Breadth of Extracurriculars

Challenges of Independent Schools

- Cost
- Transportation and scheduling
- Regulatory and Accreditation Issues

Independent versus Other Private Schools

The terms "independent school" and "private school" are often used interchangeably, but they have important distinctions in governance, funding, and autonomy.

Private schools are any educational institutions that operate outside of government funding and control. They can be run by a wide variety of entities, including religious organizations, for-profit companies, non-profit groups, or even individuals. Private schools receive their funding primarily from tuition, donations, and occasionally support from affiliated organizations, such as churches or dioceses. This broad category encompasses parochial schools (operated by religious organizations), proprietary schools (operated for profit), and other non-public institutions.

Independent schools are a specific subset of private schools. What sets them apart is their governance and funding structure. Independent schools are always non-profit and are governed by an independent board of trustees or governors, rather than by an external organization, such as a church or corporation. They are self-funded through tuition, charitable donations, and endowments. They do not receive financial or administrative support from outside organizations, including religious bodies or for-profit entities. This structure grants independent schools complete autonomy over their curriculum, admissions, and policies, enabling them to develop distinctive educational missions and respond promptly to emerging educational trends.

To clarify:

- All independent schools are private schools, but not all private schools are independent schools.
- For example, a Catholic parochial school run by a local diocese is a private school, but not an independent school. Conversely, a non-denominational school governed solely by its own board is both private and independent.

Key differences:

- Governance:
    - Private schools may be governed by outside organizations (religious groups, corporations, etc.).
    - Independent schools are governed solely by their own independent board of trustees.
- Funding:
    - Private schools may receive financial support from affiliated organizations.
    - Independent schools rely only on tuition, donations, and endowments, with no outside operational funding.
- Curriculum Autonomy:
    - Private schools may have to align with the values or requirements of their governing body.
    - Independent schools have full autonomy to design their own curriculum and educational philosophy.

Chapter 12: The College Problem

College is not the only path to success. The skills gap is real, and there are millions of jobs available that don't require a four-year degree.
- Mike Rowe

The modern American college system stands at a crossroads, facing mounting criticism over its cost, return on investment, and the state of intellectual freedom. These issues have profound implications not only for individual students but also for the broader question of educational sovereignty, who controls the purpose and direction of higher learning in a democratic society.

The Crisis of Cost and Value

The cost of a college education has soared over the past several decades, far outpacing inflation and wage growth. Tuition and fees at public and private institutions continue to rise, leaving many students and families with staggering debt burdens. Despite some stabilization and increased financial aid in recent years, the net cost of attendance remains prohibitively high for many, especially those from low-income backgrounds. For example, the average net cost for a public four-year institution can exceed $ 20,000 per year, with unmet financial need persisting even after accounting for loans and work-study programs. This financial pressure leads many to question whether the economic benefits of a degree justify the investment, a skepticism reflected in recent surveys showing that only a small minority of students believe higher education offers good value for its price.

The cost of college in America has risen dramatically over the past four decades, with tuition at public and private institutions more than doubling in that time. While many factors contribute to this increase, a critical, yet often underappreciated, driver is the guaranteed availability of federal student loans and government funding mechanisms.

The Role of Guaranteed Student Loans

The expansion of federal student loan programs has fundamentally altered the economics of higher education. When the government guarantees virtually unlimited access to student loans, it removes natural market constraints on tuition prices. Colleges know that students can borrow more to cover higher costs, so they face less resistance when raising tuition.

Research from the Federal Reserve Bank of New York found that for every dollar increase in federal subsidized loan limits, colleges raised their sticker price tuition by about 60 cents. This phenomenon, sometimes referred to as the **Bennett Hypothesis**, suggests that a significant portion of the additional borrowing capacity made available by government loans is retained by colleges themselves, rather than being passed on to students in the form of enhanced educational value. The effect is most pronounced at private institutions and for more expensive programs.

While it is often claimed that rising tuition is a response to declining state or federal funding, the data does not support this narrative. In fact, state funding for higher education has increased over the past four decades, not decreased. If tuition were simply rising to offset funding cuts, tuition should have fallen as state funding rose. Instead, both state funding and tuition have increased, meaning colleges are taking in more money from both sources.

This influx of funding has not necessarily translated into better outcomes for students. Much of the new revenue has been spent on administrative expansion, student services, and amenities, not on instruction or educational quality. As a result, the value proposition of a college degree is increasingly questioned: students are paying more, often with borrowed money, but are not always seeing commensurate returns in job market outcomes or skills.

The guaranteed flow of federal loans and grants shields colleges from competitive pressures that would otherwise force them to control costs and improve quality. Instead of focusing on efficiency or educational outcomes, institutions have incentives to expand non-essential spending, knowing that students can always borrow more to pay the bill. This dynamic creates a cycle where costs rise, loans increase, and the value of many graduates' degrees stagnates or even declines.

Overall, the combination of guaranteed student loans and ever-increasing government funding has fueled the relentless rise in college costs. Rather than improving educational outcomes, this system often transfers wealth from students and taxpayers to institutional budgets, while leaving many graduates with unsustainable debt and uncertain job prospects.

Global Comparisons: Funding Mechanisms and Their Consequences

United States: The U.S. model is characterized by high tuition, widespread access to federal student loans, and significant government and private spending. This creates a feedback loop: as government-backed loans and grants become more available, colleges raise tuition, knowing students can borrow more. This has led to some of the highest per-student spending and tuition fees in the world, with the U.S. spending nearly twice the average per student.

The result is escalating student debt and questions about the value of the investment.

The United Kingdom and Australia have moved toward high tuition, offset by government-backed, income-contingent loans. The UK, for instance, steadily increased tuition fees since the late 1990s, shifting more costs onto students while providing loans to cover them. This has resulted in a similar pattern: as loans became more accessible, tuition rose, and student debt increased.

Many European countries (e.g., Germany, Norway, France, Finland) offer free or very low tuition at public universities, funded primarily by the state. However, this model often leads to chronic underfunding: universities operate on tighter budgets, which can result in larger class sizes, fewer resources, and sometimes lower teaching quality. In Germany and Argentina, for example, free tuition is often accompanied by underfunded institutions, lengthy degree completion times, and high dropout rates. When public funding is cut or fails to keep up with enrollment, the quality of education can suffer.

Countries like Chile, Japan, and South Korea have privatized a significant portion of their higher education sector, shifting the costs to students. In Chile, high tuition relative to income and insufficient student aid have led to widespread protests and limited upward mobility for lower-income students. In these systems, government loans and scholarships are available, but coverage is often incomplete, leaving many students without adequate support.

Around the world, the percentage of students accessing loans is rising faster than other forms of aid, especially in countries that have shifted costs to students. Where loans are widely available, tuition tends to rise, mirroring the U.S. dynamic.

In countries where the government covers most higher education costs, spending per student is lower, and institutions are forced to operate more frugally. This can protect students from debt but may also limit educational resources and innovation.

Intellectual Diversity and Ideological Indoctrination

Perhaps most concerning from a sovereignty perspective is the erosion of intellectual diversity on campus. Universities, once celebrated as bastions of free inquiry and debate, are increasingly criticized for cultivating intellectual monocultures. Professors and commentators warn that many institutions now suppress dissenting viewpoints, particularly those that challenge prevailing progressive or social justice orthodoxies. The proliferation of diversity, equity, and inclusion programs has not translated into a diversity of thought; instead, it has coincided with the marginalization of conservative, libertarian, or religious perspectives.

A significant body of critique highlights the ascendancy of neo-Marxist or victim-oppressor frameworks in the humanities and social sciences. This ideology, rooted in critical theory, reframes social relations in terms of power and oppression, dividing individuals into categories of victims and oppressors based on race, gender, sexuality, and other identities. Critics argue that this approach not only distorts academic inquiry by privileging activism over scholarship but also fosters a culture of grievance, self-censorship, and intolerance toward dissent. The result is a campus environment where open debate is stifled, and students are encouraged to view themselves primarily through the lens of group identity and historical victimization.

A growing body of critique contends that higher education in the United States is increasingly marked by issues stemming from the widespread adoption of Diversity, Equity, and Inclusion (DEI) initiatives and the influence of Marxist-derived ideology. In practice, this means universities increasingly prioritize group identity over individual merit and seek to equalize outcomes through policies that favor certain groups while disadvantaging others.

Critics argue that the entrenchment of DEI and neo-Marxist ideology has led to several negative outcomes:

- Suppression of Dissent: Campuses have become intellectual monocultures where alternative viewpoints, especially those critical of DEI or leftist orthodoxy, are marginalized or actively suppressed. This stifles debate and undermines the traditional academic mission of critical inquiry and free exchange of ideas.
- Administrative Overreach: DEI bureaucracies wield significant influence over hiring, admissions, and curriculum, often imposing political criteria on faculty and students. For example, some universities have adopted explicit or implicit racial quotas in hiring and admissions, which critics argue is a form of institutionalized discrimination.
- Ideological Indoctrination: The focus on equity (as opposed to equality) and the framing of all social issues as manifestations of systemic oppression can lead to intellectual rigidity and a culture of grievance, where students are encouraged to see themselves primarily as victims or oppressors.
- Shift in Institutional Mission: Instead of prioritizing the pursuit of truth and the transmission of knowledge, universities are increasingly seen as training grounds for political activism and social change, often at the expense of academic rigor and scientific advancement.

These trends are seen by detractors as undermining the core functions of higher education. The pursuit of truth, open debate, and viewpoint diversity are compromised when institutions are captured by a single ideological perspective. Furthermore, the allocation of substantial resources to DEI initiatives is viewed as diverting attention and funding away from teaching and research.

These trends, skyrocketing costs, questionable economic returns, and the narrowing of acceptable viewpoints reflect a deeper crisis of sovereignty in American higher education. As the state, private sector, and ideological movements vie for control over curricula and campus culture, the university's traditional mission of fostering independent thought and civic responsibility is increasingly undermined. When institutions prioritize political conformity or market utility over intellectual rigor and pluralism, they risk betraying the very principles that justify their privileged status in a democratic society.

In short, the challenges facing today's colleges are not merely financial or administrative; they are fundamentally about the purpose and control of education itself. Restoring educational sovereignty will require not just policy reform but a renewed commitment to intellectual freedom, viewpoint diversity, and the cultivation of genuinely independent minds.

Declining standards

There is also growing evidence and widespread concern that academic standards in college-level education have declined both in the United States and globally. In the U.S., surveys of tenured faculty reveal that nearly half believe standards have fallen in recent years, with 37% admitting to routinely inflating grades and a third acknowledging they have reduced course rigor. Faculty cite pressures such as the corporatization of higher education, where institutions, motivated by financial insecurity and the need to attract and retain students, are incentivized to lower standards rather than risk losing tuition revenue. This has led to a system where the health of academic programs is measured more by graduation rates than by the rigor or quality of instruction, and where faculty may feel compelled to pass underprepared students to spare them further debt or to avoid program cuts.

Grade inflation is a particularly acute symptom of this trend, with many classes awarding high grades for diminishing amounts of work, resulting in degrees that carry less value and students who are less prepared for the workforce or advanced study. The lowering of expectations is compounded by a shift in institutional priorities, with universities increasingly focused on student satisfaction, emotional support, and social promotion, sometimes at the expense of academic excellence. There is also a growing politicization of academic standards, where disparities in student outcomes are attributed to systemic bias, leading some institutions to question the validity of traditional expectations such as punctuality, participation, or the use of standard English, further eroding consistent benchmarks for achievement.

Globally, similar patterns are evident. In the UK, resource constraints and funding models that tie university budgets to student retention have created a vicious cycle: institutions under financial pressure may lower entry and academic standards to maintain enrollment, which in turn puts further strain on resources and staff, leading to further compromises in quality. Surveys of academics in the UK and Europe confirm that the squeeze on resources is widely seen as having an adverse effect on standards, with declining entry qualifications and rising dropout rates contributing to a perception of systemic decline. In the developing world, large-scale studies indicate that while access to higher education has expanded, the quality of education, as measured by basic literacy and learning outcomes, has stagnated or declined over the past few decades, particularly in South Asia and sub-Saharan Africa.

International organizations, such as UNESCO and the European Union, have recognized these challenges, calling for a renewed focus on quality and relevance in higher education amid concerns about the adequacy of learning outcomes and the effectiveness of quality assurance mechanisms. The rapid growth of private and transnational institutions, especially in Africa and Asia, has further complicated oversight, with concerns about credential fraud and the difficulty of maintaining consistent standards across diverse educational systems.

The decline in academic standards in higher education is a complex, global phenomenon driven by financial pressures, changing institutional priorities, grade inflation, and, in some contexts, political and social dynamics that challenge traditional measures of academic achievement. This trend has significant implications for the value of college degrees and the preparedness of graduates for the demands of the modern workforce.

Job Market Realities

While a college degree still correlates with higher lifetime earnings and lower rates of poverty, the labor market for graduates is undergoing a shift. The job outlook for bachelor's degree holders in 2024 is relatively strong, with a modest increase in hiring opportunities. However, the demand for advanced degrees has softened, and employers increasingly prioritize practical skills and specific credentials over traditional academic qualifications. This trend suggests a disconnect between what colleges offer and what employers require, raising questions about the adaptability and relevance of current curricula.

College in the United States has undergone a dramatic transformation over the past century. Originally, higher education was an exclusive domain, reserved for a privileged few, primarily white men from affluent backgrounds, who sought preparation for specific professions, such as law, medicine, or the clergy. Over time, access broadened as social and economic changes, including the GI Bill and later financial aid programs, opened the doors to more diverse populations. This democratization of college attendance, while expanding opportunity, also shifted the function of a degree from a specialized credential to a more general requirement for entry into the middle class.

As more people earned degrees, employers began to use educational attainment as a convenient screening tool, a phenomenon known as degree inflation. Jobs that once required only a high school diploma or an associate's degree increasingly began to demand a bachelor's or even a graduate degree, regardless of whether the work itself had become more complex. For example, the proportion of jobs requiring a graduate degree nearly doubled from 8% in 1983 to 14% in 2021, with projections indicating it will reach 16% by 2031. This has led to a situation where an associate's degree, once a reliable ticket to stable employment, is often insufficient for advancement in many fields. Even bachelor's degrees can feel devalued as employers raise the bar further.

The consequences are significant. Degree inflation closes off job opportunities to the majority of Americans who lack four-year degrees, exacerbates labor shortages, and reduces the return on investment for college graduates, who may find themselves underemployed or required to pursue further education for roles that previously required less.

While associate's degrees and certificates still offer value in certain technical and healthcare fields, their labor market returns have become more variable. Many students now feel compelled to stack credentials or continue on to bachelor's or graduate programs to remain competitive. This escalation in credential requirements reflects not only changing employer expectations but also the broader social shift that has turned college from a selective gateway to a near-universal expectation, with all the attendant pressures and challenges for students, institutions, and the workforce.

This shift from college being an exclusive pathway for specific careers to a mass or near-universal experience has led to degree inflation and a relative decline in the value of credentials. It is occurring globally, not just in the United States.

Over the past two decades, access to higher education has increased dramatically in all regions of the world, with more than a third of the global population now pursuing some form of post-secondary study. This expansion has been driven by economic growth, policy initiatives, and the rise of private and distance education institutions. As a result, the number of university graduates worldwide is projected to more than double between 2013 and 2030, reaching 300 million by 2030. Across the OECD, the proportion of young adults with higher education qualifications now exceeds those with only upper secondary education.

This massification of higher education has led to a worldwide phenomenon similar to what you describe: credentials that once signaled elite or specialized training have become more common, and in many fields, higher-level degrees are now required for jobs that previously accepted lower qualifications. Where an associate's degree or its equivalent once provided reliable access to stable employment, in many countries, a bachelor's or even a master's degree is now needed for similar roles. This is often referred to as "credential inflation" or "degree inflation," and it is observed in both developed and developing economies.

Despite the increase in degree holders, the employment premium for higher education has generally remained steady: bachelor's and master's graduates still earn significantly more than those with only secondary education, on average. However, the expansion of access has not automatically translated into higher graduation rates or equitable outcomes, and concerns about the quality and relevance of education have emerged alongside these trends. In some countries, the rapid growth of higher education has outpaced improvements in primary and secondary education, resulting in challenges to student preparedness and completion rates.

Essentially, the shift from elite to mass and now toward universal access to higher education is a global trend, and with it has come a relative decline in the signaling power of lower-level degrees and an escalation in credential requirements for many jobs. The resulting degree inflation and questions about the value and quality of higher education are now common concerns in many countries, not just the U.S..

Employment trends in the U.S. show a clear and accelerating shift away from strict college degree requirements for many jobs, especially in sectors outside of those with formal licensing or regulatory demands (like medicine, law, or engineering). The share of job postings requiring at least a bachelor's degree has dropped from about 20% before the pandemic to around 17.6% in late 2024, opening up tens of thousands of additional opportunities for the roughly two-thirds of Americans without a four-year degree. This trend is driven by several factors: persistent labor shortages, the need for a larger and more diverse talent pool, and a growing recognition that practical skills, real-world experience, and the ability to self-learn are often better indicators of job performance than formal education.

Major companies, including Google, IBM, Tesla, Accenture, Walmart, Dell, Verizon, Delta, General Motors, Bank of America, and Home Depot, have publicly announced the removal of degree requirements for many high-paying office and technical jobs. This shift is most pronounced in "middle-tier" roles such as construction managers, web developers, IT help desk specialists, sales supervisors, event planners, and computer programmers, positions where skills can be demonstrated and where degreed and non-degreed workers have long worked side by side. Surveys indicate that approximately one-third of companies eliminated bachelor's degree requirements for certain roles in 2024, and another quarter plan to do so by 2025. State governments are also following suit, dropping degree requirements for most public sector jobs in places like Alaska, Maryland, Minnesota, New Jersey, Pennsylvania, Utah, and Virginia.

The move toward skills-based hiring is particularly strong in industries facing acute labor or skills shortages, such as information services, software development, construction, finance, and insurance. Employers report that removing degree requirements increases the number and diversity of applicants, helps fill open positions more quickly, and allows for more competitive selection of qualified candidates. While nearly all companies still require degrees for some roles, especially at higher levels, the overall trend is toward greater flexibility: two-thirds of employers who dropped degree requirements did so for entry-level jobs, over half for mid-level roles, and nearly a quarter for some senior positions.

At the same time, employers are placing greater value on alternative credentials, including certificate programs, associate degrees, online degrees, and apprenticeships. Approximately 75% of surveyed companies stated that they value certificate programs, and a majority now prioritize relevant work experience over formal education when evaluating candidates.

While degrees remain necessary for certain regulated professions, the U.S. job market is increasingly open to candidates who can demonstrate skills and experience through alternative pathways. The trend toward skills-first hiring is expected to continue and expand across more industries in the coming years.

Outside the United States, there is a noticeable, though uneven, trend toward relaxing degree requirements for employment, particularly in sectors where practical skills and experience are more important than formal academic credentials. This shift is influenced by similar factors as in the U.S.: labor shortages, the need for a more diverse workforce, and recognition that traditional degrees are not always the best indicator of job readiness or potential.

In the United Kingdom, Australia, and parts of Europe, employers are increasingly open to candidates with alternative qualifications such as vocational certificates, apprenticeships, and industry-recognized credentials. For example, the UK has expanded higher-level apprenticeships that combine paid work with academic study, enabling individuals to enter fields such as IT, finance, and engineering without a traditional university degree. In Germany and Switzerland, the dual education system has long provided a respected pathway into skilled professions through apprenticeships and vocational training, which employers value as much as, or more than, academic degrees for many roles.

Globally, large multinational companies, especially in technology, finance, and business services, are leading the way in skills-based hiring. Firms such as IBM, Google, and Accenture have publicly stated that they no longer require degrees for many positions, focusing instead on demonstrated skills, certifications, or relevant work experience. This is particularly evident in information technology, software development, and digital marketing, where rapid technological change makes up-to-date skills more valuable than traditional credentials. The trend is also spreading to fields such as construction, logistics, and customer service, where practical experience and on-the-job training are highly valued.

While degree requirements remain standard for regulated professions such as medicine, law, and engineering, other sectors are seeing a marked shift. Surveys in multiple countries indicate that employers are more likely to hire based on relevant experience and certifications, with many reporting increased diversity, larger applicant pools, and better retention as a result of dropping degree prerequisites.

However, the pace of change varies by country and industry. In some regions, particularly where university education is heavily subsidized or seen as a social norm, degrees still carry significant weight, especially for career advancement. However, overall, the global employment landscape is shifting toward greater flexibility, with skills-based hiring gaining momentum and alternative pathways, such as apprenticeships, online credentials, and vocational training, becoming increasingly recognized and valued by employers.

It is necessary for someone to go to college primarily when their career goals require a degree or specialized academic training that cannot be obtained elsewhere. Many professions, such as teaching, social work, engineering, healthcare, finance, and technology, require at least a bachelor's degree as a minimum qualification, making college attendance essential for entry into these fields or to meet licensing requirements. Beyond formal requirements, college is also important for those who enjoy academic life and want to explore diverse disciplines, developing critical thinking, communication, and problem-solving skills that are highly valued by employers.

College becomes necessary when individuals seek access to professional jobs that offer higher earning potential and opportunities for career advancement. Statistics show that college graduates earn significantly more on average than those with only a high school diploma, and many employers list a bachelor's degree as a prerequisite for entry-level positions. Additionally, college provides structured environments for networking, internships, and experiential learning, which can be crucial for launching and sustaining a successful career.

However, college is not universally necessary for success. For some careers, particularly in skilled trades, technology, or entrepreneurship, alternative pathways such as apprenticeships, certifications, or in-house training may be sufficient. The decision to attend college should weigh the cost, the expected return on investment, and alignment with one's career aspirations. For those uncertain about their direction, college can offer a valuable space to explore interests and develop a broad foundation before specializing.

Basically, college is necessary when a desired career requires formal credentials, when one seeks to maximize earning potential and job stability, or when one values the academic and social experiences it provides. For others, especially in fields where skills and experience trump degrees, college may be optional or one of several viable pathways to success.

Alternatives to college

Young people today have a growing array of alternatives to the traditional four-year college route, many of which offer strong career prospects, lower debt, and hands-on experience. This shift reflects both changing workforce demands and a reevaluation of what constitutes a successful and fulfilling career.

The push for four-year degrees as the default path has led to a national skills gap and soaring student debt, while millions of well-paying jobs in the trades go unfilled. Influencers like Mike Rowe and a growing number of educators and employers are working to change the narrative, encouraging young people to consider all their options and pursue careers that match their interests, talents, and values, rather than just societal expectations.

Tech Companies and In-House Training

Major technology firms and many other employers now invest heavily in in-house training and reskilling programs. Companies like Microsoft and Salesforce run robust internal learning platforms, such as Salesforce's Trailhead, which combine micro-learning modules with practical projects, allowing employees to gain new skills and certifications at their own pace. These initiatives are designed to close skills gaps quickly, often in under six months. They increasingly viewed as a viable alternative to college for entering or advancing in tech roles. Many organizations also partner with external providers, such as BrainStation, to deliver immersive boot camps and certificate courses in fields like software engineering, web development, UX design, and data science, helping both new hires and current employees transition into high-demand digital careers.

MOOCs and Online Learning (e.g., Udemy, edX, Coursera)

Massive Open Online Courses (MOOCs) have revolutionized access to education by offering affordable or free courses from top universities and industry experts. Platforms like edX and Coursera provide university-level courses and credentials, including MicroMasters and Professional Certificates, in subjects ranging from computer science to business and healthcare. Udemy, although not affiliated with a particular university, offers a vast catalog of practical, user-rated courses created by industry professionals and universities around the world, making it a popular choice for self-directed learners and corporate training alike. These platforms allow students to acquire job-ready skills, earn recognized certificates, and even pursue modular degrees, all at their own pace and often at a fraction of the cost of traditional education.

Trade Schools and Vocational Training

Trade schools, also known as vocational or technical colleges, offer specialized training in fields such as plumbing, electrical work, HVAC, welding, and more. These programs typically last from six months to two years, allowing students to enter the workforce quickly and with marketable skills. Tuition is often a fraction of the cost of a four-year degree, and graduates can expect strong job prospects and salaries, often exceeding $60,000 for many trades. The demand for skilled tradespeople is high and growing, making this a practical and respected path for young people who prefer hands-on work and want to avoid large student loans.

Apprenticeships

Apprenticeships combine paid, on-the-job training with classroom instruction, allowing participants to earn while they learn and gain industry-recognized credentials. Available in fields as diverse as construction, healthcare, IT, and marketing, apprenticeships are structured to provide real-world experience and a direct pathway to employment. They are particularly valued for their ability to fast-track participants into skilled professions without the financial burden of college tuition. In the U.S., apprenticeships are expanding beyond traditional trades to include white-collar and professional roles.

Mike Rowe, known for his television work highlighting skilled trades, has become a leading advocate for alternative career pathways. His mikeroweWORKS Foundation offers the Work Ethic Scholarship Program, which awards millions of dollars annually to students pursuing training in the skilled trades. The program emphasizes work ethic, personal responsibility, and a willingness to acquire skills in demand. Applicants must sign the S.W.E.A.T. Pledge (Skills and Work Ethic Aren't Taboo), submit references, and demonstrate a commitment to hard work. Since its inception, the foundation has awarded over $11 million in scholarships to more than 1,800 recipients across 48 states, supporting careers in fields from welding to cybersecurity. Rowe's mission is to challenge the stigma that trade jobs are "consolation prizes" and to highlight the dignity and financial stability these careers can provide.

Community Colleges and Two-Year Programs

Community colleges offer associate degrees and certificate programs that can lead directly to employment or serve as a stepping stone to a four-year degree. These institutions are often more affordable, provide flexible scheduling, and offer support services to help students transition to adult life and the workforce. Many community colleges have strong partnerships with local employers, which increases job placement opportunities for their graduates.

Military Service

Joining the military provides structured training, discipline, and access to technical education in fields such as aviation, engineering, and healthcare. Service members often receive benefits like tuition assistance, healthcare, and the opportunity to earn college credits or pursue further education after their service.

Entrepreneurship and Content Creation

With the rise of digital platforms, some students pursue entrepreneurship or careers as content creators on social media. While this path can be highly competitive and uncertain, it offers opportunities for those with creativity, technical skills, and business acumen to build independent careers.

Direct Entry into the Workforce

Some students choose to enter the workforce immediately after high school, seeking part- or full-time employment, and may pursue further training or education later as needed. This option can provide valuable experience and financial independence, especially for those who are undecided about long-term career goals.

Alternatives to College Around the World

Globally, students have access to a wide and growing range of alternatives to traditional university education, many of which are deeply integrated into national education and workforce systems. In Europe, for example, apprenticeships and vocational training are robust, highly structured, and widely respected pathways. Germany's dual education system is a standout, with approximately 60% of young people participating in programs that combine classroom instruction with paid, hands-on work experience in industries such as manufacturing, engineering, and healthcare.

This model directly addresses skills shortages, resulting in high rates of youth employment, with over 80% of apprentices being offered permanent jobs after completing their training. Switzerland's similar system covers more than 230 professions and emphasizes lifelong learning, allowing for continual upskilling and reskilling throughout one's career. The UK and Australia also have strong apprenticeship frameworks, with the UK increasingly offering higher-level apprenticeships that blend academic study with practical work, and Australia incentivizing apprenticeships in both traditional trades and emerging industries through employer subsidies.

MOOCs and online learning platforms are also expanding rapidly worldwide. Platforms like edX, Coursera, and Udemy have millions of learners in countries such as India, the UK, and Canada, offering university-level courses and professional certificates that can be completed flexibly and affordably. China, not included in Western MOOC statistics, has developed its own massive online learning ecosystem, further broadening global access to skills-based education.

Trade schools and technical colleges remain popular in many regions, offering focused, practical training for specific careers in fields such as automotive repair, construction, healthcare, and IT. These programs are often shorter and more affordable than university degrees and are closely aligned with labor market needs.

Gap years and structured international programs are another common alternative, particularly in countries such as Australia and the UK. Students may volunteer abroad, participate in adventure leadership training, or engage in service projects, gaining valuable life skills, cultural exposure, and leadership experience before committing to further education or employment.

Entrepreneurship and self-employment are increasingly viable options globally, as digital platforms and global markets make it easier to start businesses, freelance, or monetize creative skills. Many young people are turning hobbies, digital content creation, or small ventures into full-time careers without formal degrees.

Military service and direct workforce entry remain established alternatives in many countries, providing structured training, discipline, and often educational benefits or pathways to further study.

Ultimately, international universities themselves can serve as an alternative for students seeking high-quality, affordable education outside their home country. For example, public universities in Germany and Argentina offer low or no tuition, and institutions in the UK, Ireland, and Australia provide English-language instruction at a lower cost than many American universities.

Outside the United States, alternative pathways after high school are often more formalized and integrated into national education and workforce systems, particularly through apprenticeships, vocational training, and government-supported programs. The global expansion of online learning and the rise of entrepreneurship further broaden the landscape, giving students a diverse array of choices tailored to their interests, financial circumstances, and career goals.

Chapter 13: AI and education

Talk with your children about how they are using AI in their schoolwork... Don't let AI undercut learning. Explore what's possible together, exploring how AI can support learning diversity, boost creativity, and personalize learning.

- Dr. Robert Harrison, ACS International Schools

Throughout history, transformative inventions like the printing press and the internet have dramatically altered how people access and interact with information. Each of these breakthroughs was initially met with skepticism, fear, and even resistance. When the printing press was introduced, it faced backlash from authorities and segments of society who worried about the spread of uncontrolled ideas and the loss of traditional gatekeepers. Similarly, the internet, now an essential part of daily life, was once dismissed by some as a passing trend, and its early days were marked by concerns about misinformation and the overwhelming flood of data.

Today, artificial intelligence stands at a similar crossroads. Many people are skeptical or fearful of AI, uncertain about its implications, and wary of its rapid integration into daily life. Some dismiss AI as a temporary trend, while others voice concerns about its potential for misuse, lack of transparency, and the erosion of personal control.

This skepticism is fueled by both the complexity of AI systems, which can make their workings opaque even to experts, and by highly publicized incidents of AI errors or manipulation.

History confirms that such skepticism often accompanies technologies that fundamentally change how information is produced, distributed, and consumed. The printing press democratized access to books and ideas, sparking a surge in literacy and the spread of radical new thoughts. The internet has made knowledge globally accessible in real-time, transforming not just information access but also communication, commerce, and culture. In both cases, the initial fears gave way to acceptance as the benefits became apparent and the technology became integrated into everyday life.

AI is now beginning to reshape our relationship with information in equally profound ways. It personalizes content, curates news and entertainment, and mediates what we see and when we see it, often without us being fully aware of its influence. This new era of information access is likely to be even more transformative than previous ones, making knowledge more accessible but also raising new challenges around trust, critical thinking, and digital literacy.

Whether welcomed or resisted, the trajectory of history suggests that AI will transform how we interact with information and one another. Its influence will expand, making information more personalized and accessible, and changing our lives in ways we are only beginning to understand, regardless of whether we are ready for it or not.

Artificial Intelligence is fundamentally transforming the landscape of education by making learning more personalized, efficient, and accessible. One of the most significant impacts of AI is its ability to tailor educational experiences to individual students. Adaptive learning systems analyze each learner's progress and preferences, delivering customized lessons that match their pace and style. This personalization helps students stay engaged and motivated, while also ensuring that they receive the right level of challenge and support.

AI is also revolutionizing feedback and tutoring. Intelligent tutoring systems provide instant feedback, allowing students to quickly identify their strengths and areas for improvement. This immediate support encourages independent learning and enables students to progress at their own speed. For teachers, AI streamlines numerous administrative tasks, including grading, attendance, and scheduling, thereby freeing up valuable time that can be redirected toward direct interaction with students and lesson planning.

Content creation is another area where AI is making a difference. Teachers can use AI tools to generate lesson plans, quizzes, and multimedia resources, making it easier to create engaging and diverse educational materials. Additionally, AI-powered technologies such as text-to-speech and speech recognition are making learning more accessible for students with disabilities, thereby promoting inclusivity in the classroom.

AI also plays a crucial role in analyzing large sets of student data to provide actionable insights. Educators can utilize these insights to identify learning gaps, predict which students may be at risk of falling behind, and intervene early to provide targeted support. Furthermore, AI is helping teachers with their own professional development by recommending personalized training and keeping them up to date with the latest educational practices.

The rise of AI has also facilitated the growth of remote and global learning. Intelligent tools support virtual classrooms, enabling students from different locations to collaborate and learn together. This has made education more accessible to a broader audience, regardless of geographical barriers.

While the benefits of AI in education are substantial, there are also significant challenges to address, including ensuring data privacy, mitigating algorithmic bias, and providing equitable access to technology. Responsible implementation is crucial for maximizing the positive impact of AI while minimizing potential drawbacks.

Consequently, AI is enhancing education by supporting both teachers and students when used appropriately and with a critical eye. As AI continues to evolve, it holds the promise of helping students in the rapidly changing, technology-driven world, while also requiring thoughtful consideration of ethical and equity issues.

AI For Teaching

When guiding parents and educators on how to positively incorporate AI into their teaching, it's important to focus on both practical strategies and a mindset that embraces technology as a supportive tool rather than a replacement for human connection.

One effective approach is to encourage parents and teachers to explore AI-powered educational platforms together with their children or students. By doing so, they can model curiosity and digital literacy, showing that learning new technologies is a shared journey. For example, parents might sit with their children as they use an AI-driven reading app, discussing the story and asking questions to deepen comprehension. Educators can employ similar strategies in the classroom by integrating AI tools into group activities or assignments and facilitating discussions about how the technology works and how it can be used responsibly.

Another idea is to use AI to personalize learning experiences. Parents and teachers can help students set goals and track their progress with the assistance of AI tools that adapt to individual strengths and weaknesses. This not only boosts motivation but also teaches children to take ownership of their learning. Encouraging students to reflect on their progress and challenges with the help of AI-generated feedback can foster a growth mindset and resilience.

It's also valuable to promote critical thinking about AI itself. Parents and educators can have open conversations with children about how AI makes decisions, its limitations, and why it's essential to question information, even when it comes from intelligent systems. This helps students become discerning users of technology, capable of navigating the digital world thoughtfully and safely.

For teachers, professional development is key. They should seek out training opportunities to become familiar with the latest AI tools and best practices for integrating them into the curriculum. Sharing experiences and resources with colleagues can create a supportive community that stays up-to-date with technological advances.

Ultimately, both parents and educators should emphasize the importance of balance. AI can be a powerful supplement to traditional teaching, but it should not replace human interaction, creativity, or emotional support. By using AI thoughtfully and intentionally, adults can help children develop the skills they need to thrive in a world where technology and human ingenuity are intertwined.

AI is also becoming an invaluable resource for educators and parents when it comes to planning, creating assignments, and gathering information. For lesson planning, AI-powered platforms can streamline the entire process by generating customizable lesson plans that align with curriculum standards and can be differentiated to suit the needs of different students. These tools act as thought partners, helping educators brainstorm activities, refine unit plans, and focus on designing more engaging and relevant lessons. While the output from AI often requires teacher review and adaptation, it can spark new ideas and save significant time, allowing educators to devote more energy to deeper student engagement.

When it comes to creating assignments, AI tools can quickly generate a wide variety of tasks across multiple subjects and grade levels. Teachers can input prompts specifying the subject, difficulty, and format, and the AI will produce assignments that can then be reviewed and customized as needed. This not only makes the process more efficient but also enables the creation of assignments that are more varied and tailored to student interests. AI can even help design assignments that are more interactive and collaborative, making them more enjoyable for students and less tedious for teachers to grade.

The ability to personalize assignments based on student data enables tasks to be adjusted in real-time to match each learner's strengths, weaknesses, and interests, resulting in higher motivation and deeper engagement.

For gathering information, AI-powered writing and search assistants can help educators and parents quickly summarize complex topics, identify the most relevant content, and generate ideas for activities or projects. These tools are especially useful for overcoming writer's block and ensuring that lesson content is both accurate and up-to-date. AI can also aid in creating presentations by turning research and text into slides, inserting relevant images, and helping to craft visually appealing materials for lectures or parent meetings. This makes it easier to stay organized and ensures that instructional materials are engaging and accessible.

By integrating AI into planning, assignment creation, and information gathering, educators and parents can work more efficiently, personalize learning experiences, and provide richer educational opportunities for students.

Teaching Students about AI

Teaching students to use AI effectively and responsibly requires tailoring your approach to their developmental stage, setting clear boundaries, and consistently reinforcing that AI is a tool to support, not replace, critical thinking and learning.

For young children, such as those in kindergarten and early elementary grades, I personally would not use AI. However, that should be up to the family. In this case, you should introduce AI in simple, engaging ways that demystify the technology. Interactive games like Quick, Draw! can help children understand that AI learns from data and patterns, much like they do when practicing a new skill. At this age, the focus should be on helping students view AI as a smart tool, rather than a person, and on developing foundational digital literacy skills, such as distinguishing between real and fictional content and practicing basic online safety. It's important to ensure that technology use supplements, but never replaces, hands-on, sensory learning, which is critical for young children's development.

As students move into upper elementary and middle school, you can begin to introduce more hands-on activities, such as coding games, AI chatbots, and simple robotics projects. This is also the stage where students' critical thinking and abstract reasoning abilities are developing, so it's a good time to encourage them to use AI for research, brainstorming, and problem-solving, while also teaching them to question the information AI provides. For example, you might have students use a generative AI to draft an essay or answer a question, and then work together to critique the output, identify errors, and improve upon it. This helps students see AI as a partner in learning rather than a shortcut or replacement for their own reasoning.

With high school students, you can delve into more advanced uses of AI, such as exploring machine learning concepts, ethical considerations, and real-world applications. Encourage students to use AI for sophisticated research, data analysis, or creative projects, but always require them to fact-check, cite sources, and reflect on the process. Discussing the ethical implications of AI, including issues of bias, misinformation, and academic honesty, is crucial at this stage. Students should understand that while AI can enhance their work, over-reliance can erode their critical-thinking skills and undermine genuine learning.

Across all age groups, it's essential to model and reinforce responsible AI use. This includes having open conversations about how AI works, its limitations, and the importance of privacy and digital safety. Teach students to use AI to supplement their understanding, such as by asking it to explain a difficult concept or generate practice questions, but to always verify information and rely on their own judgment. Encourage them to use AI as a brainstorming partner, a tool for reflection, or a means to explore different perspectives. However, make it clear that the intellectual work of analyzing, interpreting, and creating must remain their own.

Finally, balance is key. AI should be just one part of a broader educational experience that includes offline activities, collaborative projects, and opportunities for original thought. By introducing AI in age-appropriate ways, setting clear expectations, and consistently emphasizing its role as a supportive tool, you can help students of all ages become thoughtful, ethical, and empowered users of technology.

Teaching kids to use AI as a learning partner across any subject means showing them how to leverage these tools for understanding, exploration, and skill-building, rather than simply letting AI do the work for them. This approach is valuable for parents who want to be actively involved in their child's education and for educators aiming to foster deeper learning and independent thinking.

Start by framing AI as a helper that can explain concepts, offer feedback, and generate practice questions, while emphasizing that the student remains in control of the learning process. For example, if a child is struggling with a math problem, use an AI tool to walk through the steps together, prompting the child to explain their reasoning at each stage. This way, AI provides support and clarification, while the student still undertakes the cognitive work and develops problem-solving skills.

In language arts, students can draft essays or stories and then use AI to get suggestions for improvement or to check grammar. Encourage them to review the AI's feedback critically, deciding what changes to accept and which to reject. This not only improves their writing but also teaches them to evaluate information and trust their own voice. In science or social studies, AI can help break down complex topics, summarize readings, or suggest project ideas. Ask students to use these summaries as a starting point, then research further or discuss the topic to deepen their understanding.

Parents can model this process by engaging with AI alongside their children, asking questions, exploring resources, and discussing what they learn. This shared experience helps demystify AI and shows kids that learning is an ongoing, collaborative journey. For younger children, keep activities hands-on and interactive, using AI to supplement creative projects or to answer "why" questions, always encouraging curiosity and discussion.

Set clear boundaries and expectations: AI should be used to check work, brainstorm ideas, or clarify confusing points, not to generate finished assignments or answers without the student's effort. Encourage kids to reflect on how AI helped them and what they learned in the process. This reflection reinforces that AI is a tool for learning, not a shortcut to completion.

For parents invested in their child's education, AI offers a way to stay informed and involved, even in subjects where they may not feel like experts. AI-powered platforms can provide regular updates on student progress, suggest personalized resources, and help parents spot areas where extra support is needed. By partnering with their children and schools, parents can utilize AI to enhance learning at home and ensure their child develops the skills and habits necessary for lifelong learning in an increasingly AI-rich world.

Part 3: Practical Guide for Ownschooling

Chapter 14: Supporting Your Child's Learning

For good or ill, you are always your child's most influential teacher. Even when he reaches school age, you are still the dean-at-home, the chief academic officer. The more involved you are, the better your child's chances of getting a good education. If you begin to remove yourself from the learning process, those chances start to plummet. If you turn over your most important responsibilities to others, you may doom his school career. That amounts to educational abandonment, a pernicious form of child neglect. You need to be in charge of your child's education. So take charge...

- William Bennett

Over the years working in education, I have learned as much from my students as I have taught them. Particularly valuable were the practices that their parents instilled in them to be successful in school and in life. This guide presents these as actionable steps that you can take to create an environment that fosters the development of better habits and skills for learning.

Regardless of the path, parental engagement is the cornerstone of educational autonomy. Your "proof of work" is demonstrated by meeting teachers, researching schools, asking questions, and ensuring your child's learning environment aligns with your family's values. Even if you cannot homeschool, you can be an active, informed participant in your child's education, advocating, supporting, and collaborating every step of the way.

In every educational path, the most crucial factor is active parental involvement, your proof of work. Whether you homeschool, choose public, charter, hybrid, or private school, your engagement, advocacy, and partnership with educators will shape your child's experience and success.

Supporting Your Child's Learning

Helping your child succeed in their educational journey begins with creating a supportive home environment. Whether your child is learning in a traditional classroom, through homeschooling, or in another setting, your involvement plays a crucial role in their growth and motivation. By providing a dedicated space for study, minimizing distractions, and fostering positive habits such as reading, you lay the foundation for lifelong learning.

Supporting your child's education is not just about academic achievement. It's about nurturing curiosity, building confidence, and fostering a love of learning. Simple steps, such as setting routines, showing interest in their studies, and offering encouragement, can make a significant difference. With thoughtful guidance and a supportive atmosphere, you empower your child to reach their full potential and develop skills that will serve them well throughout life.

Space

It is important to create a space where your student can work uninterrupted and without distractions. This may seem difficult or not particularly important, but it is one of the first things you should work on when considering ways to help your child succeed in school.

Having a dedicated space to work can help your student get into a focused state more quickly. Our brains naturally categorize things, and when we have a dedicated space for specific tasks, we often associate that space with that work. This space should allow them to work uninterrupted, as interruptions can be distracting and cause your student to lose motivation or focus.

There are several factors to consider when deciding where the space should be located in your home. The first thing to consider is whether the space is in a public area, such as the dining room. If this is the case, then you will need to inform the rest of the family that the room is off-limits while someone is studying. Another consideration is putting the space in your student's bedroom. This may be better in terms of interruptions, but you also need to consider distractions, such as the TV or other devices. Lying down on the bed while studying is another issue, as it can be detrimental to productivity and focus. Lying down while studying does not allow your student to get into a focused state. It is also important that they practice how they will sit when in school. When studying, your student should sit up and work in a space that is comfortable yet conducive to getting work done.

You may have to try a few areas to see which one is best for your student and the family, but hopefully, you will find a space where your student can be productive.

Reading

Although not everyone enjoys reading as a pastime, it is a good idea to encourage this habit in your students at an early age. You can do this by reading aloud to them before they can read independently, taking them to the library, or encouraging them to read when they have some downtime or are bored.

Reading regularly not only builds vocabulary but also fosters empathy. Reading about other people, whether fictional, real, historical, or current, allows your student to see different perspectives and even introduces them to foreign lands and customs. If your student reads for pleasure, then reading for school will be less of a struggle; it can even become second nature.

Communication

Open lines of communication are a key component in ensuring your child's success in school. Your student needs to know how to communicate effectively with their teachers, adults, peers of their own age, and even with you. By having regular conversations, even if just in the car or over dinner, you can help ensure your child feels comfortable discussing issues they may be facing with you. Encouraging a relationship with other adults, such as aunts, uncles, or family friends, is beneficial, as some things may be easier to discuss with them before sharing with you. It is also helpful to empower your student to speak with their teachers if they are experiencing problems or have specific questions about the class.

Teaching how to be respectful of differing ideas, even when one disagrees, is also essential in communication. This does not mean that they have to accept what everyone else is thinking, but having the ability to ask questions and work to understand people's ideas is a crucial skill in becoming an independent thinker. In addition, learning how to challenge ideas that one does not agree with while not being hostile is a much-needed skill that you can encourage in your child. This can be achieved by simply watching TV or a movie, which allows you to observe how people interact with one another and open lines of communication about your perceptions. You can point out both positive and negative examples.

Healthy Habits

Having healthy habits is not something that comes easily to most people, even adults. It seems that creating good habits is always harder than breaking bad ones. But good habits can be achieved and maintained with some encouragement from those around you.

One of the first habits any student needs is good study habits. Ensuring that your student develops a daily study routine, even when they don't have homework, is a good way to establish a habit. If they claim they have no homework, you can have them read a book related to what they are learning, or even spend some time having them teach you something they have recently learned. This will allow them to demonstrate their knowledge effectively and show that you are genuinely engaged in their education.

Electronics can be a double-edged sword in the modern world. Not only do they put a library's worth of knowledge at our fingertips in any given moment, but they can also distract students from acquiring the knowledge they need for their education. Monitoring and setting limits on devices, even phones, can be very helpful. If you are considering getting your student a phone, consider an analog phone that does not have the full capabilities of a smartphone. Your child will be less likely to become addicted to it, and they will have to use a computer or tablet (which can be easier to regulate) for social media and other web-based applications.

Sleep can make or break a student's academic performance. If they are not getting enough sleep, often due to issues arising from electronic devices, they will not be able to perform as well in school. Limiting screen time to at least an hour before bedtime allows the body to recover from blue light exposure, which can inhibit melatonin production, the primary hormone that regulates sleep. Aside from blue light, sleep can be impacted by stress or increased stimuli before bedtime. It is often recommended that reading can be helpful before going to bed, but it is best to have your child read paper books, rather than e-books, due to the light issues mentioned above.

The last thing you can do to encourage any of these things is to lead by example. It is better to be able to say, "Do as I do," rather than, "Do as I say!"

Boundaries

Boundaries can be difficult to create for anyone, particularly for your child or teenager. With increasing pressure being placed on young people these days, it is even more important to discuss setting boundaries with your student, including their interactions with friends, the activities they participate in, and the use of electronic devices such as cell phones and video games. One of the best ways to get started is to have a device-free evening once a week. This is an opportunity for the family and even your child's friends to interact with each other without the distraction of their phones or video games. You can choose to play a board game, cards, or just sit around and talk. One fun way to engage in conversation is to have everyone write down some topics and then pick them out one at a time. This allows you to create boundaries with devices in an engaging way that can help break down the barriers of screen addiction.

Additionally, you should also discuss with your child how to establish boundaries with their friends to help prevent unwanted peer pressure. With social media, it is easy for kids and teens to get wrapped up in their friends' lives 24/7. Yet, it is up to you as the parent to monitor this behavior and make sure that they are not being bullied, harassed, or even falling for social media peer pressure activities that may endanger their mental or physical well-being.

Creating boundaries for extra-curricular activities is also important. Playing different sports or participating in one sport across multiple leagues can be time-consuming and taxing on your child's study time and overall wellness. Like adults, children need downtime, especially if they tend to be introverted, so it is essential that they have regular time throughout the week to study, in addition to time to rest or play.

Executive Function

Parents have a unique opportunity and responsibility to take charge of their child's education by nurturing executive function skills within the family. Executive function refers to a set of mental processes that enable us to plan, focus attention, remember instructions, and juggle multiple tasks successfully. These core skills of working memory, cognitive flexibility, and impulse control are foundational for both academic achievement and social success, influencing everything from classroom learning to relationships with peers.

Emerging research highlights that several modern lifestyle factors are contributing to the increased prevalence of executive function challenges in children and adolescents. Among the most significant are the use of technology (including screen time and video games), sleep deprivation, and potential exposure to non-native electromagnetic fields (EMF).

Technology and Screen Time:

Excessive engagement with video games and high levels of screen time have been consistently linked to impairments in executive function. Studies show that children who spend more time playing video games or using screens tend to have lower scores in areas such as working memory, impulse control, and behavioral inhibition. The fast-paced and highly rewarding nature of digital media can condition the brain to expect constant stimulation, making it harder for children to focus, plan, and regulate their behavior in less stimulating environments, such as classrooms. Furthermore, increased screen time, especially in early childhood, is associated with slower development of executive function and self-regulation skills, with risks amplified by exposure to age-inappropriate content.

Sleep Deprivation:

Sleep plays a critical role in the development and functioning of executive skills. Chronic lack of sleep or frequent nighttime awakenings disrupt the neural connectivity in brain regions responsible for decision-making, self-control, and emotional regulation. Adolescents and children who do not get sufficient, high-quality sleep are more likely to exhibit problems with impulse control, working memory, and emotional regulation. They are at higher risk for behavioral issues and academic difficulties.

Non-Native Electromagnetic Fields (EMF):

Growing evidence suggests that exposure to non-native electromagnetic fields (EMF), the kind generated by wireless devices such as cell phones, Wi-Fi routers, tablets, and laptops, may be having a detrimental effect on children's executive function and overall brain health. Unlike the natural electromagnetic fields with which we have evolved, these man-made frequencies are relatively new to human biology and are present at levels far higher than ever before in human history.

Research and clinical observations indicate that chronic exposure to non-native EMF can disrupt the delicate electrical signaling in the brain, potentially impairing neural connectivity and communication between brain regions responsible for executive skills like attention, working memory, and impulse control. Children, whose brains and nervous systems are still developing, appear to be especially vulnerable. Symptoms linked to high EMF exposure can include difficulties with concentration, increased distractibility, memory problems, irritability, and even sleep disturbances, all of which undermine the development and functioning of executive skills.

Parents should be aware that the cumulative impact of EMF exposure is likely to be much greater for today's children than for previous generations. Reducing exposure, by limiting time spent on wireless devices, turning off Wi-Fi at night, encouraging wired connections, and keeping electronic devices out of bedrooms, can be a proactive step for families concerned about supporting healthy executive function and cognitive development.

Understanding Executive Function and Its Importance

Executive function is a set of mental skills that help us manage our thoughts, actions, and emotions to achieve goals. Executive function skills are not innate; they develop gradually throughout childhood and adolescence, shaped by both brain maturation and environmental influences. The parent-child relationship is especially crucial: positive, supportive interactions provide the cognitive scaffolding children need to develop self-regulation and executive skills. When parents model and reinforce these abilities, children are more likely to thrive academically, manage emotions effectively, and adapt to new challenges.

Below are definitions for each specific area:

Working Memory

Working memory is the ability to hold and manipulate information in your mind for short periods, allowing you to use that information to complete tasks, follow instructions, or solve problems. It is essential for activities like remembering directions, doing mental math, or recalling details from a story.

Task Initiation

Task initiation is the ability to begin tasks or activities independently and efficiently. It involves knowing where and how to start, overcoming procrastination, and taking the first step even when a task is challenging or unappealing.

Planning and Prioritizing

Planning and prioritizing involve setting goals, developing steps to achieve them, and determining the order of importance for tasks. This skill helps individuals create a roadmap for completing assignments, manage their time effectively, and focus on what matters most.

Organization

Organization refers to the ability to arrange materials, information, and tasks systematically and efficiently. It includes keeping track of belongings, maintaining orderly workspaces, and structuring activities and schedules to promote efficiency and reduce stress.

Self-Monitoring

Self-monitoring is the capacity to observe and assess your own performance and progress toward goals. It involves recognizing when strategies are not working, making adjustments, and reflecting on your actions to improve outcomes.

Impulse Control and Inhibition

Impulse control (inhibition) is the ability to resist immediate temptations, distractions, or urges in order to stay focused on long-term goals. It helps individuals pause before acting, follow rules, and manage emotions and behaviors appropriately.

Developmental Expectations

Executive function develops in stages, with different skills emerging at different ages. For example, preschoolers begin to follow simple routines and rules, while elementary-aged children start to organize materials and manage multi-step tasks more independently. Understanding these developmental milestones helps parents set realistic expectations and provide appropriate support.

Actionable Steps for Building Executive Function at Home

Working Memory:

To strengthen working memory, break tasks into smaller, manageable steps and establish consistent routines. Use visual aids, such as checklists or planners, to help your child keep track of information and tasks. Encourage your child to teach you what they've learned or play memory-based games together, which can reinforce retention in a fun, low-pressure way.

Task Initiation:

Many children struggle to get started. Teach your child to identify the simplest first step of a task, sometimes called the "KISS" (Keep It Super Simple) approach. Use interactive checklists and timers to create a sense of momentum and accomplishment. Offering choices about how to begin can also foster autonomy and engagement.

Planning and Prioritizing:

Introduce tools like daily to-do lists or the Eisenhower Matrix to help your child distinguish between urgent and important tasks. Practice prioritizing together by discussing which homework assignments or chores should come first and why. This helps build decision-making skills and reduces feelings of overwhelm.

Organization:

Create clear, repeatable systems for organizing school materials, sports equipment, and personal belongings. Label storage areas and use visual supports to remind your child where things belong. Consistency is key; when organizational systems are simple and predictable, children are more likely to follow through independently.

Self-Monitoring:

Help your child set specific goals for each work session and check in periodically to reflect on progress. Teach simple mindfulness techniques, such as pausing to take deep breaths and noticing their current activity or feelings, to build awareness and self-regulation.

Impulse Control and Inhibition:

Games like "Freeze" or "Simon Says" can make practicing self-control fun and interactive. These activities teach children to pause before acting, follow directions, and manage impulses in a supportive environment.

Cognitive Flexibility:

Encourage your child to adapt to changes by introducing small variations in daily routines or playing games that require shifting strategies, such as obstacle courses with changing rules. Role reversal games and imaginative play can also foster flexible thinking and empathy.

Emotional Control:

Model healthy emotion regulation by managing your own reactions and discussing emotions openly. Teach your child strategies for calming down, such as deep breathing, taking a break, or using a "calm corner." These practices help children build resilience and navigate emotional challenges.

Assessment and Identification

Pay attention to patterns of difficulty with organization, memory, or self-control. If you notice persistent challenges, consider informal tools like checklists or formal assessments through your child's school or a specialist. Early identification allows for targeted support and intervention. Parents who are concerned about their child's executive function can access support and assessment through several pathways:

1. Consult School Professionals

Start with Teachers and School Psychologists: Teachers can share observations about your child's organization, attention, and task management. School psychologists can conduct classroom observations and administer executive function questionnaires or recommend a formal evaluation if necessary.

Request Formal Assessments: If executive function challenges are significantly affecting school performance, a comprehensive assessment by a school psychologist or educational specialist may be beneficial.

2. Use Standardized Assessment Tools

Parent Rating Scales: Tools such as the BRIEF2 (Behavior Rating Inventory of Executive Function) and the Conners 3 Parent Rating Scale enable parents to assess their child's executive function skills across various areas, including working memory, organization, and impulse control. Psychologists often use these assessments and can be requested through schools or private practitioners.

Online Screeners: Some organizations offer free online executive function assessments for parents to complete, providing immediate feedback about strengths and challenges.

3. Seek Professional Evaluation

Child Psychologists and Neuropsychologists: If concerns persist, a licensed psychologist or neuropsychologist can conduct a thorough evaluation, using interviews, standardized tests, and behavioral observations to assess executive function.

Pediatricians: Your child's doctor can help rule out medical causes and refer you to specialists if necessary.

4. Observe and Track at Home

Keep a Journal: Note patterns in your child's ability to start tasks, remember instructions, stay organized, and manage time. This information is valuable for professionals conducting assessments.

Use Self-Assessment Tools: Some experts provide self-assessment questionnaires that help children and parents identify specific strengths in executive function and areas for growth.

5. Access Community and Online Resources

Support Groups and Workshops: Many communities offer parent workshops or support groups focused on executive function.

Educational Websites: Reputable sites offer valuable resources, including tips, checklists, and guidance on supporting executive function at home.

Integrate executive function skills into everyday routines, setting the table, planning a family outing, or managing homework time. Utilize visual supports, technology tools, and metacognitive strategies (such as thinking aloud about your own planning and problem-solving) to make these skills explicit and accessible.

By embracing your role as an active guide and advocate, you empower your family to become more sovereign, capable of navigating both academic and life challenges with confidence, adaptability, and resilience.

Chapter 15: Resources for Ownschooling

The more risks you allow your children to make, the better they learn to look after themselves.

- Roald Dahl

This chapter aims to equip parents with practical tools and information to make informed educational choices with confidence and clarity. Whether your family is considering traditional schooling, homeschooling, online learning, or a blended approach, access to high-quality resources can make a significant difference in your child's academic and personal growth.

Among the most valuable tools are student success questionnaires, which help parents identify their child's unique learning styles, strengths, and areas for improvement. These assessments provide a foundation for making informed decisions about curriculum and teaching methods that best suit individual needs. In addition, a variety of reputable websites and companies offer support, information, and community for families exploring different educational paths. These platforms can connect parents with expert advice, peer experiences, and up-to-date research.

Comprehensive guides are also essential, offering step-by-step instructions on navigating the legal, academic, and social aspects of alternative education. General resources such as podcasts, forums, and blogs provide ongoing inspiration and practical tips, fostering a sense of community and shared learning. For those considering or currently homeschooling, organizations like the Home School Legal Defense Association (HSLDA) offer legal guidance and advocacy, ensuring families understand their rights and responsibilities.

Ultimately, exploring curriculum options is a crucial aspect of the educational landscape. Understanding the variety of available curricula and how to adapt materials to fit your child's needs empowers parents to create a personalized and effective educational plan. By leveraging these resources, families can take an active, informed role in their child's education, ensuring that learning is both meaningful and successful.

Student Success Checklist

Checklist to get the whole family on board for success.

☐ Have a family meeting

- ☐ Talk about everyone's needs.
- ☐ What does each family member need to succeed in order to maximize time and get their work done?
- ☐ Develop a sort of contract or policy for the family to follow
- ☐ Have everyone contribute to get buy-in

☐ Determine how the schoolwork is to be done

- ☐ Online platform from school
- ☐ Emailed assignments
- ☐ Have not yet been informed
- ☐ Realize this may change so you will need to adapt

☐ Come up with degrees of problems so you can work without interruptions

☐ What constitutes an emergency so you can be interrupted?
☐ What can be written down and dealt with in a few hours?
☐ Are there homework issues that can be addressed later?
☐ Explain that everyone has to get their work done so everyone will need to be a little more independent (again ages of children will impact this)

☐ Work out a schedule

☐ Keep the same schedule that they have during the regular school day, e.g. math first, then history, then recess, etc.
☐ Keep as much "normal" as possible
☐ Keep the children focused on learning, this is not a vacation!
☐ It may seem easier, but do not fall into the Disney+, Netflix, or Video Game trap. See below for examples of alternatives.

☐ Keep them writing to build skills

☐ Have them write on assigned topics
☐ These can be fun such as a description of their favorite video game or movie
☐ Give them a time frame to write continuously
☐ Have them practice their penmanship or cursive
☐ Have them watch a documentary and then write an essay or report on it

Questions to consider if you are thinking about Homeschooling

1. Do you need both parents to work full-time, or is it possible to have one parent or family member (e.g., grandparent) conduct the bulk of the homeschooling?

    a. Homeschooling requires a lot of attention and dedication when done correctly. If both parents work, you may need to decide whether it is feasible for one parent to stay home and homeschool.
    b. So, suppose you decide to reduce the household income to homeschool. In that case, there are creative ways to supplement the lost income. Several families I know in the United States have figured out how to supplement their income by selling used books or vintage items they source from thrift stores online. You can also sell handmade wares or homemade food at farmers' markets. These ways of earning extra income can involve the whole family, and children can learn entrepreneurial skills while participating.
    c. If you have a degree or job skills, consider ways to earn an income using them online. Perhaps you can find ways to earn money without a specific timeframe, so you can work while the children sleep or when you have help. For instance, if you know how to write, consider being a part-time editor or content writer. The main point is to think out of the box and find ways to be independent of the education system while being more financially secure and ultimately, towards the goal of sovereignty.
2. Can you set aside time to homeschool?
    a. Unlike traditional schools, which run from about 8 am to 3 pm, or thereabouts, homeschooling does not require as much time each day. You can homeschool for a few hours each day.
    b. You can also schedule those hours to fit with your schedule. So, if you have a regular meeting at noon on Wednesdays, you know not to schedule homeschool during that time. That's one of the nice things about homeschooling. You control the schedule.
    c. However, homeschool parents who have been homeschooling for a while often recommend having a somewhat regular schedule for "school" hours each week. That does not mean you have to be completely

regimented; there is still flexibility. But there should be designated learning hours each week.

3. Do you enjoy explaining things to people and learning new things?
    a. These are traits that make the transition to homeschooling easier. If you enjoy explaining how to cook something or helping learn a new skill, then you may find it easy to help your kids understand things they are studying.
    b. If you enjoy learning something new, you may find it easy to share that enthusiasm with your kids when they need to learn something new. You can make learning a common occurrence in any situation.
4. Do homeschooled children learn what they need to?
    a. Studies in recent years have shown that homeschool children typically outperform students educated in public schools when evaluated on standardized tests.
    b. These tests indicate that elementary-aged children are one year ahead of their peers, with eighth graders being up to four years ahead of their peers who have been educated in traditional schools.
2. Is it expensive to homeschool?
    a. The cost will vary a lot. It all depends on the method and curriculum you choose.
    b. Some homeschool families use private tutors for some subjects, such as math. This is more costly than finding a curriculum or online programs.
    c. Some curriculum packages are costly, as they require families to purchase all their materials, whereas others offer more affordable options or even free materials.

Get Started Homeschooling Guide

Step 1: DISCUSS

1. Discuss the idea of homeschooling with your spouse, partner, or close family.

    a. Determine who will take on most of the teaching responsibility.
    b. Discuss financial issues if one person has to stop working or reduce hours.
2. Talk to your close friends. (These are the people who will likely offer you emotional support when you need it.)
3. Find your support system through conversations with relatives (grandparents, siblings, etc.) who may be able to lend a helping hand with the teaching and supervising of the children.
4. Talk to your children about homeschooling, particularly if they are in higher grades of elementary, middle, or high school.
    a. Note, they may have a lot of anxiety, or they may be relieved to make this change.
    b. They will want to have a voice, and this can make the transition easier.

Step 2: RESEARCH

Start with the Home School Legal Defense Association, https://hslda.org/

1. Find out your state or country requirements.
2. Parent qualifications to homeschool, if any?
3. Who do you notify to declare you are homeschooling?
4. What are the curriculum standards for my area?
5. Are there other requirements?

Step 3. NETWORK

1. Find homeschool groups near you that can offer advice and support.
    a. Your state or local organization is a good place to start.
    b. Check for local Facebook homeschool and parenting groups, as many are now using the social media platform to connect with each other and new homeschool families.
2. If you want to join a co-op, research local co-ops that fit into your lifestyle.
    a. There are various religious-based co-ops, secular co-ops, and more informal meet-up groups.
3. Search for Homeschool podcasts and social media outlets that may have useful information or ways to network.

4. Check out the Ownschooling webpage to find some of our free resources and podcasts that can help you get started.

4. HOMESCHOOL LIFESTYLE

This is tricky because it will likely turn out very differently from what you imagine. But you can make some decisions that will likely stick.

1. Decide who will be the primary teacher?
    a. You or your spouse/partner
    b. Family members
    c. Homeschool co-op
    d. Tutors
    e. Other:
2. Where will you be homeschooling?
    a. Do you have a space you can use as a classroom?
    b. Will you be working at the dining room table?
3. What supplies do you need to get started that you do not already have? (One quick word of advice - try not to make too many big investments here, as you will likely change your mind on some things.)
4. How will you manage more than one child?
    a. Teach them together
    b. Have the older kids help the younger kids?
    c. Get a nanny or babysitter for really young children who are not in school yet?

5. CURRICULUM

For some, this is the most daunting; for others, the most fun. But you are now in charge of your child's education, which means finding the materials you will be using to teach them. Luckily, there are so many more resources today than a few decades ago.

1. If you are joining a co-op or sharing the responsibility with other families, you will likely have discussions on the curriculum that will be used or the classes your student will take at the co-op. Then, you can fill in other materials to use on your own.
2. If you are homeschooling on your own, then you can find a lot of resources online. There is something for everyone, from religious to secular, from STEM to a classical education focus. Some

websites serve as a repository for resources for parents to look through.

3. We recommend starting with https://www.homeschool.com, as it offers a comprehensive but not exhaustive list of curriculum options.

CURRICULUM CHECKLIST (Check the boxes you want to focus on)

☐ Religious ☐ Secular ☐ Either

Subjects:

☐ History ☐ Math ☐ English ☐ Literature ☐ Science

☐ Art ☐ Music ☐ Drama ☐ Civics ☐ Philosophy

☐ Physical Education ☐ Foreign Language ☐ Technology

☐ ________________ ☐ ________________ ☐ ____________________

Curriculum companies to remember

Company name Website

Company name Website

Company name Website

6. YOUR HOMESCHOOL ROUTINE

Everyone's homeschool journey is different. You may want to set some ground rules on what homeschooling will look like and what everyone can expect, particularly if you are transitioning your kids from being in public or private school to homeschooling.

You may need to set some boundaries for electronic devices, particularly with older kids who may be used to playing a game or watching videos online in their free time.

You should NOT try to mirror the traditional classroom day.

Homeschooling takes far less time for organized learning. School is now a lifestyle where anything becomes a learning opportunity, from cooking (math) to taking a walk (botany).

You may want to make a plan of what your homeschool day would look like, but know this will change. You may need to work with your kids individually, and each one may have different learning needs. There WILL be a time of adjustment. One thing you can do is to think about each child and what you anticipate their learning routine will be.

In the next section, you can jot down some notes on the following topics for each child.

- Learning style: self-motivated, needs motivation, independent, prefers audio or visual, etc.
- Interests: Math, Science, Nature, Reading, Literature, etc.
- Needs: Any special needs such as assistance with reading, extra attention on specific subjects, or needs more checking in

1. Child's name:

Learning style, interests, and needs:

2. Child's name:

Learning style, interests, and needs:

3. Child's name:

Learning style, interests, and needs:

4. Child's name:

Learning style, interests, and needs:

7. SCHEDULE OR ROUTINE

In this space, think about what your vision of homeschooling will look like. This is a great exercise to consider, as there is a 99% chance that this will not happen. But write it out anyway, so you can talk about it with other homeschool parents you meet, your support system, and even your children.

8. ADJUST

Please note that there will be an adjustment period for everyone. Everyone will have to go through a de-schooling phase where educational expectations are shifted from what the child had in public or private school to what is expected in a homeschool environment. Every family is unique, and even within a family, each child is distinct.

Think about some of the things you anticipate during this adjustment period and ways that you can help you and your children get through it.

There is no way to predict everything, but this will put you in the right mindset for adapting this new form of education to fit your family's needs.

1. Anticipated issue:

Possible solutions:

2. Anticipated issue:

Possible solutions:

3. Anticipated issue:

Possible solutions:

4. Anticipated issue:

Possible solutions:

9. HAVE FUN

Make learning fun for everyone! Education does not have to be droll; in fact, it can be an enriching experience when the traditional classroom and expectations that ensue (sitting still and being obedient for hours on end) are no longer put upon children.

The first step is to encourage your children to be active participants in their own education. This does not mean that they are completely in the driver's seat, but it does mean that you can cater to their interests and use those as a way to have them engage with material they may not be interested in. For example, if a middle school student aspires to be an architect, you can inform them that they will need to develop a strong understanding of math to achieve that goal.

You can also spark interest in learning by engaging your kids with activities outside of the home. Think about places you can visit that facilitate learning. This can be a museum, zoo, aquarium, nature preserve, or historic site, all of which usually have an online learning presence as well. Many even have a curriculum you can use.

List some ideas on how to make learning more engaging and interactive.

1. Place:

☐ Online ☐ In person ☐ Either

Subject(s):

☐ Curriculum provided ☐ Create a lesson

Notes:

2. Place:

☐ Online ☐ In person ☐ Either

Subject(s):

☐ Curriculum provided ☐ Create a lesson

Notes:

3. Place:

☐ Online ☐ In person ☐ Either

Subject(s):

☐ Curriculum provided ☐ Create a lesson

Notes:

Note: More resources and these templates are available on the book website: www.ownschooling.com.

Glossary of Terms

Accounting System: An accounting system is a ledger that records all transactions. For Bitcoin, it is the distributed ledger and is a transparent and immutable system that maintains a public record of all Bitcoin transactions.

Bands: A band or band-level society is the simplest form of human social organization, consisting of a small, kin-based group that is egalitarian, highly mobile, and relies on hunting and gathering for subsistence. Leadership is informal, and decisions are made by group consensus rather than by a formal authority or inherited position.

Barter: Barter is an economic system where goods and services are exchanged directly for other goods and services without the use of money.

Bennett Hypothesis: The Bennett Hypothesis posits that increases in federal student aid, such as loans and grants, enable colleges and universities to raise tuition prices. Proposed by William J. Bennett in 1987, this theory suggests that increased government aid leads to higher college costs because schools capture the additional funding by increasing their tuition charges to students.

Bitcoin and bitcoin: "Bitcoin" with a capital "B" refers to the decentralized digital currency and network as a whole, while "bitcoin" with a lowercase "b" refers to the individual units of the currency.

Bitcoin Wallet: A Bitcoin wallet is a digital tool that allows users to store, send, and receive bitcoins. It consists of a public key (for receiving funds) and a private key (for authorizing transactions).

Bills of Sale: A bill of sale is a legal document that records the transfer of ownership of property or goods from a seller to a buyer in exchange for payment, serving as official proof of the transaction.

Block: A block in the Bitcoin distributed ledger is a collection of transactions. These blocks are inked together in chronological order to form a continuous chain.

Blockchain: A decentralized record of transactions that is maintained across computers through a peer-to-peer network.

Bridewealth: Bridewealth is a cultural practice in which the groom or his family gives money, goods, or other valuables to the bride's family as part of the marriage process. It serves to formalize the marriage, compensate the bride's family, and create bonds between the two families.

Bretton Woods Agreement: An international monetary agreement established in 1944 that fixed exchange rates to the U.S. dollar and tied the dollar to gold. It played a significant role in the global monetary system.

Central Bank: A central bank is a national financial institution that manages a country's currency, money supply, and interest rates, and typically oversees the commercial banking system. It also acts as a lender of last resort to the government and other banks and is responsible for implementing monetary policy.

Central Bank Digital Currencies (CBDCs): A Central Bank Digital Currency (CBDC) is a digital form of a country's official currency issued and regulated by the central bank, designed for digital transactions and financial inclusion.

Chiefdoms: Chiefdoms are hierarchical, kin-based societies led by a chief who holds authority over multiple communities or villages. These societies typically feature social ranking, centralized leadership, and often manage resources and redistribution through the chief's leadership.

Circular Economies: Economic systems that focus on using Bitcoin for transactions. These economies help promote the spread of Bitcoin and its use as currency.

City-state: A city-state is an independent political entity that consists of a single city and sometimes its surrounding territory.

Cold Storage: A method of storing bitcoins offline, typically on a hardware wallet or paper wallet, to protect them from online threats.

Commodity: A tangible good or product that has intrinsic value.

Commodity Money: Money that is backed by a tangible commodity with intrinsic value, such as grain or gold.

Consensus: In the context of Bitcoin, consensus is the agreement among network participants (nodes and miners) on the validity of transactions and the state of the ledger.

Counterfeiting: The act of producing fake or fraudulent currency or assets to deceive others.

Credit: In banking and economics, "credit" refers to the trust which allows one party to provide money or resources to another party wherein the second party does not reimburse the first party immediately but promises either to repay or return those resources at a later date.

Cuneiform: Cuneiform is one of the earliest known systems of writing, developed by the ancient Sumerians of Mesopotamia around 3200 BCE. It involved pressing a stylus into soft clay tablets to create wedge-shaped symbols representing words or sounds.

Debasement: The intentional reduction in the value or purity of a currency, often achieved by adding less valuable materials to it.

Deflation: A decrease in the general price level of goods and services in an economy, often accompanied by an increase in the value of money.

Denarius: The denarius was a silver coin that served as the principal currency of ancient Rome for several centuries, beginning in the 3rd century BCE. It functioned both as a standard unit of value and a common medium of exchange throughout the Roman Empire.

Devaluation: A deliberate reduction in the official exchange rate of a country's currency relative to other currencies.

Distributed Ledger: A decentralized digital record-keeping system for Bitcoin where multiple copies of a ledger are maintained across a network of computers.

Divisibility: The property of being easily divisible into smaller units, allowing for flexibility in transactions.

Double-entry Accounting Method: A method of accounting that records every financial transaction with a column for both debits and credits.

Dowry: A dowry is property, money, or gifts given by the bride's family to the groom or his family as part of a marriage arrangement. It is intended to support the new household or strengthen family alliances.

Egalitarian: Egalitarian describes a society or group where all members are considered equal, and there are few or no social hierarchies or differences in wealth, power, or status.

Electrum: Electrum is a naturally occurring alloy of gold and silver used by ancient civilizations to make some of the earliest known coins. Its unique blend gave it a pale yellow color and variable intrinsic value.

Exchange of Value: The process of transferring one form of value, such as money or goods, for another.

Exogamous: Exogamous refers to the social practice of marrying outside one's specific social group, clan, or tribe. This custom helps create alliances and relationships between different groups.

Federal Reserve Act: The Federal Reserve Act is the 1913 U.S. law that established the Federal Reserve System as the central bank of the United States. It created a national system to regulate currency, monetary policy, and banking.

Fiat Money: Currency that has value because a government declares it to be legal tender, even though it is not backed by a physical commodity.

Floating Exchange Rates: Exchange rates that fluctuate based on supply and demand in the foreign exchange market, as opposed to fixed exchange rates.

Fractional Reserve System: A banking system where banks only hold a fraction of their customers' deposits in reserve, lending out the rest.

Gold Standard: A monetary system where a country's currency is backed by and can be exchanged for a specific amount of gold.

High Time Preference: A preference for immediate consumption over saving or investing for the future.

Horticulture: Horticulture is the practice of small-scale, simple cultivation of crops using hand tools rather than plows or machinery. It is often associated with subsistence farming rather than large-scale agriculture.

Hot Storage: Storing Bitcoin in a digital wallet that is connected to the internet, making it more susceptible to hacking.

Hyperinflation: Hyperinflation is an extremely rapid and out-of-control price inflation, typically exceeding 50% per month, where a country's currency loses its value at an accelerated rate, leading to a severe decline in purchasing power and often resulting in economic instability and societal challenges. This phenomenon is typically caused by excessive growth in the money supply, and it often occurs during periods of significant political or economic upheaval.

Inflation: An increase in the general price level of goods and services in an economy, often accompanied by a decrease in the purchasing power of money.

Intrinsic value: Intrinsic value refers to the actual, inherent worth of an object, commodity, or asset, usually based on its material or essential qualities. It contrasts with value assigned by external factors like markets or governments.

Interest: The cost of borrowing money or the return on investment for lending or investing money.

Keynesian Economics: Keynesian economics is an economic theory developed by John Maynard Keynes, emphasizing the role of government intervention and fiscal policy to manage economic cycles and combat unemployment. It advocates increasing public spending during recessions to boost demand and stimulate growth.

Lender of Last Resort: A central bank or institution that provides emergency loans to financial institutions in times of crisis to prevent systemic collapse.

Lightning Network: A second-layer scaling solution for Bitcoin that enables faster and cheaper transactions by conducting most transactions off-chain. Eventually, transactions are put onto the chain.

Liquidity: The ease with which an asset can be quickly converted into cash without significantly affecting its price.

Low Time Preference: A preference for saving and investing for the future over immediate consumption.

Medium of Exchange: Something that is widely accepted as a means of payment in transactions, like money.

Mempool: The memory pool of pending transactions in the Bitcoin network waiting to be confirmed by miners.

Mining: Individuals or entities that use computational power to validate transactions and add them to the distributed ledger in exchange for rewards.

Nodes: Computers or devices on the Bitcoin network that maintain a copy of the distributed ledger and validate transactions.

Off-chain: Off-chain transactions in Bitcoin occur outside of the blockchain network, where the transfer of Bitcoin or Bitcoin data is executed through secondary channels and is not immediately recorded on the blockchain. They offer faster and potentially more private transfers without directly impacting the main distributed ledger, such as the Lightning Network.

On-chain: On-chain transactions in Bitcoin refer to transactions that are recorded and verified on the Bitcoin blockchain, involving the transfer of Bitcoin between wallets, which become irreversible once they are confirmed and added to the blockchain after being validated by network participants, known as miners. These transactions are publicly visible and a part of the permanent, decentralized ledger, providing transparency and security inherent to the blockchain technology.

Pastoralist: A pastoralist is someone who raises and herds domesticated animals as their main source of livelihood. Pastoralist societies often migrate seasonally to find fresh grazing land for their livestock.

Portability: The ease with which a currency or asset can be carried and transferred.

Proof of Work (PoW): A consensus mechanism in the Bitcoin infrastructure where miners must perform computational work (guessing random numbers) to validate transactions and add blocks to the ledger.

Precious Metals: Rare and valuable metals, such as gold and silver, often used as stores of value.

Private Key: A secret cryptographic key that allows the owner to access and control their Bitcoin holdings.

Public Key: A cryptographic key that is publicly shared and used to receive Bitcoin.

Reciprocity: Reciprocity is the mutual exchange of goods, services, or favors between individuals or groups, which helps maintain social and economic relationships. It exists in various forms, including generalized, balanced, and negative reciprocity.

Reserve Currency: A widely accepted currency that is held in significant quantities by governments and institutions as part of their foreign exchange reserves.

Reserves: Assets held by banks or financial institutions to meet potential future liabilities.

Risk: The uncertainty associated with the potential for loss or gain in an investment or decision.

Scarcity: The limited availability of a resource or asset relative to the demand for it.

Sound Money: Money that maintains its value over time and is not subject to significant inflation or devaluation.

Stability: The quality of being resistant to sudden and unpredictable changes.

Standard of Value: A function of money that allows it to be used as a common measure of the value of goods and services.

State-backed currency: State-backed currency is money issued by a government or central authority whose value is supported not by physical commodities but by trust in the state's stability and legal declaration. Most modern money, known as fiat currency, is state-backed.

Store of Value: A function of money that allows it to maintain its value over time and serve as a repository of wealth.

Time Preference: An individual's preference for consuming resources and goods either in the present (high time preference) or in the future (low time preference).

Transaction: An exchange of goods, services, or assets between two or more parties.

Transaction Fees: Fees paid by users of the Bitcoin network to miners for processing transactions.

Tribes: Tribes are larger-than-band, kin-based societies that are organized around extended families or clans and often led by informal leaders without centralized authority. They commonly practice agriculture or pastoralism and maintain social cohesion through shared customs and traditions.

Unit of Account: A function of money that allows it to serve as a standard measure for pricing and comparing goods and services.

Value: The perceived worth or utility of a good, service, or asset in an economic context.

Volatility: The degree of variation in the price or value of an asset over time, often used to describe the price fluctuations of Bitcoin.

World Reserve Currency: A world reserve currency is a foreign currency held in large quantities by governments and central banks to facilitate international trade, investments, and payments, often serving as a benchmark for valuing other currencies. Throughout history, this role has shifted with global economic power: the Spanish silver dollar dominated from the sixteenth to nineteenth centuries, the Dutch guilder rose in the seventeenth and eighteenth centuries, the British pound sterling took precedence in the nineteenth and early twentieth centuries, and the U.S. dollar has held the position since the mid-twentieth century.

References by Chapter

A note on the sources in this section. Numerous sources were used throughout the chapters. For brevity, I have chosen to list them only in the chapter where they were first used.

Chapter 1 References

Henderson, A. T., & Mapp, K. L. (2002). "A New Wave of Evidence: The Impact of School, Family, and Community Connections on Student Achievement." *Southwest Educational Development Laboratory*.

Jeynes, W. H. (2007). "The Relationship between Parental Involvement and Urban Secondary School Student Academic Achievement: A Meta-Analysis." *Urban Education*, 42, 82-110. https://doi.org/10.1177/0042085906293818

Chapter 2 References

Fried, Morton H. (1967). *The Evolution of Political Society: an Essay in Political Anthropology*. Random House.

Service, Elman R. (1962). *Primitive Social Organization: An Evolutionary Perspective*. Random House.

Chapter 3 References

Allen, Lindsay. (2005). *The Persian Empire*. British Museum Press.

Barlow, Charles. (1980). "The Roman Government and the Roman Economy, 92-80 B.C." *The American Journal of Philology* 101 (2),: 202-219.

Baron, J.P. (2018). "Making Money in Mesoamerica: Currency Production and Procurement in the Classic Maya Financial System." *Economic Anthropology* 5: 210-223.

Bellinger, Alfred R. (1956). "The Coins and Byzantine Imperial Policy." *Speculum* 31 (1): 70–81.

Boomgaard, Peter. (2008). "Early Globalization: Cowries as Currency, 600 BCE-1900." In *Linking Destinies*. Brill: 13-27.

Boyle, David, ed. (2015). *The Money Changers: Currency Reform from Aristotle to E-Cash*. Routledge.

Bromberg, Benjamin. (1942). "The Origin of Banking: Religious Finance in Babylonia." *The Journal of Economic History* 2 (1): 77-88.

Butcher, Kevin. (2015)"Debasement and the Decline of Rome." *Studies in Ancient Coinage in Honor of Andrew Burnett*: 181-205.

Dalton, George. (1965). "Primitive Money." *American Anthropologist*. 66: 44–65.

Darr, Alan P. (2202). "The Medici and the Legacy of Michelangelo in Late Renaissance Florence: An Introduction." In *The Medici, Michelangelo, and the Art of Late Renaissance Florence*, New Haven: Yale University Press.

Davies, Glyn. (2002). *A History of Money: From Ancient Times to the Present Day*. University of Wales Press.

De Roover, Raymond. (1963). *The Rise and Decline of the Medici Bank, 1397-1494*. Harvard University Press.

Elliott, Colin P. (2014). "The Acceptance and Value of Roman Silver Coinage in the Second and Third Centuries AD." *The Numismatic Chronicle* 174: 129-152.

Fazzini, Marco, Luigi Fici, Alessandro Montrone, and Simone Terzani. (2016). "A Modern Look At The Banco De' Medici: Governance And Accountability Systems In Europe's First Bank Group." *International Business & Economics Research Journal* 15 (6): 271-286.

Ferguson, Niall. (2008). *The Ascent of Money: A Financial History of the World.* Penguin Books.

Finley, Moses. (1974). *The Ancient Economy.* University of California Press.

Fitzpatrick, S. (2004). "Banking on Stone Money." *Archaeology* 57 (2): 18-23.

Galbraith, John Kenneth. (1975). *Money: Whence It Came, Where It Went.* Princeton University Press.

Gensheimer, Thomas R. (1984). "The role of Shells in Mesopotamia: Evidence for Trade Exchange with Oman and the Indus Valley." *Paléorient*: 65-73.

Goetzmann, William N. (2016). *Money Changes Everything: How Finance Made Civilization Possible.* Princeton University Press.

Goldthwaite, Richard A. (1987). "The Medici Bank and the World of Florentine Capitalism." *Past and Present* 114: 3-31.

Graeber, David. (2001*Towards an Anthropological Theory of Value.* Palgrave.

Harl, K.W. (1996). *Coinage in the Roman Economy: 300 BC to AD 700.* Johns Hopkins University Press.

Head, Barclay Vincent. (1877). *The Coinage of Lydia and Persia; from the Earliest Times to the Fall of the Dynasty of the Achaemenidae.* Trübner.

Heikkinen, Deanna and Joel Marquez. (2024). *Shells to Satoshi: The Story of Money and the Rise of Bitcoin.* Self-published.

Herodotus. *Herodotus: The Histories.* (1996). Penguin Books.

Holland, Tom. (2006). *Persian Fire: The First World Empire and the Battle for the West.* Doubleday.

Hollingsworth, Mary. (2018). *The Family Medici: The Hidden History of the Medici Dynasty.* London: Pegasus Books, 2018.

Horesh, Niv. (2013). "Cannot Be Fed On When Starving: An Analysis Of The Economic Thought Surrounding China's Earlier Use Of Paper Money." *Journal of the History of Economic Thought* 35 (3): 373-395.

Jarrett, J.A. (2015). "*Small Change and Big Changes: Minting and Money After the Fall of Rome.*" Unpublished. https://eprints.whiterose.ac.uk/90089/.

Martin, Thomas R and John. Lescault. (2017). *Ancient Greece: From Prehistoric to Hellenistic Times.* Blackstone Publishing.

Melitz, Jacques. (2017). "A Model of the Beginnings of Coinage in Antiquity." *European Review of Economic History* 21 (1): 83–103.

Metcalf, William E. (2016). *The Oxford Handbook of Greek and Roman Coinage.* Oxford University Press.

Mundell, Robert A. (2002). "The Birth of Coinage." *Columbia University Department of Economics Discussion Paper Series,* 102 (8).

Menger, Carl. (1950). *Principles of Economics.* Free Press.

Naik, Jimuta. (2014). "Beginning of the Early Banking Industry in Mesopotamia Civilization from 8th Century BCE," *Social Science Research Network.*

Polo, Marco. (1974). *Marco Polo: The Travels*, trans. Nigel Cliff. Penguin.

Schaps, David M. (2004). *The Invention of Coinage and the Monetization of Ancient Greece*. University of Michigan Press.

Sehgal, Kabir. (2015). *Coined: The Rich Life of Money and How Its History Has Shaped Us*. Grand Central Publishing.

Simmel, Georg. (1978). *The Philosophy of Money*, trans. Tom Bottomore and D. Frisby. Routledge.

Stojanović, Biljana. (2006). "Monetary Stability: The Byzantine Model" *Megatrend Review* 231: 57-88.

Temen, Peter. "The Economy of the Early Roman Empire." *The Journal of Economic Perspectives* 20 (1): 133-151.

Thornton, M.K. and R.L. Thornton. (1990). "The Financial Crisis of A.D. 33: A Keynesian Depression?" *The Journal of Economic History* 50 (3): 655-662.

Tzilla Eshel, Ayelet Gilboa, Ofir Tirosh, Yigal Erel, Naama Yahalom-Mack. (2023). "The Earliest Silver Currency Hoards in the Southern Levant: Metal trade in the Transition from the Middle to the Late Bronze Age." *Journal of Archaeological Science* 149.

Van De Mieroop, Marc. (2015). *A History of the Ancient Near East, ca. 3000- 323 BC*. Blackwell.

Verboven, Koenraad. (2007). "Demise and Fall of the Augustan Monetary System." In *Crises and the Roman Empire* :245-257.

Verhagen, Hendrik L. E. (2022). *Security and Credit in Roman Law: The Historical Evolution of Pignus and Hypotheca*. Oxford University Press.

Wallace, Robert W. (1987). "The Origin of Electrum Coinage." *American Journal of Archaeology* 91 (3): 385–97.

Weatherford, Jack. (1997). The History of Money. Three Rivers Press.

Yang, Liansheng. (1952). *Money and Credit in China: A Short History.* Cambridge: Harvard University Press.

Chapter 4 References

Alden, Lyn. (2023). *Broken Money: Why Our Financial System is Failing Us and How We Can Make It Better.* Timestamp Press.

Bloomfield, A. (1959). "Monetary Policy Under the International Gold Standard," *Federal Reserve Bank of New York.*

Bojanic, Antonio N. (2018). "The Impact of Fiscal Decentralization on Accountability, Economic Freedom, and Political and Civil Liberties in the Americas." *Economies* 6 (1): 8-28.

Bordo, Michael D. (1993). "The Bretton Woods International Monetary System: A Historical Overview *" A Retrospective on the Bretton Woods System: Lessons for International Monetary Reform*, edited by Michael D. Bordo and Barry Eichengreen, University of Chicago Press.

Bretton Woods Agreement. *Avalon Project*, Yale University. https://avalon.law.yale.edu/20th_century/decad047.asp.

British Parliamentary Papers. (1819). "The Gold Standard Act." https://www.gold.org/sites/default/files/documents/1819may21.pdf.

Brunton, Bruce. (2013). "The East India Company: Agent of Empire in the Early Modern Capitalist Era." *Social Education* 77 (2): 78–81.

Cassis, Youssef, Richard S. Grossman and Catherine R. Schenk, eds. (2016). "Private banks and private banking." In *The Oxford Handbook of Banking and Financial History*, Oxford: Oxford University Press.

Cooper, Richard N., et al. (1982). "The Gold Standard: Historical Facts and Future Prospects." *Brookings Papers on Economic Activity* 1: 1–56.

Devereux, Michael B, et al. (2010). "Oil Currency and the Dollar Standard: A Simple Analytical Model of an International Trade Currency." *Journal of Money, Credit, and Banking* 42 (4): 521–550.

Edvinsson, Rodney, Tor Jacobson, Daniel Waldenström, eds. (2018). *Sveriges Riksbank and the History of Central Banking*. Cambridge University Press.

Eichengreen, Barry. (2004). "Global imbalances and the Lessons of Bretton Woods." *Economy International* 4 (100): 39-50.

Ellen, Roy F. (1977). "The Trade in Spices." *Indonesia Circle* 5 (12): 21-25.

Forbes, BC. (1916). "Men Who Are Making America." *Leslie's Weekly*, Oct. 19, 1916. https://archive.org/downloadmenwhoaremakinga00for/menwhoaremakinga00for.pdf

Forbes, Kristin J. (2004). "Strengthening Banking Systems: Lessons from Around the World and Across the Ages." *Trabajo presentado en la Conferencia sobre Reforma Estructural de la APEC.*

Goldberg, Linda, and Cedric Tille. (2009) "Macroeconomic Interdependence and the International Role of the Dollar." *Journal of Monetary Economics* 56 (7): 990-1003.

Gortsos, Christos V. (2022). "On the Cypriot 2012-2013 Banking Crisis and the 2013 Banking Resolution." *Banking & Finance Law Review* 38: 271-284.

Gowa, Joanne. (2019) *Closing the Gold Window: Domestic Politics and the End of Bretton Woods.* Cornell University Press.

Griffin, Edward. (1998). *The Creature from Jekyll Island: A Second Look at the Federal Reserve.* 3rd ed. American Media.

Gwertzman, Bernard. (1974). "'Milestone' Pact Is Signed By U.S. and Saudi Arabia," *New York Times,* June 9, 1974. https://www.nytimes.com/1974/06/09/.

Hayek, Friedrich A. von. (2006). *The Road to Serfdom.* Taylor and Francis.

Hayek, Friedrich A. von. (1948). *Individualism and Economic Order.* University of Chicago Press.

Helleiner, Eric. (1996). *States and the Reemergence of Global Finance: from Bretton Woods to the 1990s.* Cornell University Press.

Hetzel, Robert L. (2008). *The Monetary Policy of the Federal Reserve: A History.* Cambridge University Press.

Horwitz, Stephen. (2010). *Austrian Economics: An Introduction.* Cato Institute.

Keynes, John Maynard. (1936). *The General Theory of Employment, Interest and Money.* New York: Macmillan, 1936. https://www.hetwebsite.net/het/texts/keynes/gt/gtcont.htm.

Knafo, Samuel. (2006). "The Gold Standard and the Origins of the Modern International Monetary System." *Review of International Political Economy* 13 (1): 78-102.

Lamoreaux, Naomi R, and Ian Shapiro, eds. (2019). *The Bretton Woods Agreements: Together with Scholarly Commentaries and Essential Historical Documents.* Yale University Press.

Liu ZZ, Papa M. (2022). *Can BRICS De-Dollarize the Global Financial System?* Cambridge University Press.

Minas, Renate, Sharon Wright, and Rik van Berkel. (2012). "Decentralization and Centralization." *International Journal of Sociology and Social Policy* 32 (5-6): 286–98.

Minsky, Hyman P. (2008). *Stabilizing an Unstable Economy.* McGraw-Hill.

Mises, Ludwig von. (1981). *The Theory of Money and Credit*, trans. H.E. Batson. Liberty Fund.

Pearson, Michael Naylor, ed. (2017*). Spices in the Indian Ocean World.* Routledge.

Pihl, Christopher. (2024). "A Bank in a Monarchy: An Early Modern Anomaly? The Swedish Bank of the Estates of the Realm." *Scandinavian Journal of History*, 49 (1): 1-23.

Redish, Angela. (2000). *Bimetallism: An Economic and Historical Analysis.* Cambridge University Press.

Rodney, Edvinsson, et al. (2018). "Introduction." Sveriges Riksbank and the History of Central Banking," *Studies in Macroeconomic History*, Cambridge University Press: 1–25.

Rothbard, Murray. (2009). *Man, Economy, and State.* Ludwig von Mises Institute.

Roosevelt, Franklin D. "Executive Order 6102." https://archive.org/details/pdfy-MHvlymfJYU05yELW/mode/2up.

Singh, Anjana. (2019). "Early Modern European Mercantilism and Indian Ocean Trade," In *Maritime Power Networks in World History*, Brill: 245–262.

United States Congress. (1873-1875). "Specie Resumption Act," 296. *The Statutes at Large and Proclamations of the United States of America*, vol. XVIII, part 3.

Warburg, Paul M. (1930). *The Federal Reserve System. Its Origin and Growth. Reflections and Recollections.* Macmillan.

Chapter 5 References

Ammous, Saifedean. (2018). *The Bitcoin Standard: Sound Money in a Digital Age.* John Wiley & Sons.

Balaji, K. C., and K. Balaji. (2017). "A Study on Demonetization and Its Impact on Cashless Transactions." *International Journal of Advanced Scientific Research and Development* 4 (3): 58-64.

Bardhan, Pranab. (2002). "Decentralization of Governance and Development." Journal of *Economic Perspectives* 16 (4): 185–205.

Elliott, Francis. (2009). "Chancellor on brink of second bailout for banks." *The Financial Times*, January 3, 2009.

Franco, Pedro. (2014). *Understanding Bitcoin: Cryptography, Engineering and Economics.* Wiley & Sons.

Fritzner, Yan. (2019). *Inventing Bitcoin.* Self-published.

Fuller, Bruce. (2015). *Organizing Locally: How the New Decentralists Improve Education, Health Care, and Trade.* The University of Chicago Press.

Goyal, P., Chakrabarti, A. (2021). "Banking the Unbanked: The Fintech Revolution." *Intelligent Engineering and Management for Industry 4.0*: 91-105.

Grable, J., Kwak, E.J. and Archuleta, K. (2023). "Distrust of Banks Among the Unbanked and Banked." *International Journal of Bank Marketing* 41 (6): 1498-1520.

Greene, Claire, and Oz Shy. (2024). "Unbanked Consumers and How They Pay." *Journal of Economics and Finance* 48: 186-195.

Kinney, Alexander B. (n.d.). "Embedding into an Emerging Money System: The Case of Bitcoin." *Sociological Focus* 54 (1): 77–92.

Nakamoto, Satoshi. (2008). "Bitcoin: A Peer-to-Peer Electronic Cash System." *Bitcoin.org*. https://bitcoin.org/ bitcoin.pdf.

Nakamoto, Satoshi. (2009). "Cypherpunks online forum post." *P2P Foundation*. https://p2pfoundation.ning.com/forum/topics/bitcoin-open-source.

Williams, Jason A. (2020). *Bitcoin: Hard Money You Can't Fuck With*. Going Parabolic Publishing.

Wong, Paul and Jesse Leigh Maniff. "Comparing Means of Payment: What Role for a Central Bank Digital Currency?" https://www.federalreserve.gov/econres/notes/feds-notes/comp Aring-means-of-payment-what-role-for-a-central- bank-digital-currency-0200813.html./appendiox.

Chapter 6 References

Bitty, Yehuda. (2019). "Reflections on Jewish Education." *Journal of Education, Innovation, and Communication*, 1 (2): 15–20.

Chazan, B., Chazan, R., & Jacobs, B. M. (2017). *Cultures and Contexts of Jewish Education*. Palgrave Macmillan.

Cohen, E., & Rocklin, M. (n.d.). "The Spirit of Jewish Classical Education." Tikvah Fund.

Fitzpatrick, A., & Sabapathy, J. (Eds.). (2020). *Individuals and Institutions in Medieval Scholasticism.* University of Chicago Press.

Heikkinen, Deanna. "Seeking Intellectual Diversity: A Narrative of Using Ayn Rand in Higher Education." Unpublished dissertation.

Hoffman, J. (1992). "The Organization and Administration of Schools in Classical Judaism." *Religious Education*, 87 (3): 416–434.

Kadish, A., Shmidman, M., & Fishbane, S. (2021). *The Jewish Intellectual Tradition: A History of Learning and Achievement.* Academic Studies Press.

Johnson, M. S., & Stearns, P. N. (2012). *Education in World History.* Routledge.

Laes, C. (2017). *A Cultural History of Education in Antiquity.* Bloomsbury Academic.

Law, S., Freeman, C., & Fowler, J. (Eds.). (2015). *The Wiley Blackwell Handbook of Humanism.* Wiley-Blackwell.

Mamadaliev, A. M., Svechnikova, N. V., Miku, N. V., & Médico, A. (2019). "The German System of Public Education in the Period Between the 15th and early 20th Centuries. Part 2." *European Journal of Contemporary Education,* 8 (3): 646–654

Marrou, H. I. (1956). *A History of Education in Antiquity.* Sheed & Ward.

Rury, J. L. (Ed.). (2019). *The Oxford Handbook of the History of Education.* Oxford University Press.

Schwarz, B. B., & Bekerman, Z. (2021). "Learning Practices and Development in Yeshivas: Historical, Social, and Cultural Perspectives." *European Journal of Psychology of Education*, 36(4): 1181–1198.

Sharpes, Donald K. *Education and the US Government.* Routledge, 2020.

Spencer, H. (1859). *Education: Intellectual, Moral and Physical.* Burt.

Wilkinson, L. (2019). *History of Education in Ancient Greece.* Routledge.

Zaman, M., & Memon, N. (Eds.). (2020). *Philosophies of Islamic Education: Historical Perspectives and Emerging Discourses.* Routledge.

Chapter 7 References

Demiashkevich, M.J. (1935). *An Introduction to the Philosophy of Education.* American Book Company.

Dewey, John. (1915). *The School and Society.* Chicago University Press.

Harris, W. T. (1902). "How the School Strengthens the Individuality of the Pupils." *National Educational Association Proceedings*: 118-125.

Mann, H., & Massachusetts Board of Education. (1957). *The Republic and the School: Horace Mann on the Education of Free Men.* Teachers College, Columbia University.

Miller, K.S. (2012). "Fine Print, Restrictive Grants, and Academic Freedom." *Academe* 98 (3): 17-21.

Ravitch, D. (2000). *Left Back A Century of Battles over School Reform.* Touchstone.

Chapter 9 References

Arment, A. (2019). The Call of the Wild and Free: Reclaiming Wonder in Your Child's Education. HarperOne.

Bauer, S. W., & Wise, J. (2020). The Well-trained Mind: A Guide to Classical Education at Home (4th ed.). W. W. Norton & Company.

Bentley, Rachael Rettner. (2024). "Worldschooling Is Catching On. Here's What You Need to Know." Scientific American, October 21, 2024.

Bogart, J. (2019). The Brave Learner: Finding Everyday Magic in Homeschool, Learning, and Life. TarcherPerigee.

Dobson, L. (2001). The First Year of Homeschooling Your Child: Your Complete Guide to Getting Off to the Right Start. Prima Publishing.

Dobson, L. (2002). The Ultimate Book of Homeschooling Ideas: 500+ Fun and Creative Learning Activities for Kids Ages 3–12. Prima Publishing.

Duvall, S. F., Delquadri, J. C., & Ward, D. L. (2004). "A Preliminary Investigation of the Effectiveness of Homeschool Instructional Environments for Students with Attention-deficit/Hyperactivity Disorder." School Psychology Review, 33 (1): 140–158.

Gray, Peter, and Gina Riley. (2013). "The Challenges and Benefits of Unschooling According to 232 Families Who Have Chosen That Route." Journal of Unschooling and Alternative Learning, 7 (14): 1–27.

Griffith, M. (1999). The Homeschooling Handbook: How to Make Homeschooling Simple, Affordable, Fun, and Effective. Prima Publishing.

Murphy, J. (2012). Homeschooling in America: Capturing and Assessing the Movement. Corwin Press.

Richards, Akilah S. (2020). Raising Free People: Unschooling as Liberation and Healing Work. PM Press

Riley, G. M. (2025). The Homeschooling Starter Guide: How to Create and Adapt the Best Education Action Plan for Your Needs. Sourcebooks.

Rupp, R. (2000). Home Learning Year by Year: How to Design a Homeschool Curriculum from Preschool through High School. Three Rivers Press.

Thompson, Lainie Liberti. (2023). Wonder Year: A Guide to Long-Term Family Travel and Worldschooling. LifeTree Media.

Chapter 10 References

Center on Education Policy. (2020). "History and Evolution of Public Education in the US." (ERIC Document ED606970).

Berner, A. R. (2017). *Pluralism and American public education: No One Way to School.* Palgrave Macmillan.

Cohn, D. N. (Ed.). (2021). *International Education at the Crossroads.* Indiana University Press.

Gross, R. N. (2018). *Public vs. Private: The Early History of School Choice in America.* Oxford University Press.

Reese, W. J. (2011). *America's Public Schools: From the Common School to "No Child Left Behind."* Johns Hopkins University Press.

Tyack, D., & Cuban, L. (1995). *Tinkering Toward Utopia: A Century of Public School Reform.* Harvard University Press.

Zimmerman, J. (2002). *Whose America?: Culture Wars in the Public Schools.* Harvard University Press.

Chapter 11 References

Ee, J., Orfield, G., & Teitell, J. (2018). "Private Schools in American Education: A Small Sector Still Lagging in Diversity." *The Civil Rights Project at UCLA.*

FutureEd. (2024). "Public Funds, Private Schools: A New Analysis of the Early Returns in Eight States." *The 74 Million.*

Kane, P. R. (1992). "Emerging Issues in K-12 Independent School Governance. "AGB Occasional Paper No. 14. *Association of Governing Boards of Universities and Colleges.*

Lubienski, C., & Lubienski, S. T. (2006). "Charter, Private, Public Schools and Academic Achievement: New Evidence from NAEP Mathematics Data." *National Center for Education Statistics.*

Samuel, L. R. (2024). *The American Private School: A Cultural History.* Rowman & Littlefield.

Sargent, P. (Ed.). (2013). *The Handbook of Private Schools* (94th ed.). Porter Sargent Publishers.

Chapter 12 References

"Academic Freedom and Educational Responsibility: A Statement of the Board of Directors of the Association of American Colleges and Universities." (2006). *Liberal Education*, 92 (2): 6-13.

American Council of Trustees and Alumni. (2005). "Intellectual Diversity Time for Action." *American Council of Trusties and Alumni.*

Diaz, S., H. Lakemacher, C. Mitchell, and American Council of Trustees. (2010). "At a Crossroads: A Report Card on Public

Higher Education in Minnesota." *American Council Of Trustees and Alumni.*

Diaz, S, H. Lakemacher, C. Mitchell and American Council of Trustees. (2009). "For the People: A Report Card on Public Higher Education in Illinois." *American Council Of Trustees and Alumni.*

Horrowitz, D. (2006). *The Professors: The 101 Most Dangerous Academics in America.* Regnery Publishing.

Jones, G. H. (2010). "Universities, the Major Battleground in the Fight for Reason and Capitalism." *Academe*, 96(4): 34-37.

La Falce, D. & Gomez, S. P. (2007). "Political Attitudes in the Classroom: Is Academia the Last Bastion of Liberalism?" *Journal of Political Science Education*, 3 (1): 1-20.

Lakemacher, H., Markley, E., & The American Council of, Trustees, & Alumni. (2011). "Here we have Idaho: A State Report Card on Public Higher Education." *The American Council of Trustees and Alumni.*

Linvill, D. L. (2011). "The Relationship Between Student Identity Development and the Perception of Political Bias in the College Classroom." *College Teaching*, 59 (2): 49-55.

Losco, J., and DeOllos, I. (2007). "Fear and loathing in college classrooms: A survey of political science department chairs regarding political bias." *Journal of Political Science Education*, 3 (3): 251-264.

Mintz, S., A. Savage, and R. Carter. (2010). "Commercialism and universities: An Ethical Analysis." *Journal of Academic Ethics*, 8: 1-19.

Nieli, R. K. (2005). "Enhancing Intellectual Diversity on Campus, The James Madison Program at Princeton." *Academic Questions*, 18(2): 20-48.

Palmiero, P. and Alumni American Council of Trustees. (2008) "Shining The Light: A Report Card On Georgia's System Of Public Higher Education." *American Council of Trustees and Alumni.*

Paulsen, M. S. (2014). "The Uneasy Case for Intellectual Diversity." *Harvard Journal Of Law & Public Policy*, 37(1): 145-164.

Resz, M. (2016, January 7). "Corrosion of Conformity." *The Times Higher Education Supplement.*

Rochester, J. M. (2007). Remarks Made During "Dialogue on Intellectual Diversity, A Forum Held 11 October 2007 at the University of Missouri, St. Louis." *Academic Questions,* 20: 366-369.

Rosenkranz, N. (2014). Intellectual diversity in the Legal Academy. *Harvard Journal Of Law & Public Policy*, 37(1): 137-142.

Chapter 13 References

Chichekian, T., & Benteux, B. (2022). "The Potential of Learning with (and not from) Artificial Intelligence in Education." *Frontiers in Artificial Intelligence*, 5.

Durak, G., Çankaya, S., Özdemir, D., & Can, S. (2024). "Artificial Intelligence in Education: A Bibliometric Study on Its Role in Transforming Teaching and Learning." *International Review of Research in Open and Distributed Learning*, 25(3).

Schiff, D. (2021). "Out of the Laboratory and Into the Classroom: The Future of Artificial Intelligence in Education." *AI & Society*, 36(1), 331–348.

UNESCO. (2019–2025). "Artificial Intelligence in Education: Guidance for Policy-makers & Related Materials." https://unesdoc.unesco.org/ark:/48223/pf0000376709

U.S. Department of Education, Office of Educational Technology. (2023). "Artificial Intelligence (AI) and the Future of Teaching and Learning: Insights and Recommendations." https://www.ed.gov/about/ed-overview/artificial-intelligence-ai-guidance

Wang, S., Wang, F., Zhu, Z., Wang, J., Tran, T., & Du, Z. (2024). "Artificial intelligence in education: A systematic literature review." Expert Systems with Applications, 2 (34).

Zhang, B., & Aslan, S. (2021). "AI technologies for education: Recent research & future directions." Computers and Education: Artificial Intelligence, 2.

Made in the USA
Monee, IL
04 November 2026

67382300R00164